HEAVEN'S DESIGN TEAM

VOL.04

BY ► HEBI-ZOU & TSUTA SUZUKI

ART BY ► TARAKO

CHARACTER PROFILES

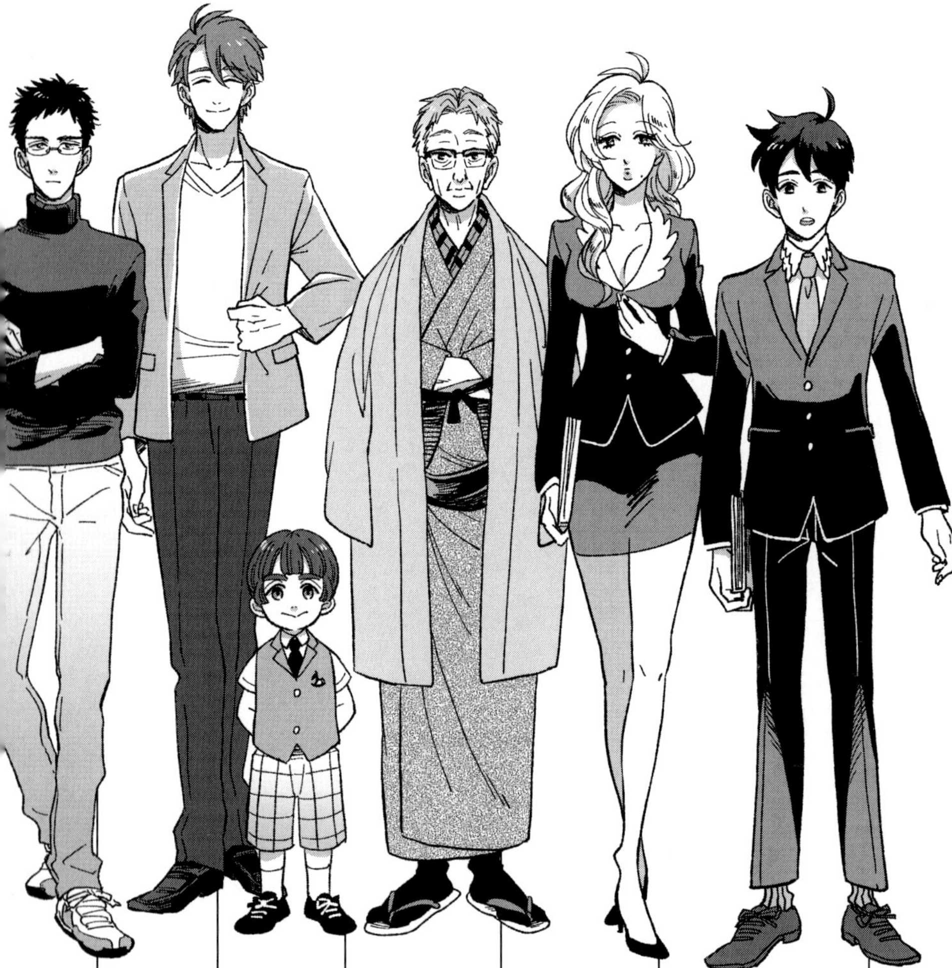

MERCURY

designer. lis master-iece: the nake.

JUPITER

A designer. His master-piece: the cow.

MR. SATURN'S GRANDSON

Mr. Saturn's grandson, Kenta. A horse fan, just like his grandpa.

MR. SATURN

A designer and the head of the Design Department. His master-piece: the horse.

UEDA

Shimoda's supervisor. An angel who acts as a liaison between God and the Design Department.

SHIMODA

The new angel. Serves as the liaison between God (the client) and the Design Department.

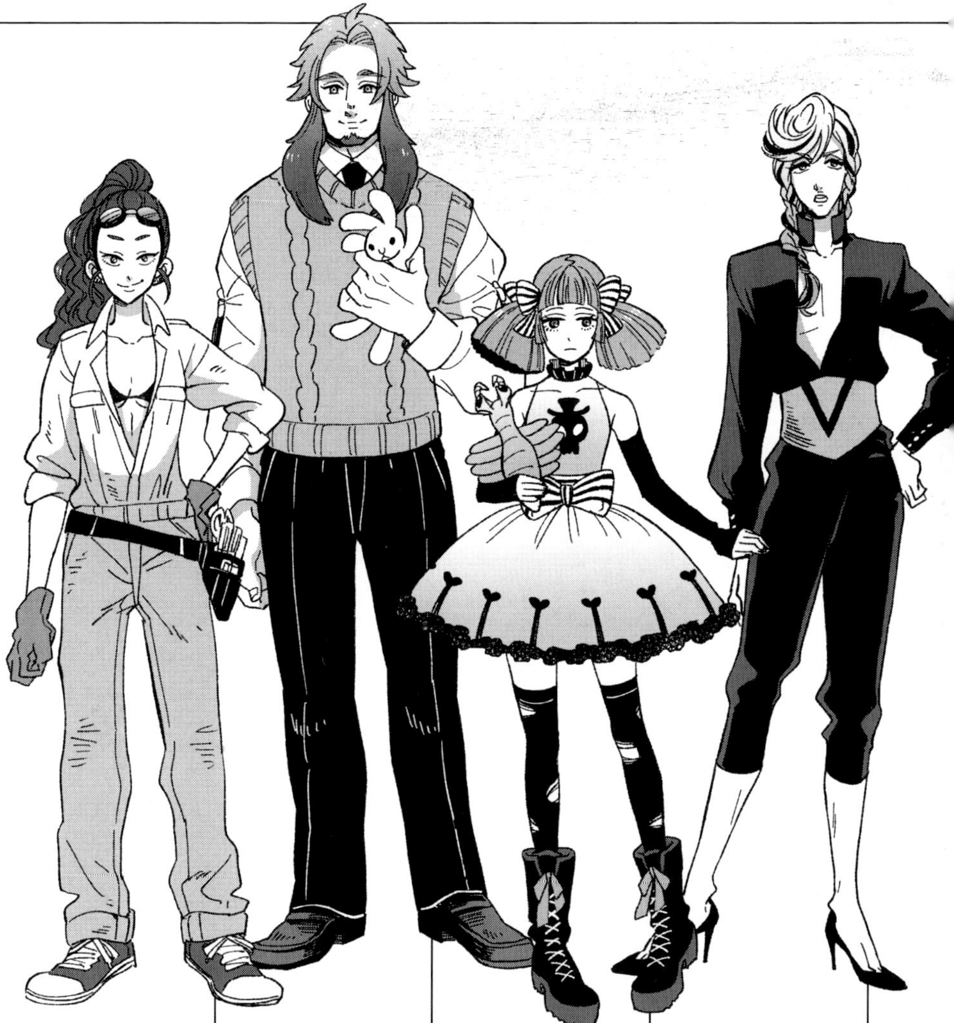

MARS

An engineer.
Tests whether the animal designs will actually function in the physical world.
The hardest worker in the office.

NEPTUNE

A designer.
His masterpiece: the kangaroo.

PLUTO

A designer.
Her masterpiece: the poisonous frog.

VENUS

A designer.
Nicknamed "Ven." Their masterpiece: the bird.

HEAVEN'S DESIGN TEAM

CONTENTS

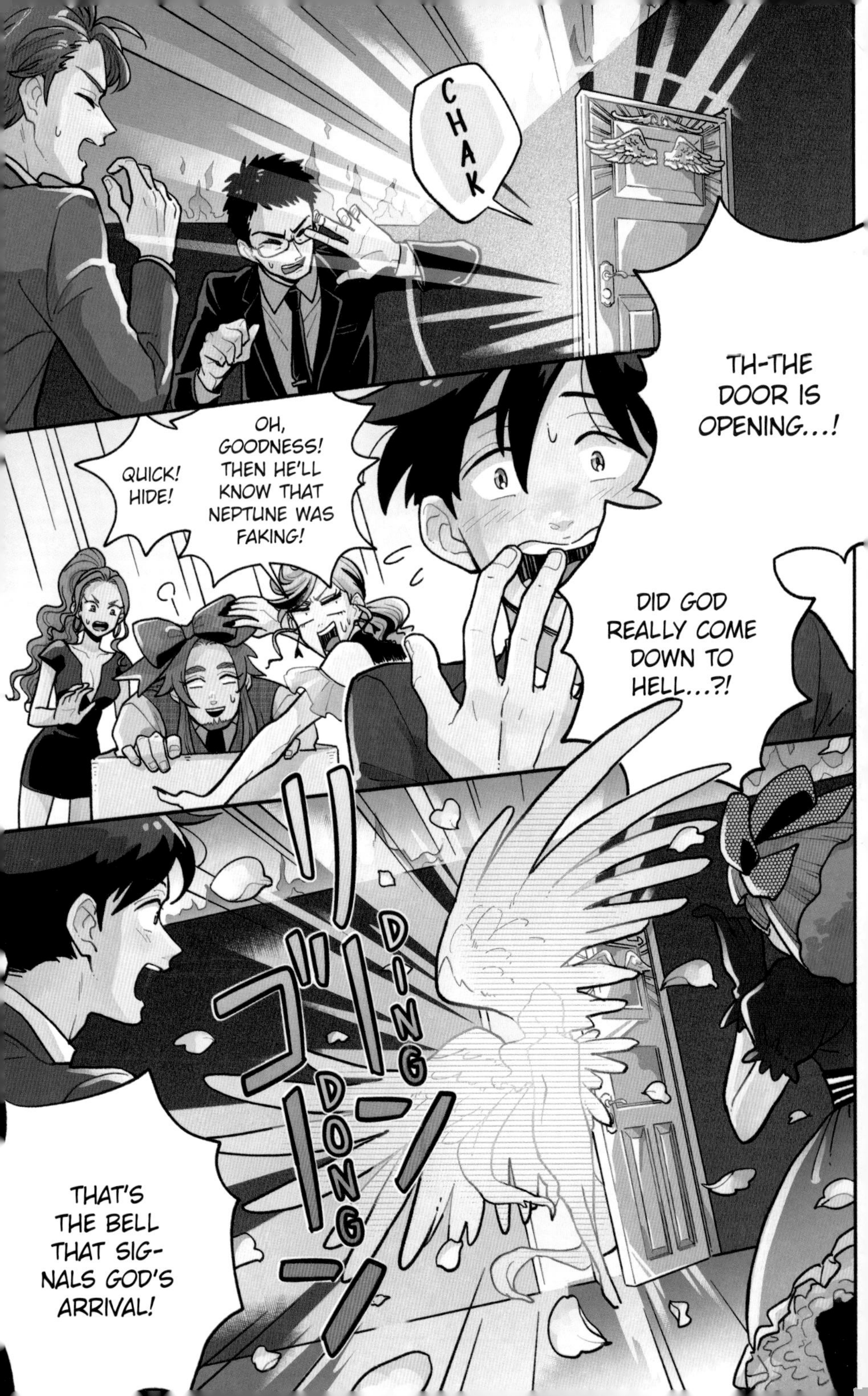
CHAK
TH-THE DOOR IS OPENING...!
DID GOD REALLY COME DOWN TO HELL...?!
OH, GOODNESS! THEN HE'LL KNOW THAT NEPTUNE WAS FAKING!
QUICK! HIDE!
DING DONG
THAT'S THE BELL THAT SIG-NALS GOD'S ARRIVAL!

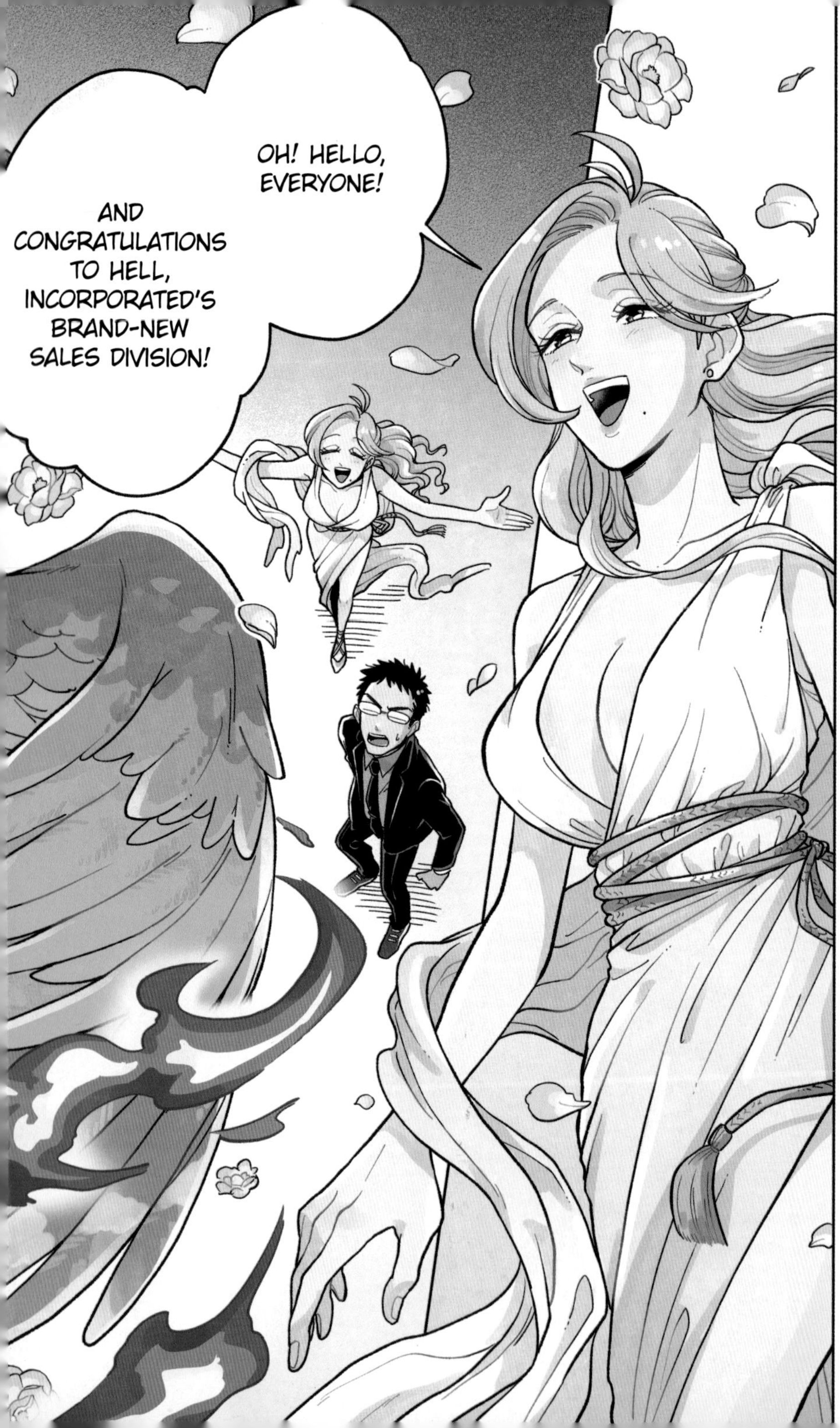
OH! HELLO, EVERYONE!
AND CONGRATULATIONS TO HELL, INCORPORATED'S BRAND-NEW SALES DIVISION!

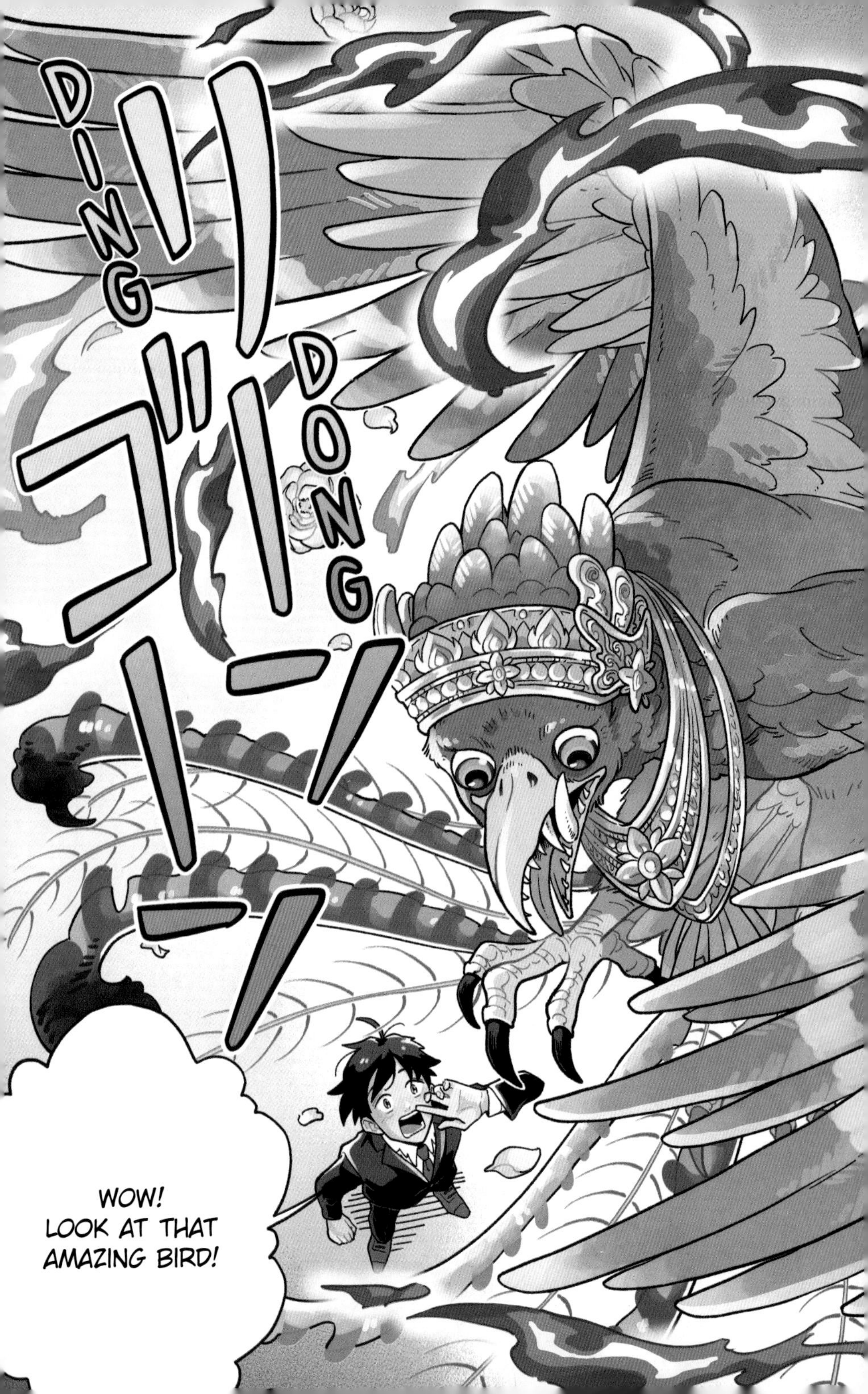
DING
DONG
ゴーーーン
WOW! LOOK AT THAT AMAZING BIRD!

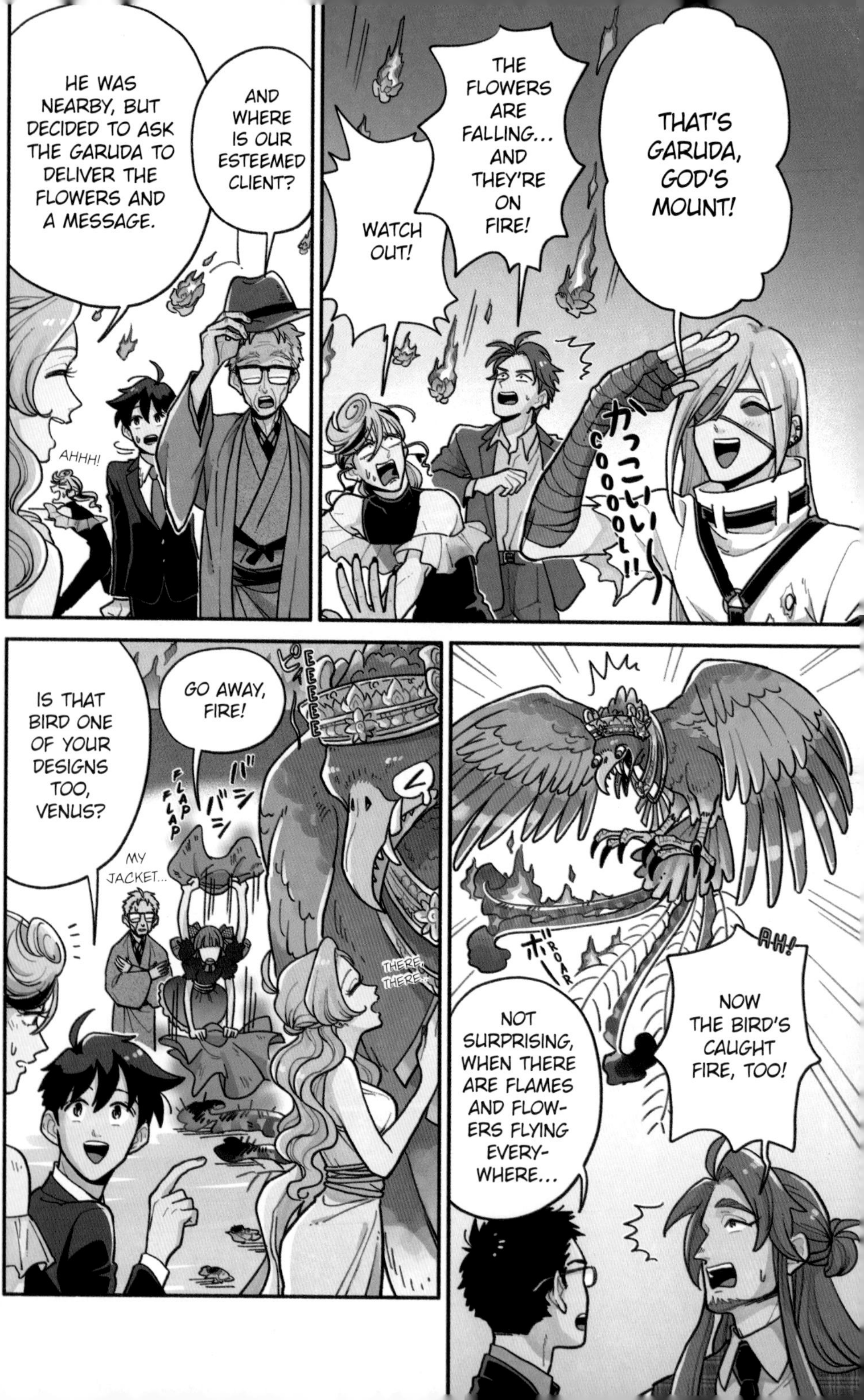
THAT'S GARUDA, GOD'S MOUNT!
THE FLOWERS ARE FALLING… AND THEY'RE ON FIRE!
WATCH OUT!
かっこいい
COOOOOL!!
AND WHERE IS OUR ESTEEMED CLIENT?
HE WAS NEARBY, BUT DECIDED TO ASK THE GARUDA TO DELIVER THE FLOWERS AND A MESSAGE.
AHHH!
ボ ROAR
AH!
NOW THE BIRD'S CAUGHT FIRE, TOO!
NOT SURPRISING, WHEN THERE ARE FLAMES AND FLOW-ERS FLYING EVERY-WHERE…
ピィ EEEEEE
GO AWAY, FIRE!
バシバシ FLAP FLAP
IS THAT BIRD ONE OF YOUR DESIGNS TOO, VENUS?
MY JACKET…
THERE, THERE…

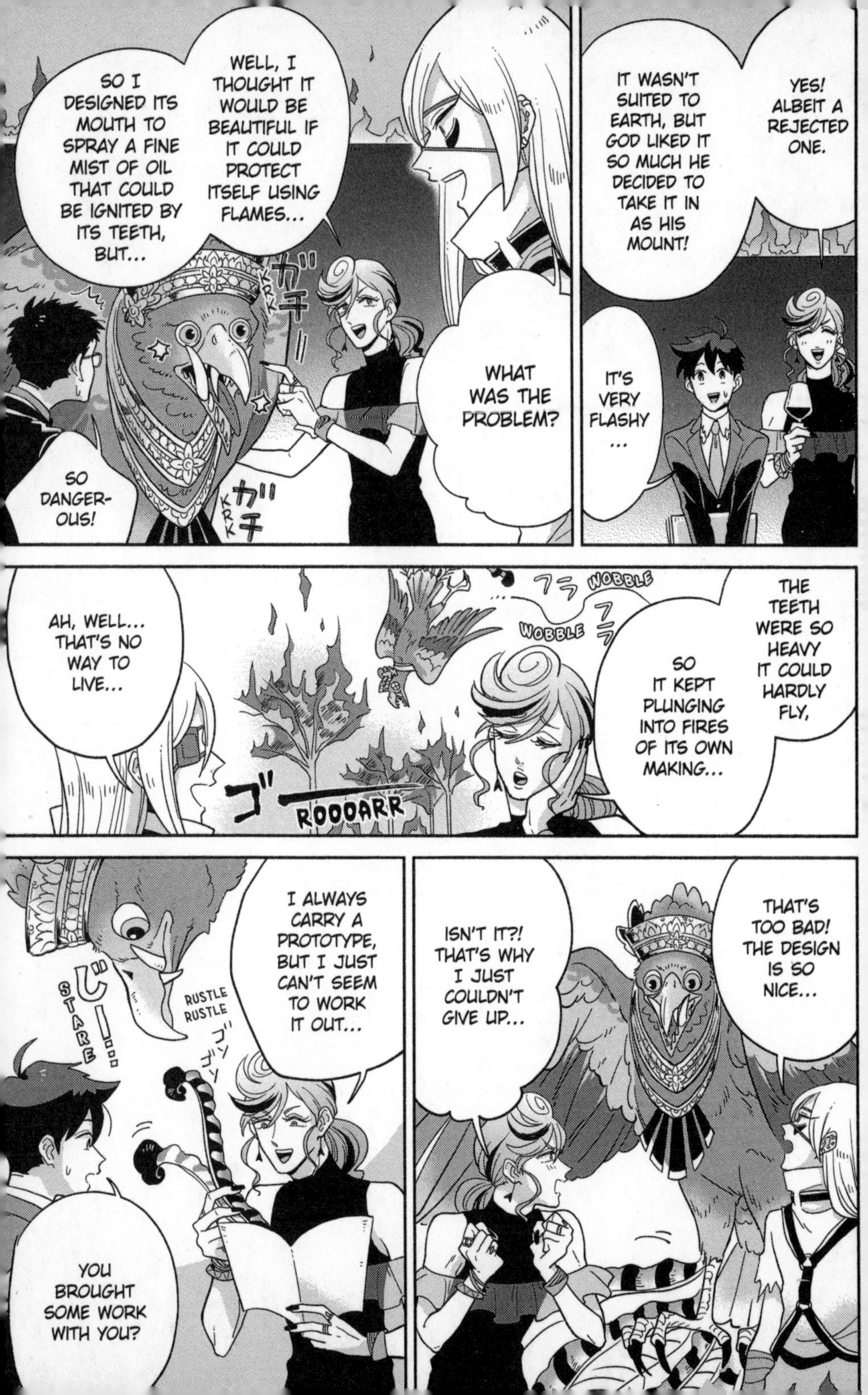
YES! ALBEIT A REJECTED ONE.
IT WASN'T SUITED TO EARTH, BUT GOD LIKED IT SO MUCH HE DECIDED TO TAKE IT IN AS HIS MOUNT!
IT'S VERY FLASHY …
WELL, I THOUGHT IT WOULD BE BEAUTIFUL IF IT COULD PROTECT ITSELF USING FLAMES…
SO I DESIGNED ITS MOUTH TO SPRAY A FINE MIST OF OIL THAT COULD BE IGNITED BY ITS TEETH, BUT…
KRK
WHAT WAS THE PROBLEM?
KRK
SO DANGER-OUS!
THE TEETH WERE SO HEAVY IT COULD HARDLY FLY,
SO IT KEPT PLUNGING INTO FIRES OF ITS OWN MAKING…
WOBBLE
WOBBLE
ROOOARR
AH, WELL… THAT'S NO WAY TO LIVE…
THAT'S TOO BAD! THE DESIGN IS SO NICE…
ISN'T IT?! THAT'S WHY I JUST COULDN'T GIVE UP…
I ALWAYS CARRY A PROTOTYPE, BUT I JUST CAN'T SEEM TO WORK IT OUT…
RUSTLE RUSTLE
STARE
YOU BROUGHT SOME WORK WITH YOU?

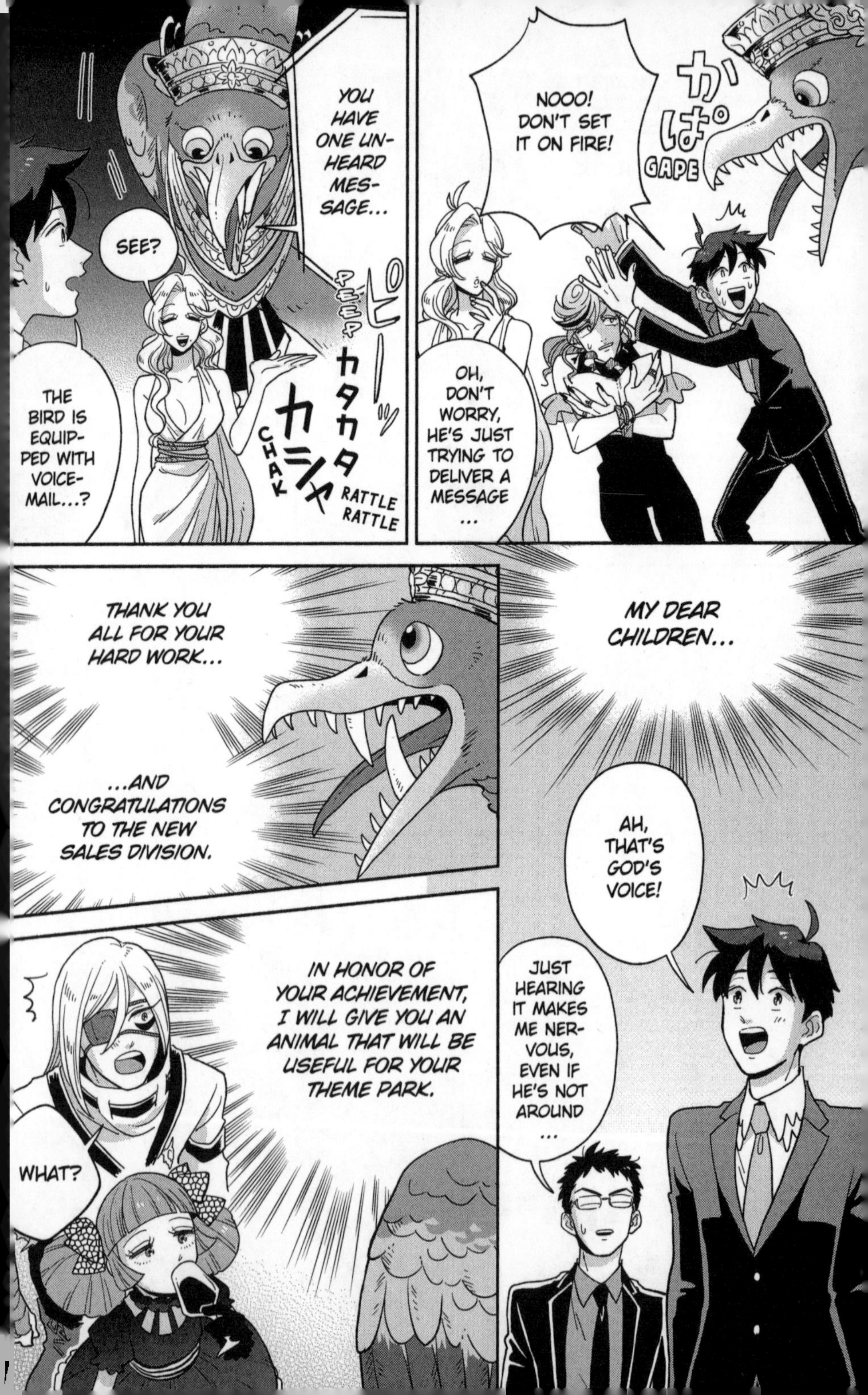
かぱ
GAPE
NOOO! DON'T SET IT ON FIRE!
OH, DON'T WORRY, HE'S JUST TRYING TO DELIVER A MESSAGE...
YOU HAVE ONE UNHEARD MESSAGE...
SEE?
ピーッ
PEEP
カタカタ
RATTLE RATTLE
カシャ
CHAK
THE BIRD IS EQUIPPED WITH VOICEMAIL...?
MY DEAR CHILDREN...
THANK YOU ALL FOR YOUR HARD WORK...
...AND CONGRATULATIONS TO THE NEW SALES DIVISION.
AH, THAT'S GOD'S VOICE!
JUST HEARING IT MAKES ME NERVOUS, EVEN IF HE'S NOT AROUND...
IN HONOR OF YOUR ACHIEVEMENT, I WILL GIVE YOU AN ANIMAL THAT WILL BE USEFUL FOR YOUR THEME PARK.
WHAT?

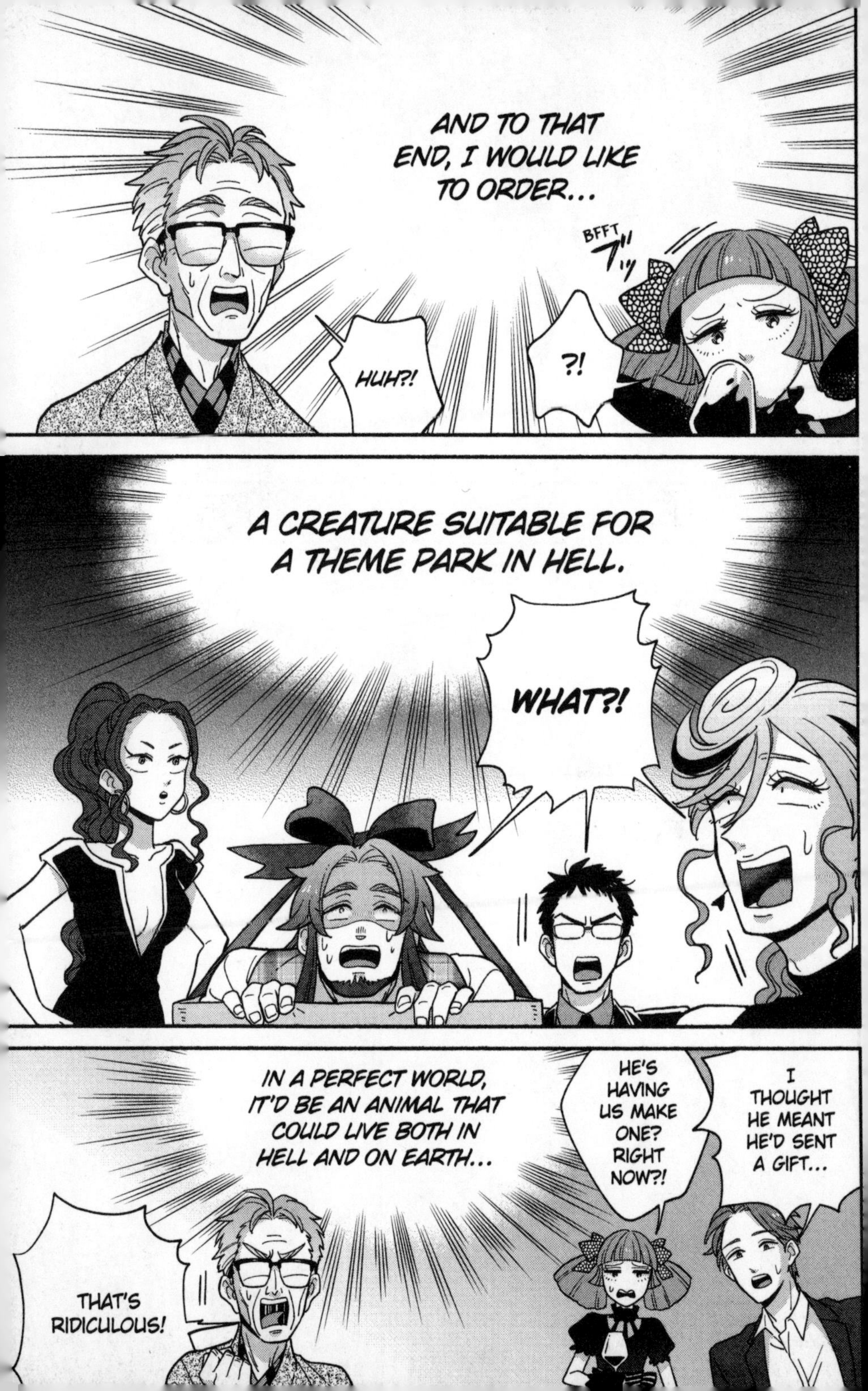
AND TO THAT END, I WOULD LIKE TO ORDER...
BFFT
ブッ
?!
HUH?!
A CREATURE SUITABLE FOR A THEME PARK IN HELL.
WHAT?!
I THOUGHT HE MEANT HE'D SENT A GIFT...
HE'S HAVING US MAKE ONE? RIGHT NOW?!
IN A PERFECT WORLD, IT'D BE AN ANIMAL THAT COULD LIVE BOTH IN HELL AND ON EARTH...
THAT'S RIDICULOUS!

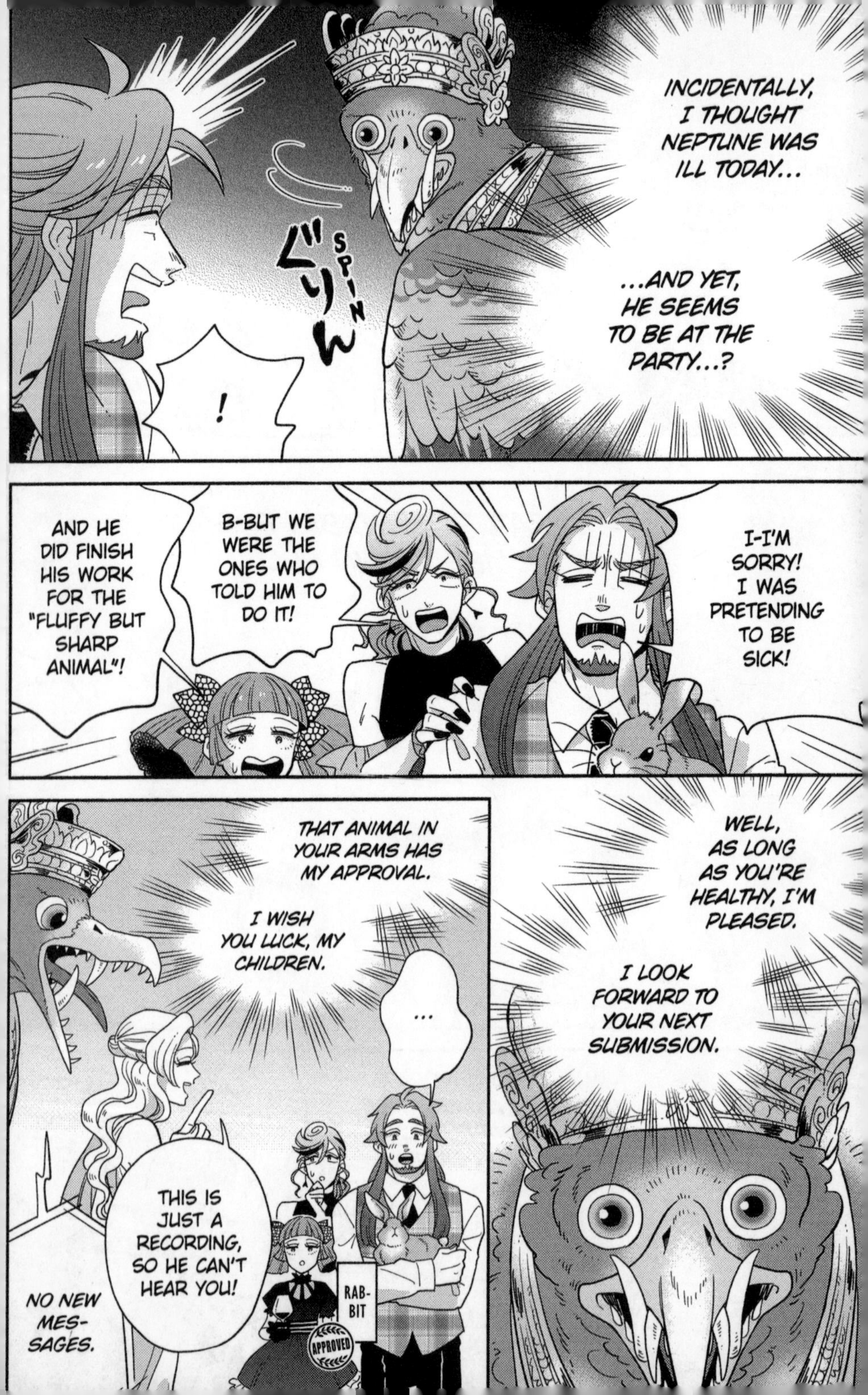
INCIDENTALLY, I THOUGHT NEPTUNE WAS ILL TODAY...
...AND YET, HE SEEMS TO BE AT THE PARTY...?
ぐりん
SPIN
!
I-I'M SORRY! I WAS PRETENDING TO BE SICK!
B-BUT WE WERE THE ONES WHO TOLD HIM TO DO IT!
AND HE DID FINISH HIS WORK FOR THE "FLUFFY BUT SHARP ANIMAL"!
WELL, AS LONG AS YOU'RE HEALTHY, I'M PLEASED.
I LOOK FORWARD TO YOUR NEXT SUBMISSION.
THAT ANIMAL IN YOUR ARMS HAS MY APPROVAL.
I WISH YOU LUCK, MY CHILDREN.
...
THIS IS JUST A RECORDING, SO HE CAN'T HEAR YOU!
RAB-BIT
APPROVED
NO NEW MES-SAGES.

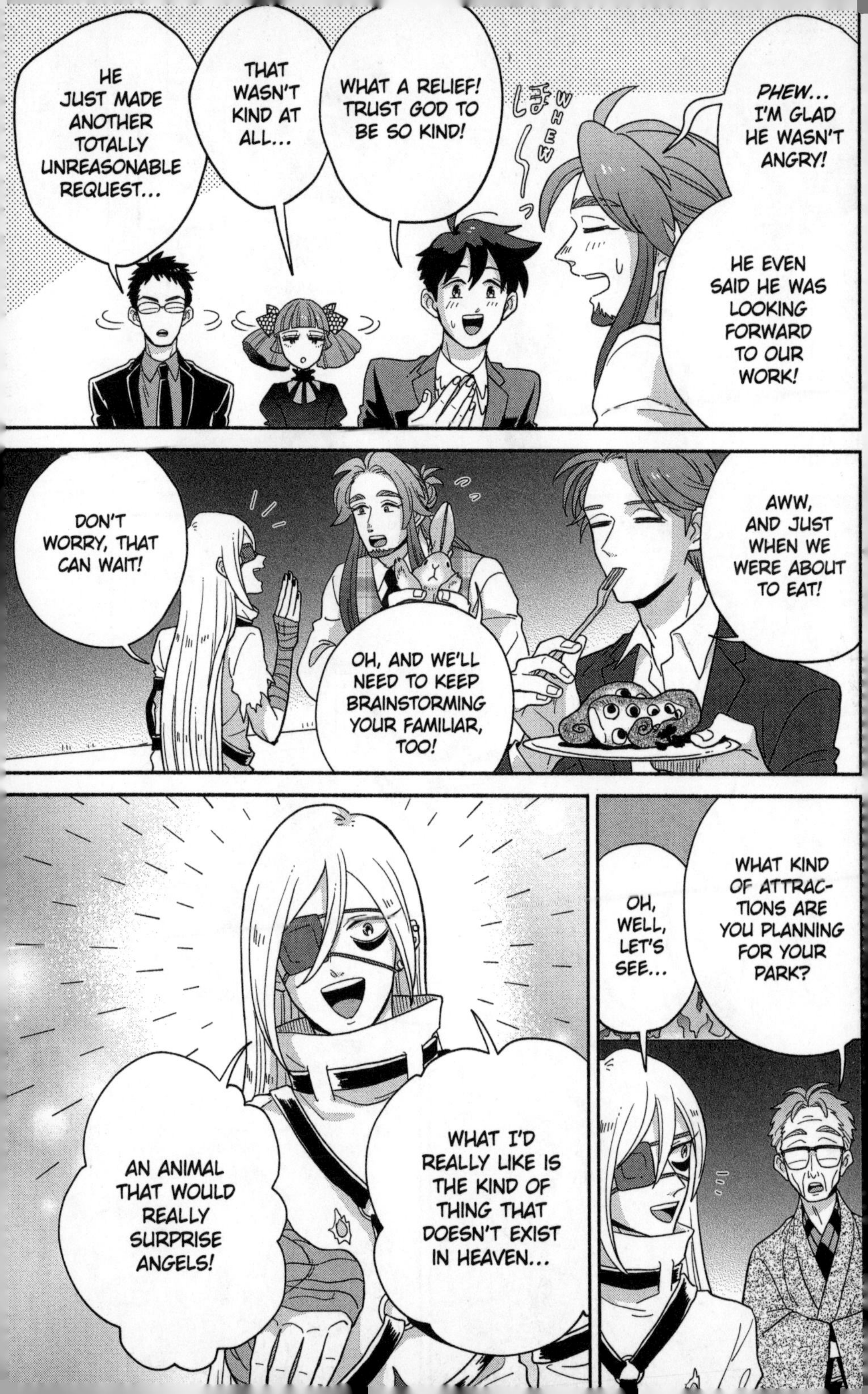
PHEW... I'M GLAD HE WASN'T ANGRY!
HE EVEN SAID HE WAS LOOKING FORWARD TO OUR WORK!
WHEW
WHAT A RELIEF! TRUST GOD TO BE SO KIND!
THAT WASN'T KIND AT ALL...
HE JUST MADE ANOTHER TOTALLY UNREASONABLE REQUEST...
AWW, AND JUST WHEN WE WERE ABOUT TO EAT!
OH, AND WE'LL NEED TO KEEP BRAINSTORMING YOUR FAMILIAR, TOO!
DON'T WORRY, THAT CAN WAIT!
WHAT KIND OF ATTRACTIONS ARE YOU PLANNING FOR YOUR PARK?
OH, WELL, LET'S SEE...
WHAT I'D REALLY LIKE IS THE KIND OF THING THAT DOESN'T EXIST IN HEAVEN...
AN ANIMAL THAT WOULD REALLY SURPRISE ANGELS!

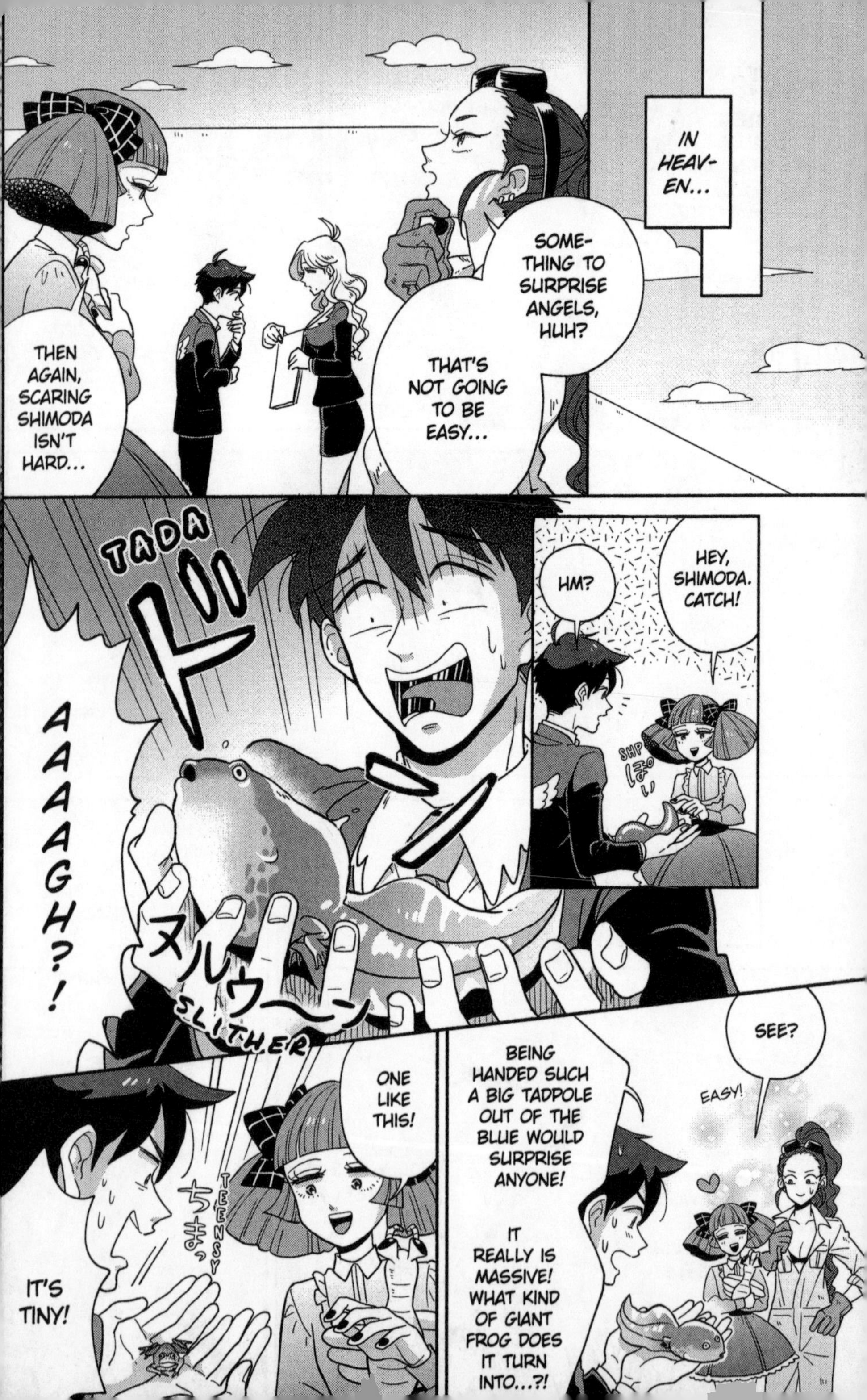
IN HEAVEN...
SOMETHING TO SURPRISE ANGELS, HUH?
THAT'S NOT GOING TO BE EASY...
THEN AGAIN, SCARING SHIMODA ISN'T HARD...
HEY, SHIMODA. CATCH!
HM?
SHP ぽい
TADA ドッ
AAAAAGH?!
ヌルウ〜〜 SLITHER
SEE?
EASY!
BEING HANDED SUCH A BIG TADPOLE OUT OF THE BLUE WOULD SURPRISE ANYONE!
IT REALLY IS MASSIVE! WHAT KIND OF GIANT FROG DOES IT TURN INTO...?!
ONE LIKE THIS!
TEENSY ちまっ
IT'S TINY!

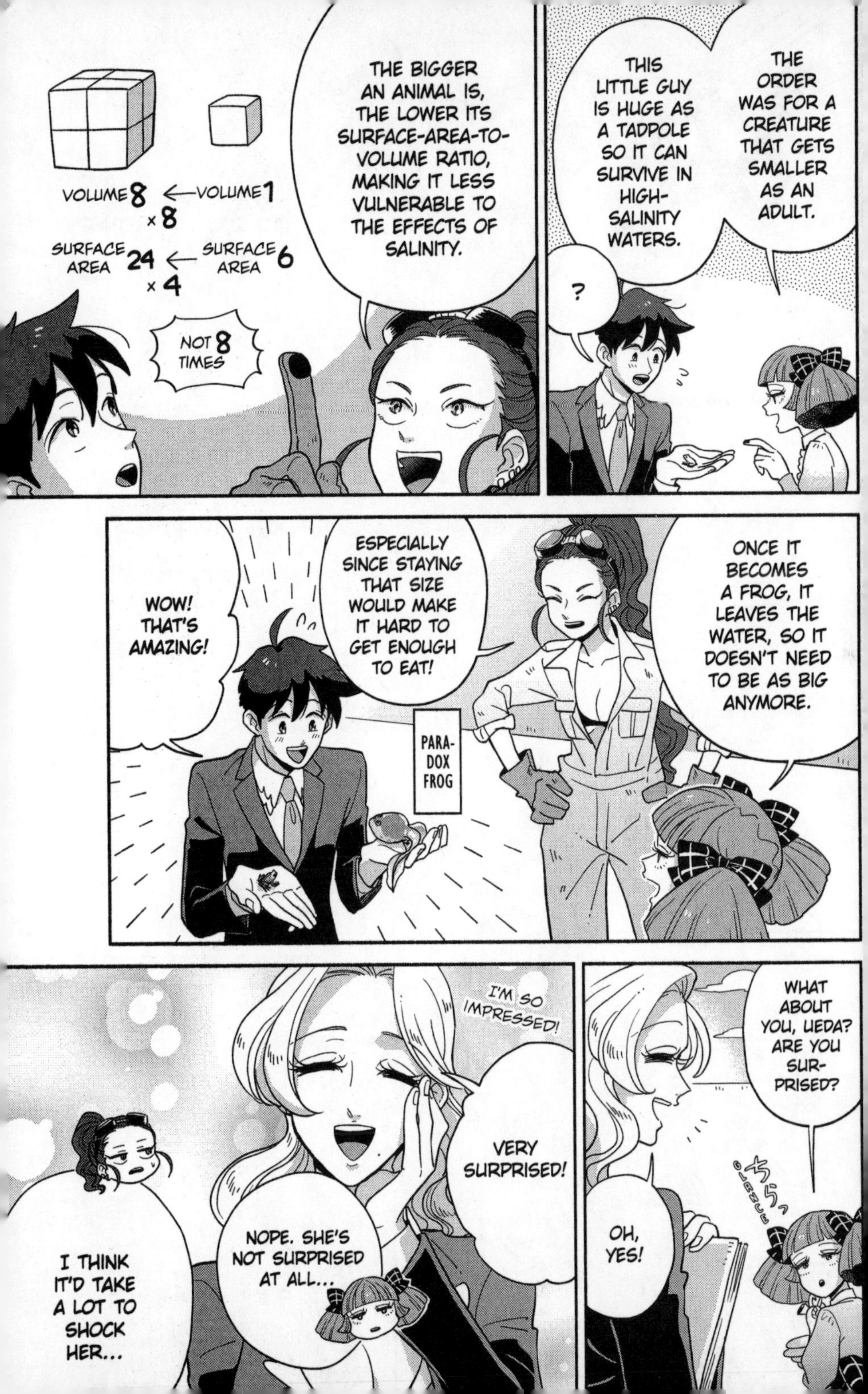
THE ORDER WAS FOR A CREATURE THAT GETS SMALLER AS AN ADULT.
THIS LITTLE GUY IS HUGE AS A TADPOLE SO IT CAN SURVIVE IN HIGH-SALINITY WATERS.
?
THE BIGGER AN ANIMAL IS, THE LOWER ITS SURFACE-AREA-TO-VOLUME RATIO, MAKING IT LESS VULNERABLE TO THE EFFECTS OF SALINITY.
VOLUME 8 ← VOLUME 1
×8
SURFACE AREA 24 ← SURFACE AREA 6
×4
NOT 8 TIMES
ONCE IT BECOMES A FROG, IT LEAVES THE WATER, SO IT DOESN'T NEED TO BE AS BIG ANYMORE.
ESPECIALLY SINCE STAYING THAT SIZE WOULD MAKE IT HARD TO GET ENOUGH TO EAT!
WOW! THAT'S AMAZING!
PARA-DOX FROG
WHAT ABOUT YOU, UEDA? ARE YOU SUR-PRISED?
ちらっ GLANCE
OH, YES!
I'M SO IMPRESSED!
VERY SURPRISED!
NOPE. SHE'S NOT SURPRISED AT ALL...
I THINK IT'D TAKE A LOT TO SHOCK HER...

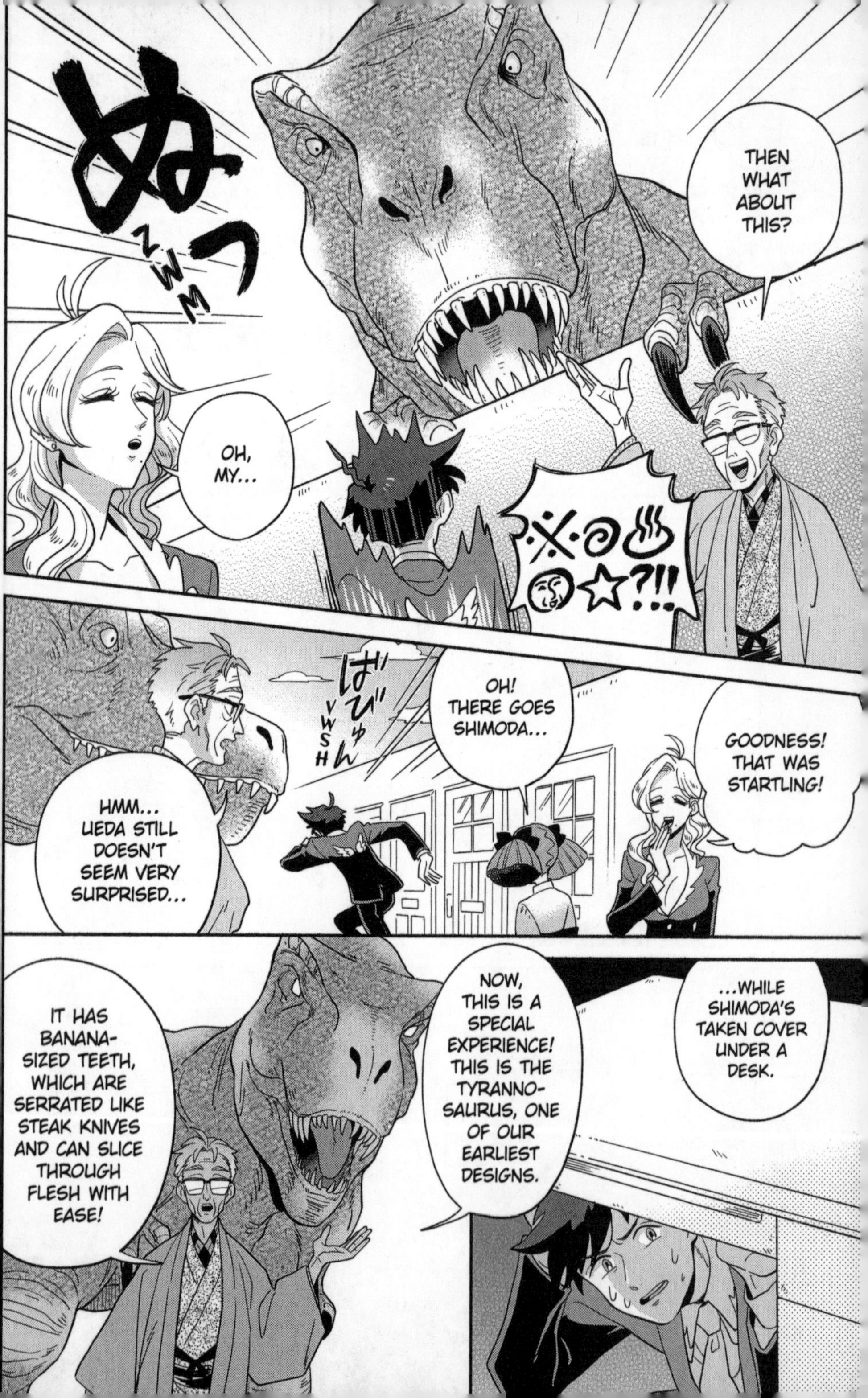
THEN WHAT ABOUT THIS?
ぬっ
ZWM
OH, MY...
※・◎♨☆?!!
GOODNESS! THAT WAS STARTLING!
OH! THERE GOES SHIMODA...
ばびゅん
VWSH
HMM... UEDA STILL DOESN'T SEEM VERY SURPRISED...
...WHILE SHIMODA'S TAKEN COVER UNDER A DESK.
NOW, THIS IS A SPECIAL EXPERIENCE! THIS IS THE TYRANNO-SAURUS, ONE OF OUR EARLIEST DESIGNS.
IT HAS BANANA-SIZED TEETH, WHICH ARE SERRATED LIKE STEAK KNIVES AND CAN SLICE THROUGH FLESH WITH EASE!

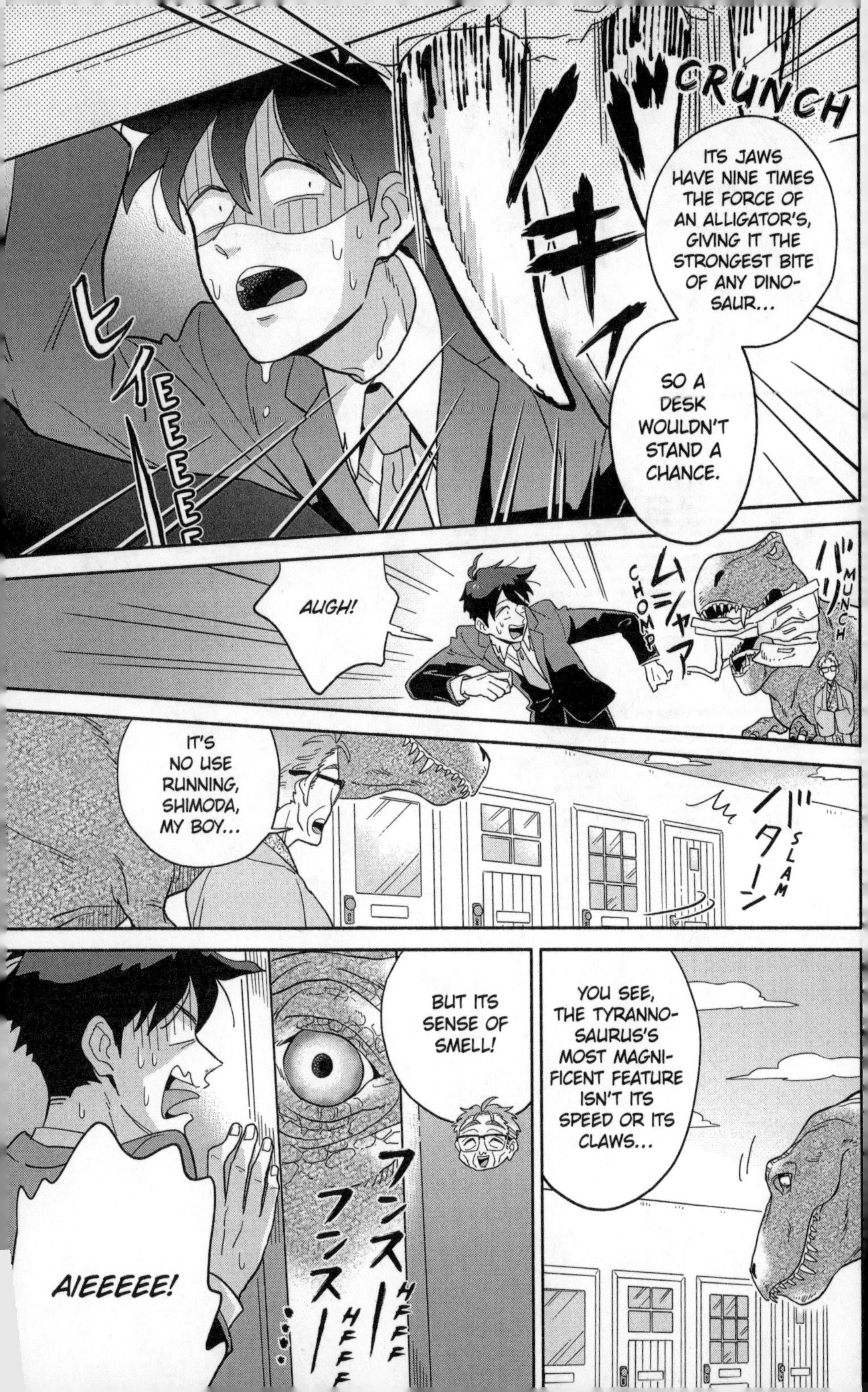

CRUNCH
ITS JAWS HAVE NINE TIMES THE FORCE OF AN ALLIGATOR'S, GIVING IT THE STRONGEST BITE OF ANY DINO-SAUR...
SO A DESK WOULDN'T STAND A CHANCE.
MUNCH
CHOMP
AUGH!
SLAM
IT'S NO USE RUNNING, SHIMODA, MY BOY...
YOU SEE, THE TYRANNO-SAURUS'S MOST MAGNI-FICENT FEATURE ISN'T ITS SPEED OR ITS CLAWS...
BUT ITS SENSE OF SMELL!
HFFF
HFFF
AIEEEEE!

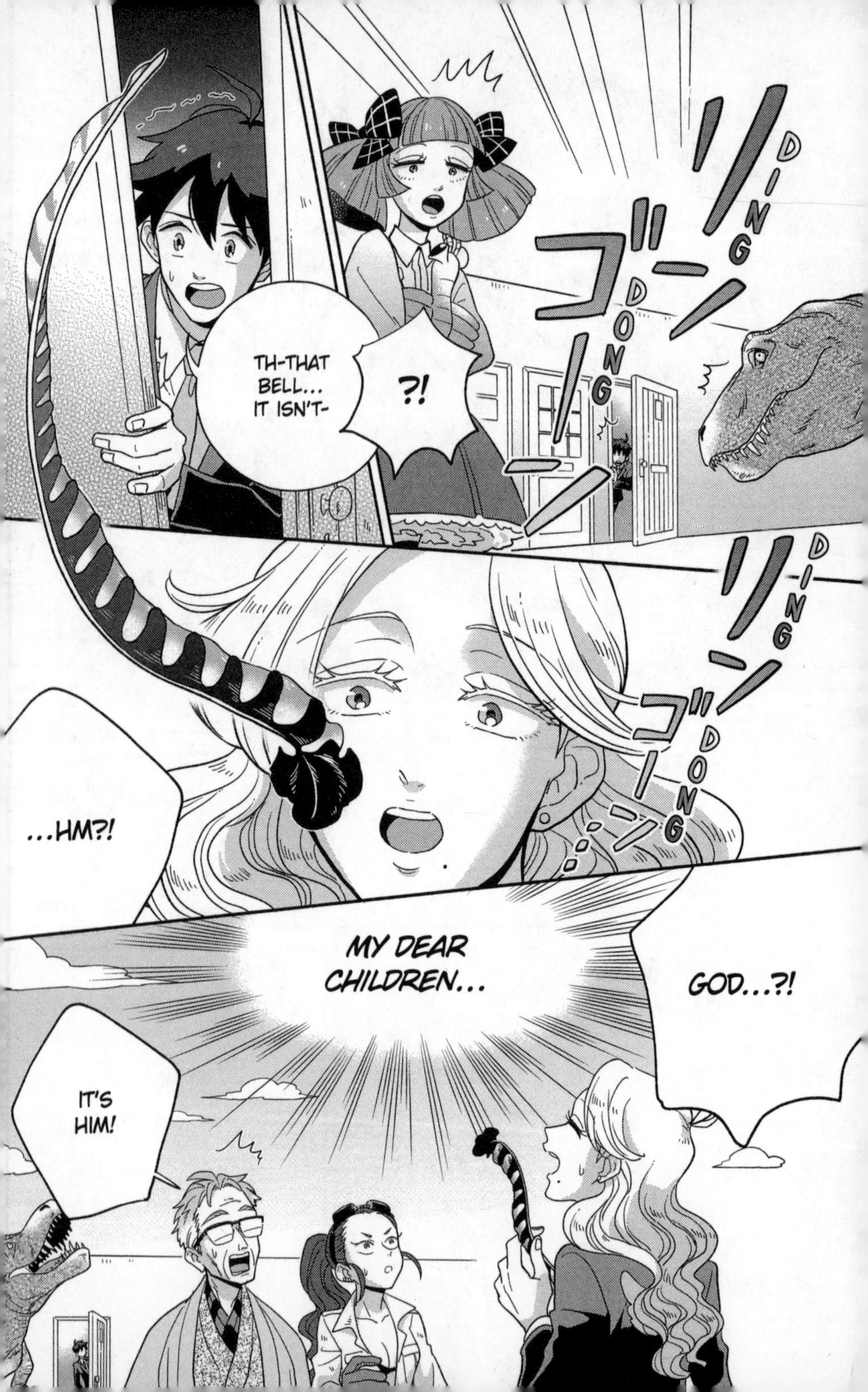
DING DING DONG DONG
?!
TH-THAT BELL... IT ISN'T-
DING DING DONG DONG
...HM?!
GOD...?!
MY DEAR CHILDREN...
IT'S HIM!

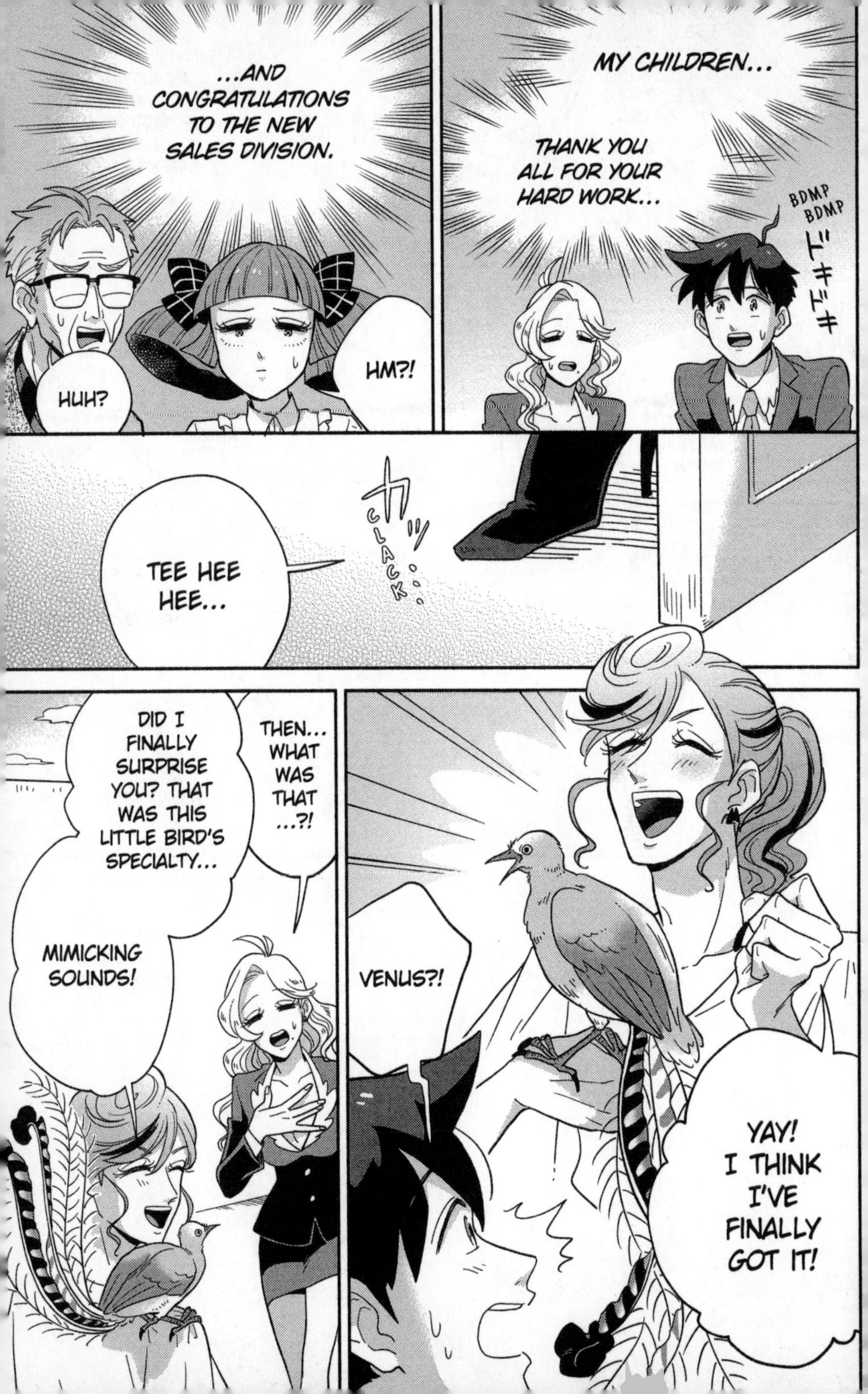
MY CHILDREN...
THANK YOU ALL FOR YOUR HARD WORK...
BDMP BDMP
ドキドキ
...AND CONGRATULATIONS TO THE NEW SALES DIVISION.
HM?!
HUH?
カッ
CLACK
TEE HEE HEE...
YAY! I THINK I'VE FINALLY GOT IT!
VENUS?!
THEN... WHAT WAS THAT...?!
DID I FINALLY SURPRISE YOU? THAT WAS THIS LITTLE BIRD'S SPECIALTY...
MIMICKING SOUNDS!

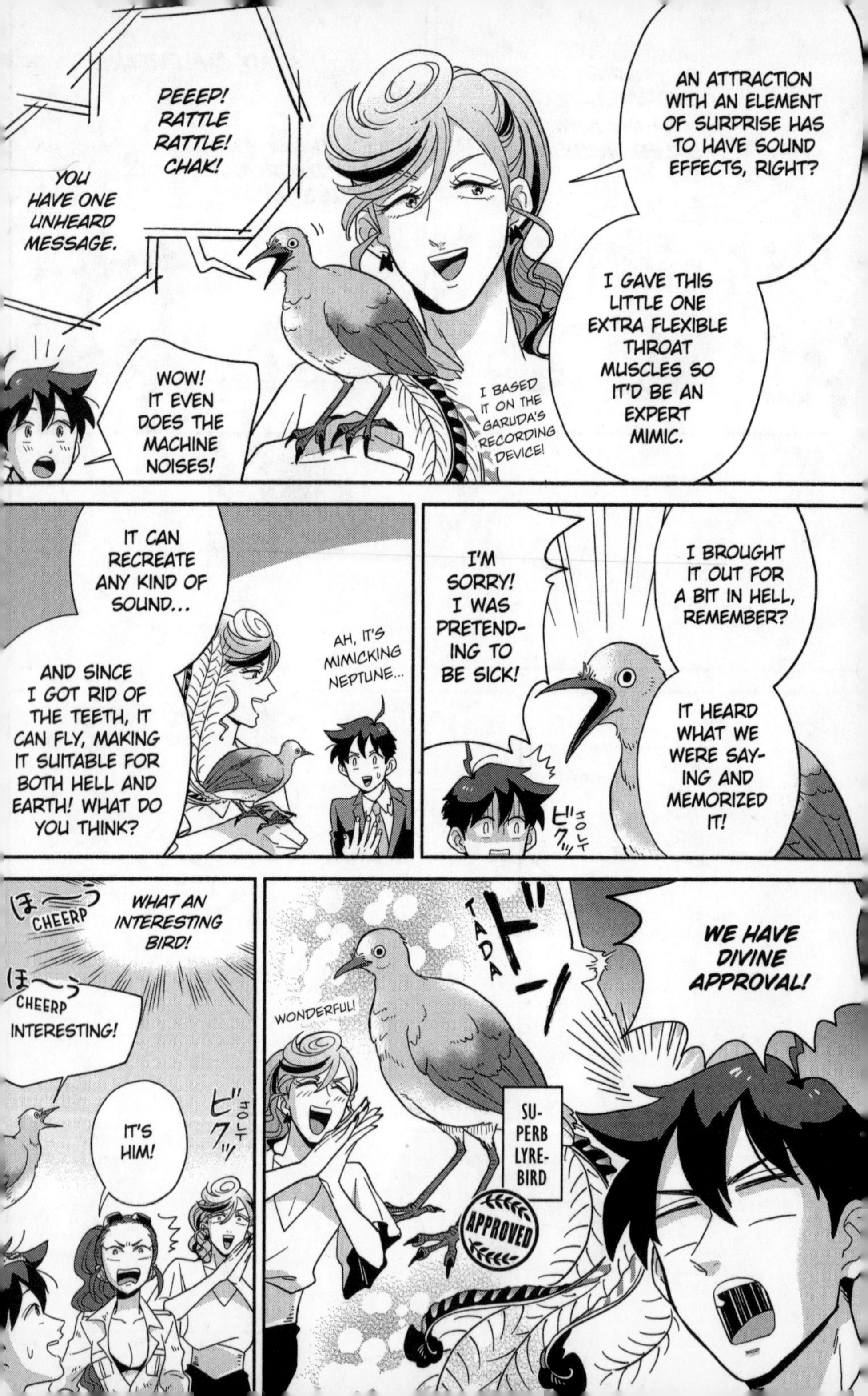
AN ATTRACTION WITH AN ELEMENT OF SURPRISE HAS TO HAVE SOUND EFFECTS, RIGHT?
I GAVE THIS LITTLE ONE EXTRA FLEXIBLE THROAT MUSCLES SO IT'D BE AN EXPERT MIMIC.
I BASED IT ON THE GARUDA'S RECORDING DEVICE!
PEEEP! RATTLE RATTLE! CHAK!
YOU HAVE ONE UNHEARD MESSAGE.
WOW! IT EVEN DOES THE MACHINE NOISES!
I BROUGHT IT OUT FOR A BIT IN HELL, REMEMBER?
I'M SORRY! I WAS PRETEND-ING TO BE SICK!
IT HEARD WHAT WE WERE SAY-ING AND MEMORIZED IT!
ビクッ JOLT
IT CAN RECREATE ANY KIND OF SOUND...
AH, IT'S MIMICKING NEPTUNE...
AND SINCE I GOT RID OF THE TEETH, IT CAN FLY, MAKING IT SUITABLE FOR BOTH HELL AND EARTH! WHAT DO YOU THINK?
WE HAVE DIVINE APPROVAL!
ドーン TADA
WONDERFUL!
SU-PERB LYRE-BIRD
APPROVED
WHAT AN INTERESTING BIRD!
ほ〜う CHEERP
ほ〜う CHEERP
INTERESTING!
ビクッ JOLT
IT'S HIM!

THE ENCYCLOPEDIA OF REAL ANIMALS 22

ANIMAL 56 | SUPERB LYREBIRD

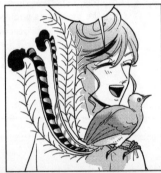

THE REAL THING

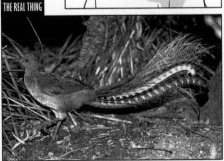

The superb lyrebird is also known for its extremely long tail feathers.

Photo: Jeurgen & Christine Sohns/Aflo

[Name] *Menura novaehollandiae*
[Classification] Class: Aves
Order: Passeriformes
Family: Menuridae
Genus: *Menura*
[Habitat] Eastern Australia
[Length] 100 cm (3.3 ft) (including the tail)

The largest bird in the order Passeriformes, the superb lyrebird is known for its exceptional mimicry, and can mimic sounds ranging from the songs of other bird species to mechanical noises including camera shutters and car alarms. Though theories regarding this level of accuracy are still being studied, it is thought that the simplicity of the bird's syrinx (vocal organ) may be a factor—instead of the four sets of syringeal muscles typical in other bird species, the lyrebird has only three. Combining several different songs from its repertoire, the superb lyrebird generally sings for 20 minutes at a time.

During mating season, the females of the species are drawn to the males that perform the most sophisticated songs. Males also create territorial dancing mounds where they stage elaborate courtship displays involving fanning out their tails to cover their heads and performing a peculiar dance.

ANIMAL 57 TYRANNOSAURUS REX

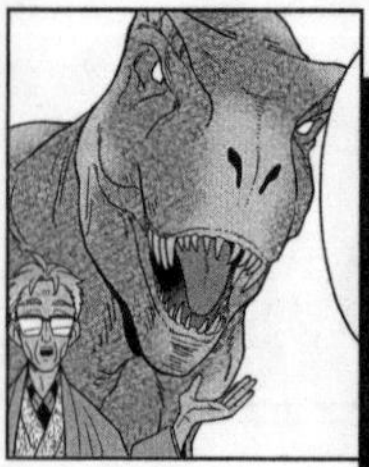

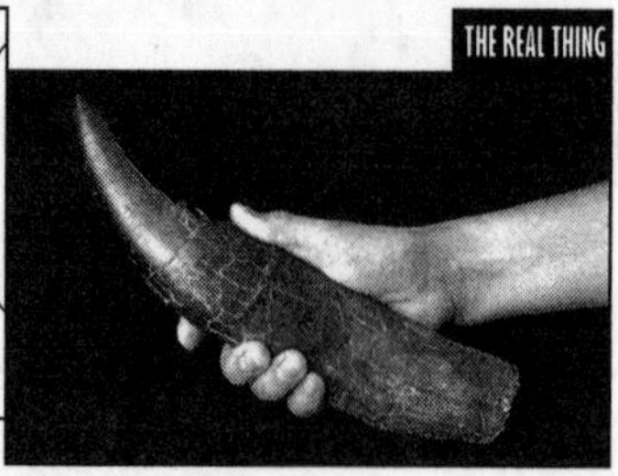
THE REAL THING

Tyrannosaurus rex teeth reach up to 25 cm (10 in) in length, with serrated edges like a steak knife.

Photo: Ardea/Aflo

[Name] *Tyrannosaurus rex*
[Classification] Class: Reptilia
Order: Saurischia
Family: Tyrannosauridae
Genus: *Tyrannosaurus*
[Habitat] North America
[Length] 12-13 m (39-42 ft)

The largest carnivorous dinosaur, the Tyrannosaurus rex ate mainly large herbivores using jaws nine times more powerful than those of an alligator. Its olfactory bulb comprised around 70% of its brain, giving it an extremely keen sense of smell. Opinions are divided as to whether or not the T. rex had feathers, and some scientists have theorized that the dinosaur's young may have had them as protection against the cold.

ANIMAL 58 PARADOX FROG

The paradox frog measures up to 25 cm (10 in) as a tadpole, and then shrinks to a fourth of that size once it becomes an adult. The reason for this change in size isn't clear, but one theory posits that the large size of the tadpole makes it less affected by factors like water quality and salinity, thus allowing it to thrive in brackish waters.

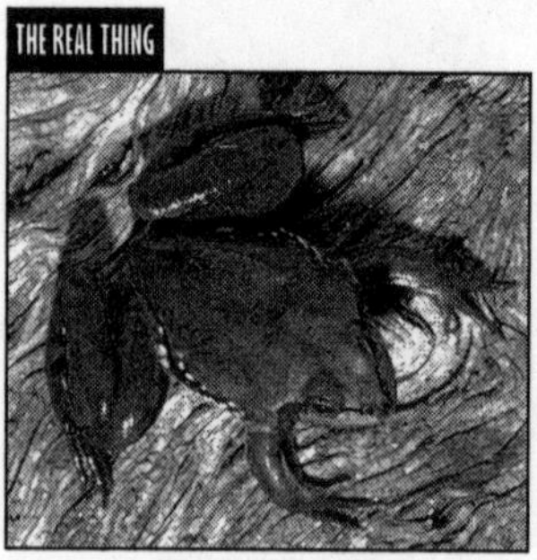
THE REAL THING

Photo: Science Source/Aflo

Because of the energy inefficiency of its large size, the paradox frog shrinks when it becomes an adult.

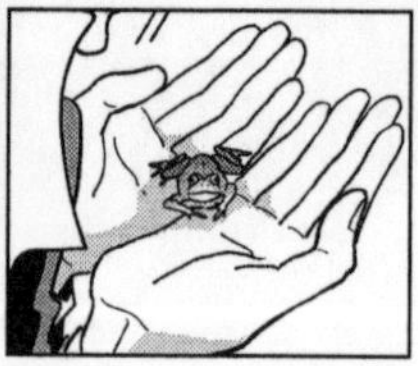

[Name] *Pseudis paradoxa*
[Classification] Class: Amphibia
Order: Anura
Family: Hylidae
Genus: *Pseudus*
[Habitat] South America
[Length] 6.5-7.5 cm (2.6-2.8 in)

HEAVEN'S DESIGN TEAM

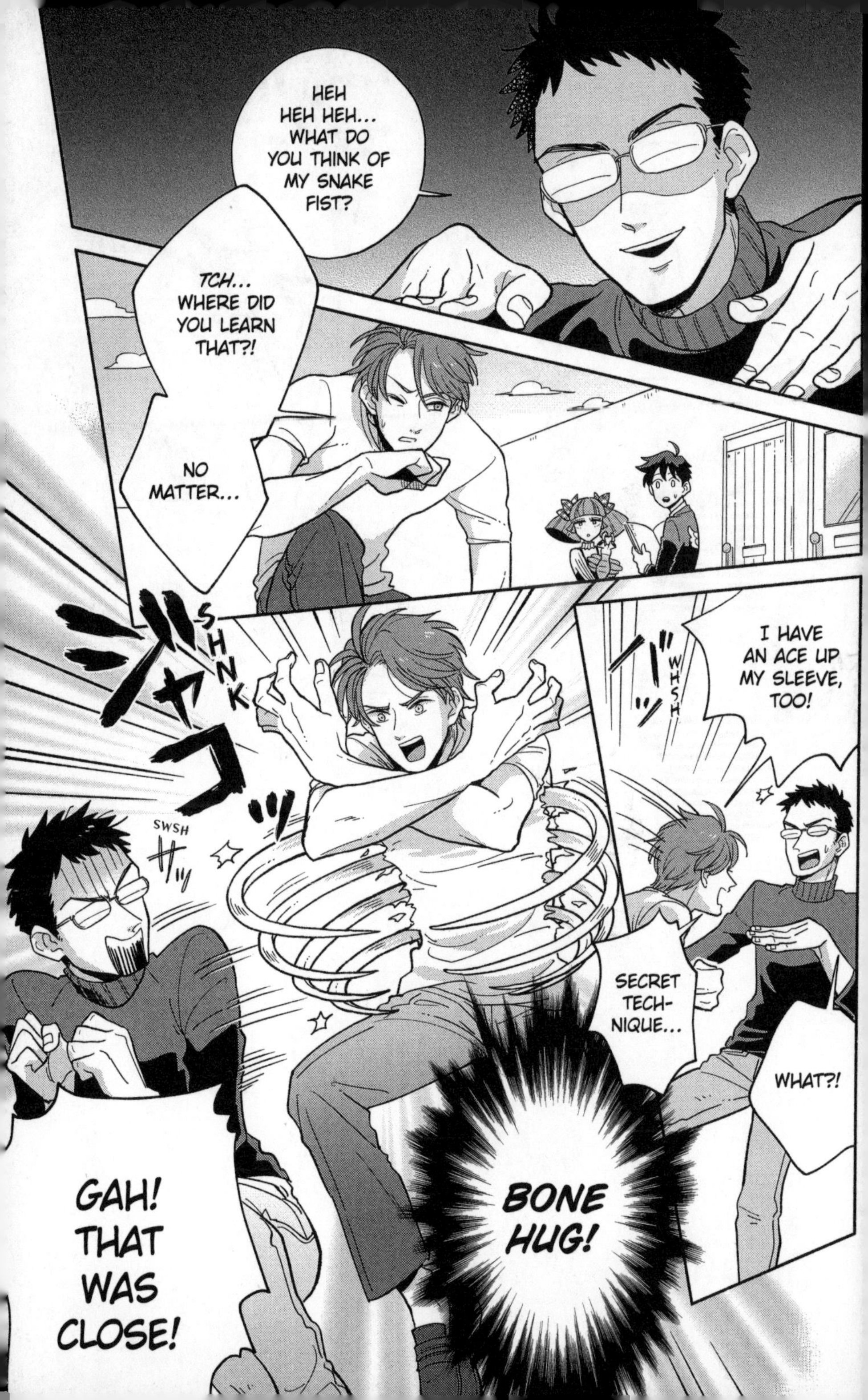
HEH HEH HEH... WHAT DO YOU THINK OF MY SNAKE FIST?
TCH... WHERE DID YOU LEARN THAT?!
NO MATTER...
I HAVE AN ACE UP MY SLEEVE, TOO!
WHSH
WHAT?!
SHNK
SECRET TECH-NIQUE...
BONE HUG!
SWSH
GAH! THAT WAS CLOSE!

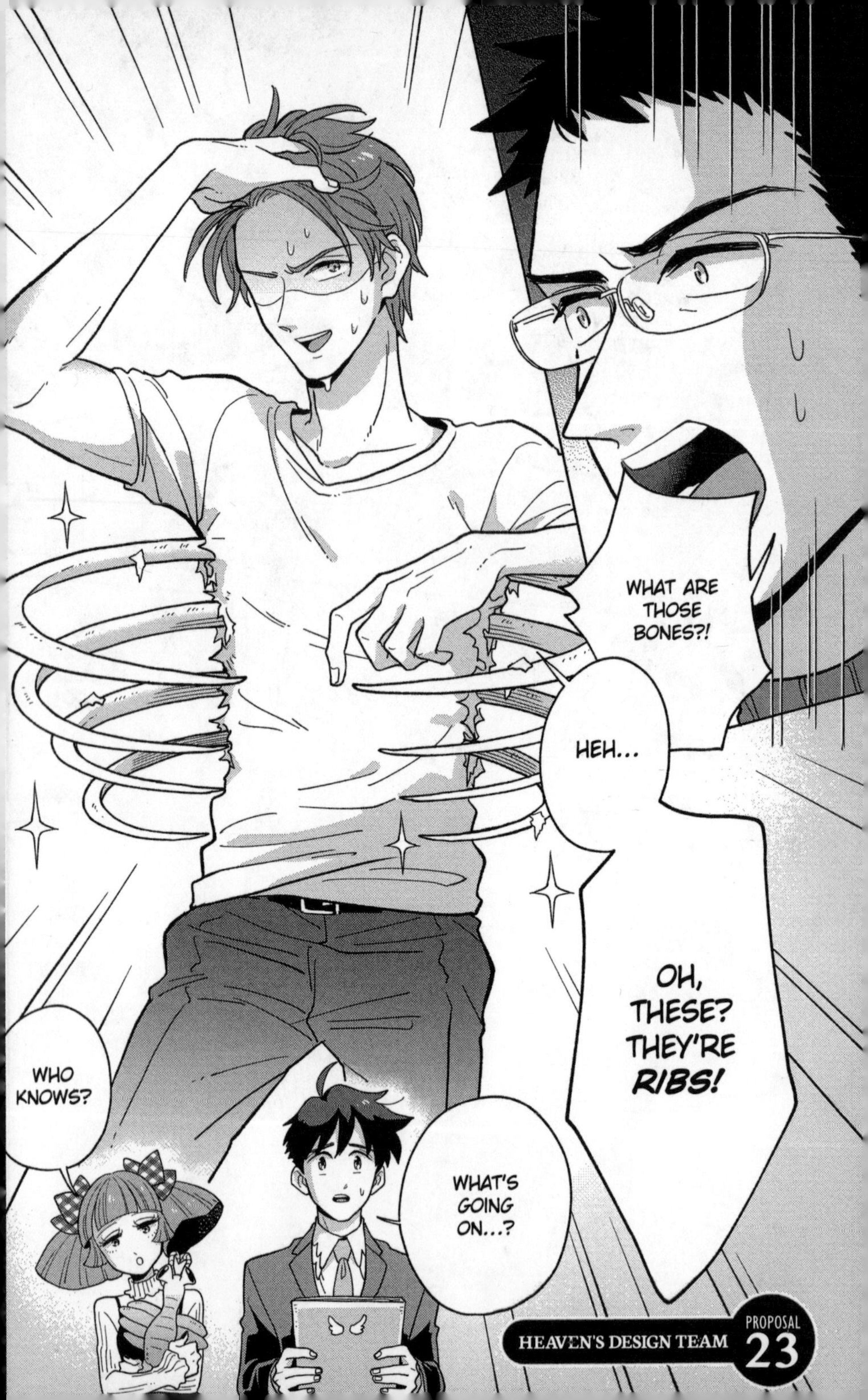
WHAT ARE THOSE BONES?!
HEH...
OH, THESE? THEY'RE *RIBS!*
WHAT'S GOING ON...?
WHO KNOWS?
HEAVEN'S DESIGN TEAM
PROPOSAL 23

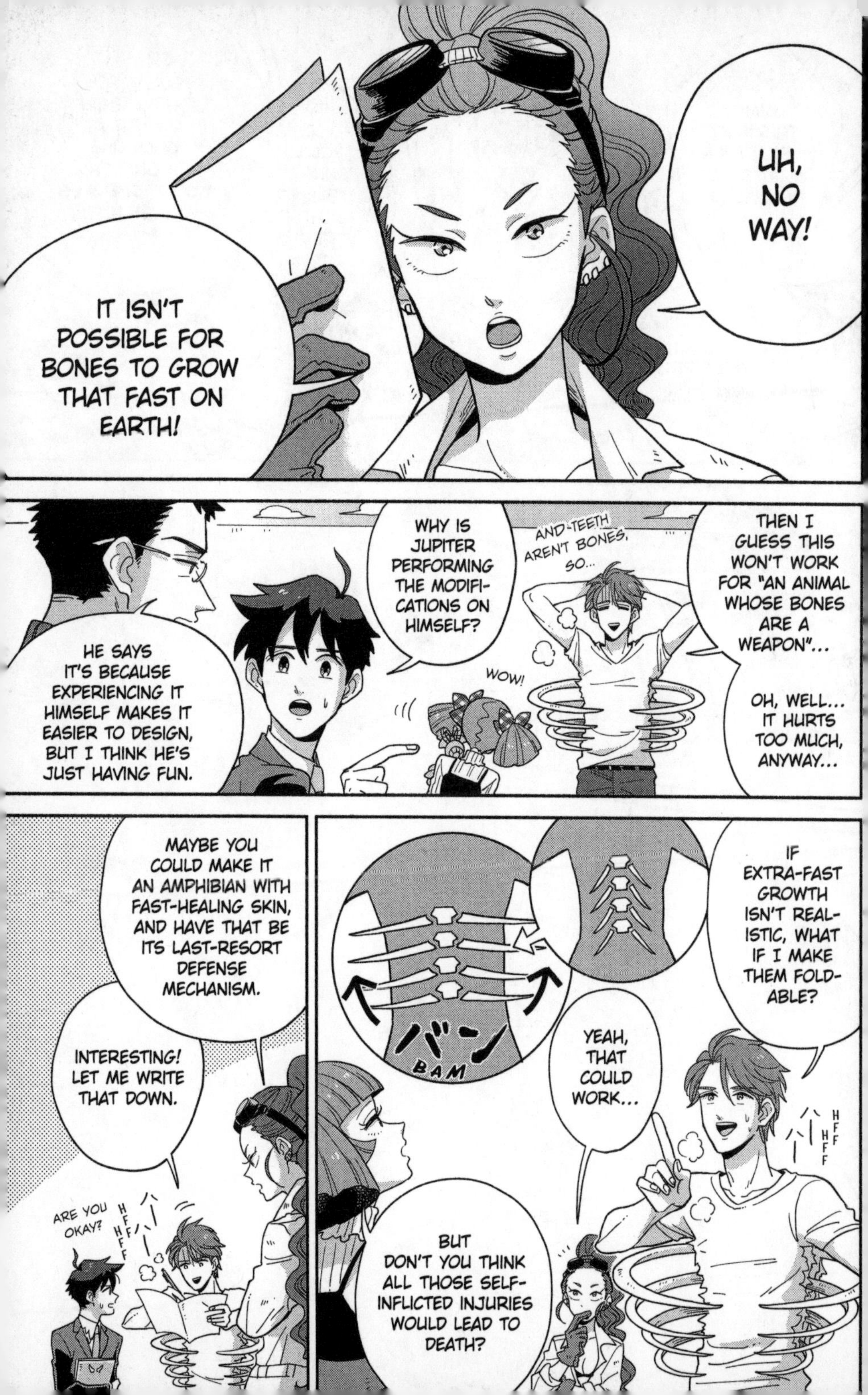
UH, NO WAY!
IT ISN'T POSSIBLE FOR BONES TO GROW THAT FAST ON EARTH!
THEN I GUESS THIS WON'T WORK FOR "AN ANIMAL WHOSE BONES ARE A WEAPON"...
OH, WELL... IT HURTS TOO MUCH, ANYWAY...
AND TEETH AREN'T BONES, SO...
WOW!
WHY IS JUPITER PERFORMING THE MODIFICATIONS ON HIMSELF?
HE SAYS IT'S BECAUSE EXPERIENCING IT HIMSELF MAKES IT EASIER TO DESIGN, BUT I THINK HE'S JUST HAVING FUN.
IF EXTRA-FAST GROWTH ISN'T REALISTIC, WHAT IF I MAKE THEM FOLDABLE?
バーン
BAM
YEAH, THAT COULD WORK...
HFF HFF
BUT DON'T YOU THINK ALL THOSE SELF-INFLICTED INJURIES WOULD LEAD TO DEATH?
MAYBE YOU COULD MAKE IT AN AMPHIBIAN WITH FAST-HEALING SKIN, AND HAVE THAT BE ITS LAST-RESORT DEFENSE MECHANISM.
INTERESTING! LET ME WRITE THAT DOWN.
HFF HFF
ARE YOU OKAY?

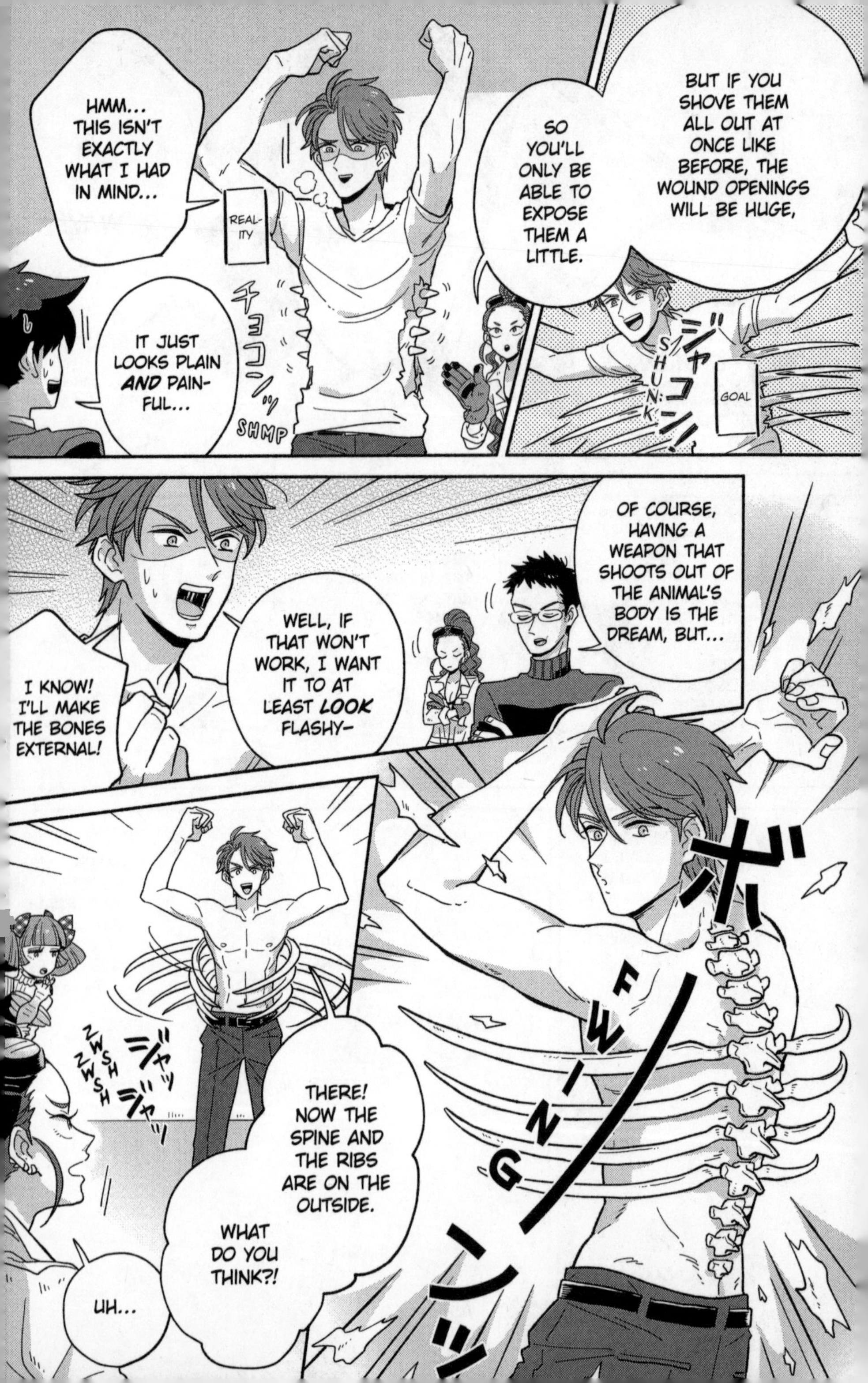
BUT IF YOU SHOVE THEM ALL OUT AT ONCE LIKE BEFORE, THE WOUND OPENINGS WILL BE HUGE,
SO YOU'LL ONLY BE ABLE TO EXPOSE THEM A LITTLE.
GOAL
ジャコン!
SHUNK
HMM... THIS ISN'T EXACTLY WHAT I HAD IN MIND...
REAL-ITY
チョコン
SHMP
IT JUST LOOKS PLAIN AND PAIN-FUL...
OF COURSE, HAVING A WEAPON THAT SHOOTS OUT OF THE ANIMAL'S BODY IS THE DREAM, BUT...
WELL, IF THAT WON'T WORK, I WANT IT TO AT LEAST LOOK FLASHY-
I KNOW! I'LL MAKE THE BONES EXTERNAL!
ズバン
FWING
THERE! NOW THE SPINE AND THE RIBS ARE ON THE OUTSIDE.
WHAT DO YOU THINK?!
ジャッ
ジャッ
ZWSH
ZWSH
UH...

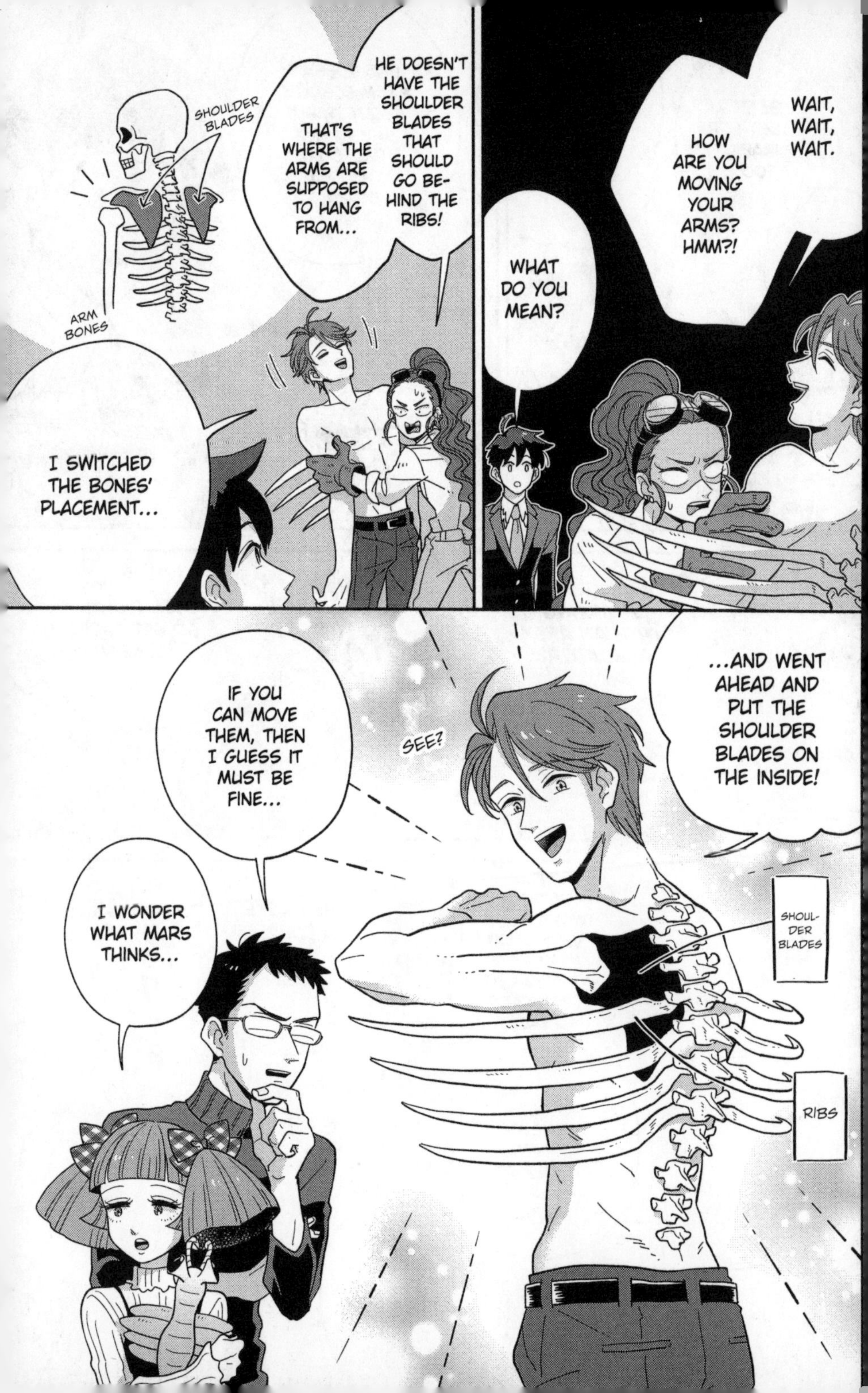
WAIT, WAIT, WAIT.
HOW ARE YOU MOVING YOUR ARMS? HMM?!
WHAT DO YOU MEAN?
HE DOESN'T HAVE THE SHOULDER BLADES THAT SHOULD GO BE-HIND THE RIBS!
THAT'S WHERE THE ARMS ARE SUPPOSED TO HANG FROM...
SHOULDER BLADES
ARM BONES
I SWITCHED THE BONES' PLACEMENT...
...AND WENT AHEAD AND PUT THE SHOULDER BLADES ON THE INSIDE!
SEE?
SHOUL-DER BLADES
RIBS
IF YOU CAN MOVE THEM, THEN I GUESS IT MUST BE FINE...
I WONDER WHAT MARS THINKS...

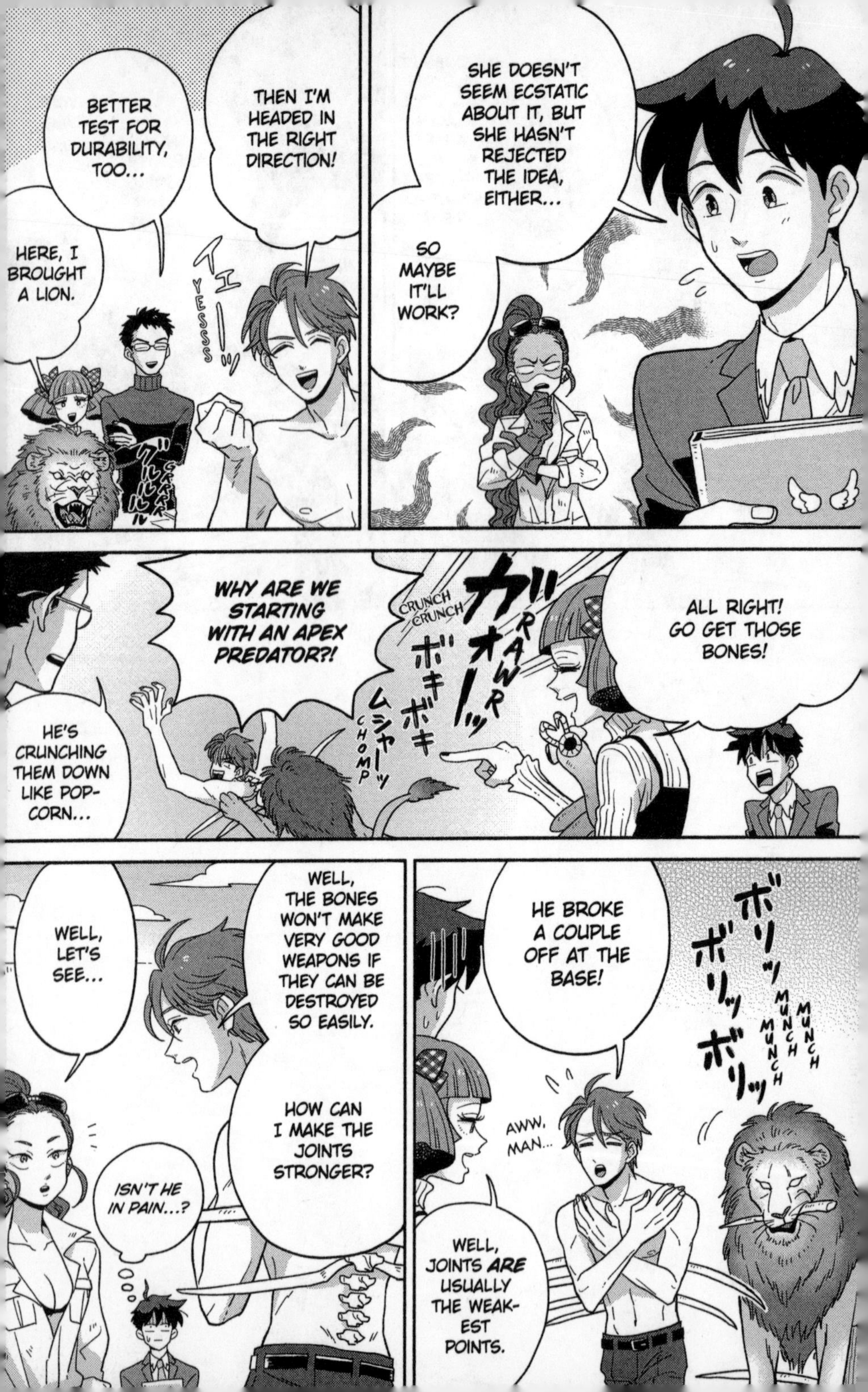

SHE DOESN'T SEEM ECSTATIC ABOUT IT, BUT SHE HASN'T REJECTED THE IDEA, EITHER...
SO MAYBE IT'LL WORK?
THEN I'M HEADED IN THE RIGHT DIRECTION!
イエー!! YESSS!!
BETTER TEST FOR DURABILITY, TOO...
HERE, I BROUGHT A LION.
グルルル GRRR
ALL RIGHT! GO GET THOSE BONES!
ガオーッ RAWR
CRUNCH CRUNCH
ボキボキ
ムシャーッ CHOMP
WHY ARE WE STARTING WITH AN APEX PREDATOR?!
HE'S CRUNCHING THEM DOWN LIKE POP-CORN...
ボリッ ボリッ ボリッ MUNCH MUNCH MUNCH
HE BROKE A COUPLE OFF AT THE BASE!
AWW, MAN...
WELL, JOINTS *ARE* USUALLY THE WEAK-EST POINTS.
WELL, THE BONES WON'T MAKE VERY GOOD WEAPONS IF THEY CAN BE DESTROYED SO EASILY.
WELL, LET'S SEE...
HOW CAN I MAKE THE JOINTS STRONGER?
ISN'T HE IN PAIN...?

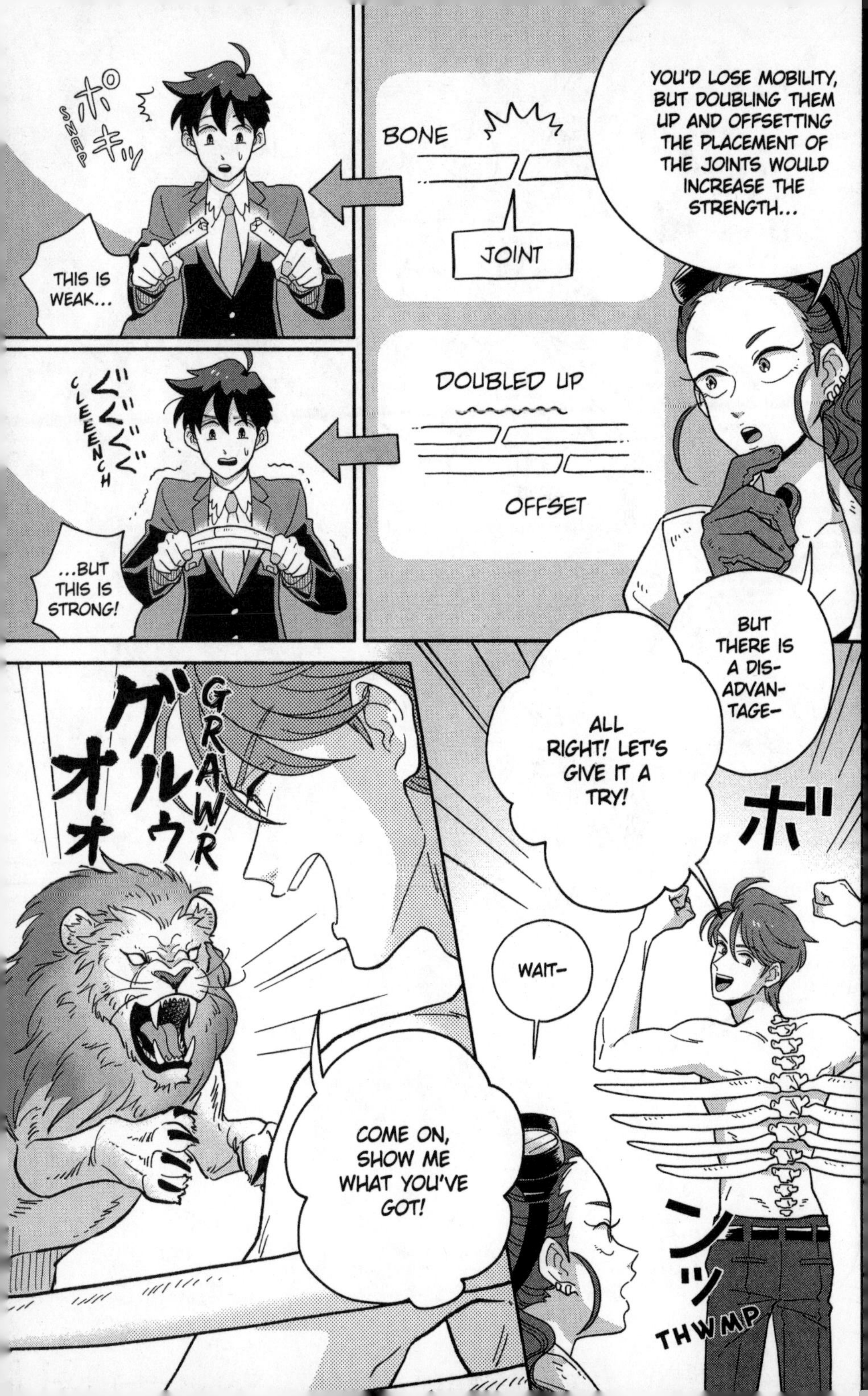
YOU'D LOSE MOBILITY, BUT DOUBLING THEM UP AND OFFSETTING THE PLACEMENT OF THE JOINTS WOULD INCREASE THE STRENGTH...
BONE
JOINT
ポキッ
SNAP
THIS IS WEAK...
DOUBLED UP
OFFSET
ぐぐぐぐ
CLEEENCH
...BUT THIS IS STRONG!
BUT THERE IS A DIS-ADVAN-TAGE-
ALL RIGHT! LET'S GIVE IT A TRY!
ボ
WAIT-
ンッ
THWMP
グルウオオ
GRAWR
COME ON, SHOW ME WHAT YOU'VE GOT!

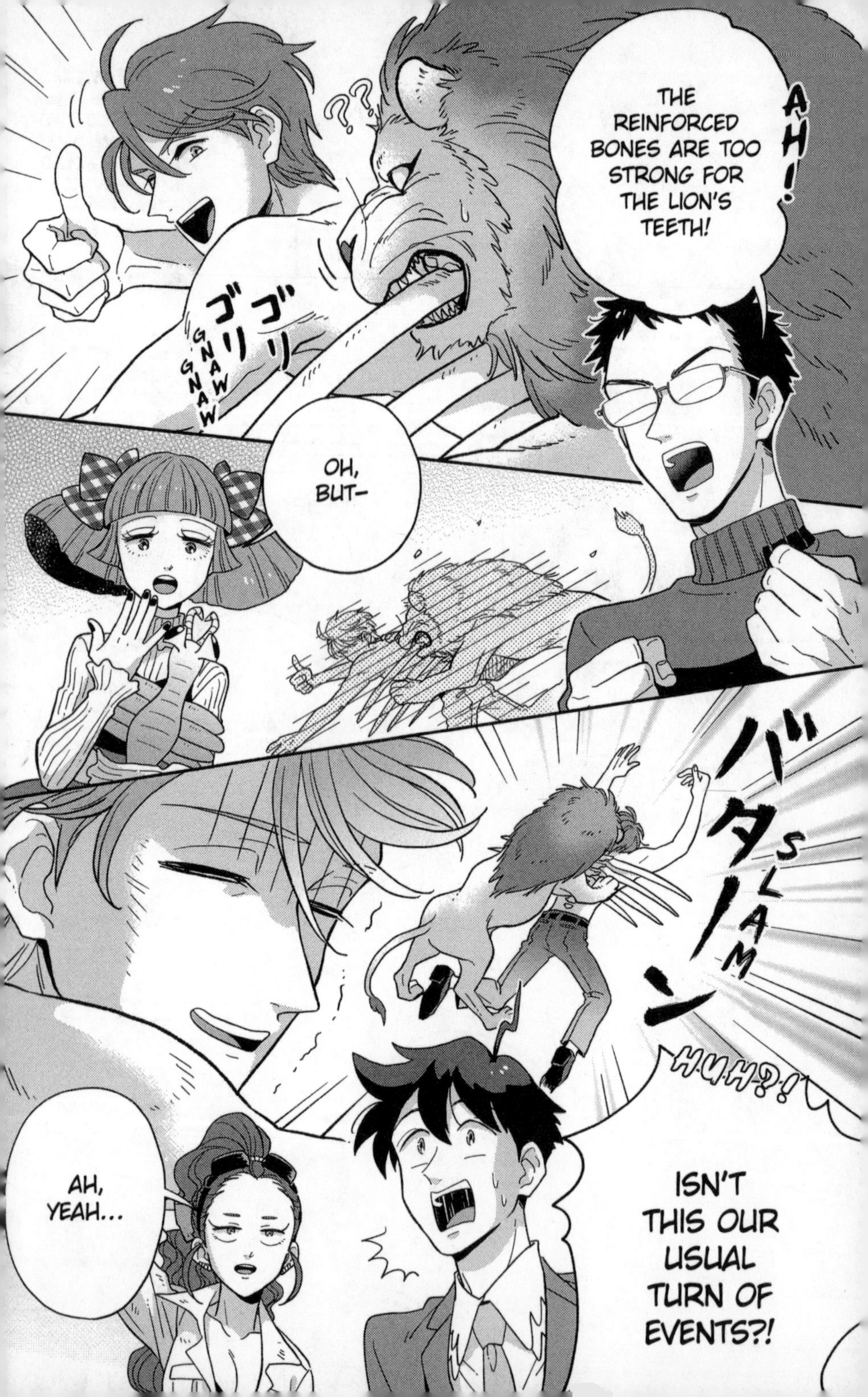
AH!
THE REINFORCED BONES ARE TOO STRONG FOR THE LION'S TEETH!
ゴリゴリ
GNAW GNAW
OH, BUT-
バタン
SLAM
HUH?!
ISN'T THIS OUR USUAL TURN OF EVENTS?!
AH, YEAH...

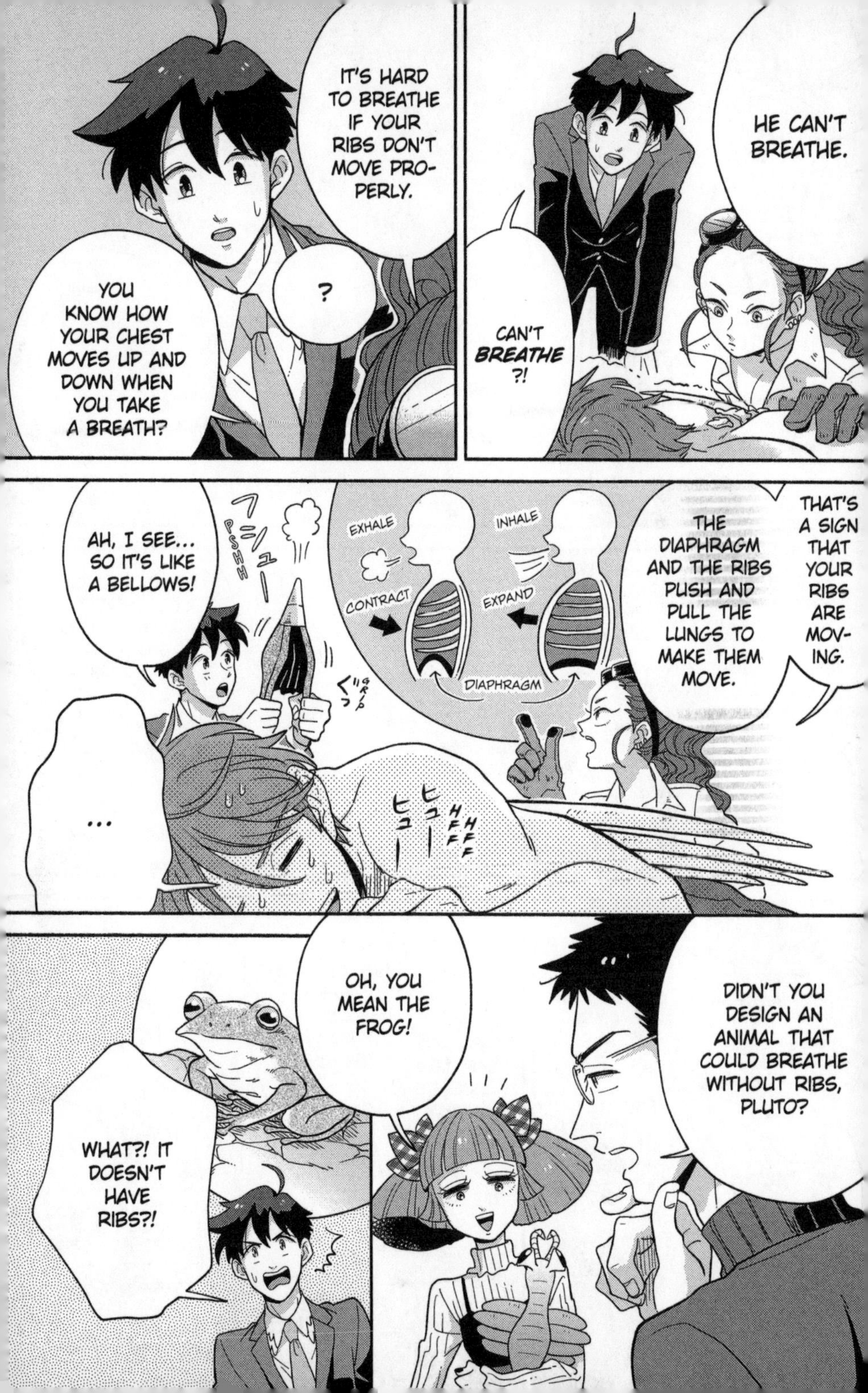
HE CAN'T BREATHE.
CAN'T *BREATHE*?!
IT'S HARD TO BREATHE IF YOUR RIBS DON'T MOVE PRO-PERLY.
?
YOU KNOW HOW YOUR CHEST MOVES UP AND DOWN WHEN YOU TAKE A BREATH?
THAT'S A SIGN THAT YOUR RIBS ARE MOV-ING.
THE DIAPHRAGM AND THE RIBS PUSH AND PULL THE LUNGS TO MAKE THEM MOVE.
INHALE
EXPAND
EXHALE
CONTRACT
DIAPHRAGM
HFFF
HFFF
GRIP
PSHH
AH, I SEE... SO IT'S LIKE A BELLOWS!
...
DIDN'T YOU DESIGN AN ANIMAL THAT COULD BREATHE WITHOUT RIBS, PLUTO?
OH, YOU MEAN THE FROG!
WHAT?! IT DOESN'T HAVE RIBS?!

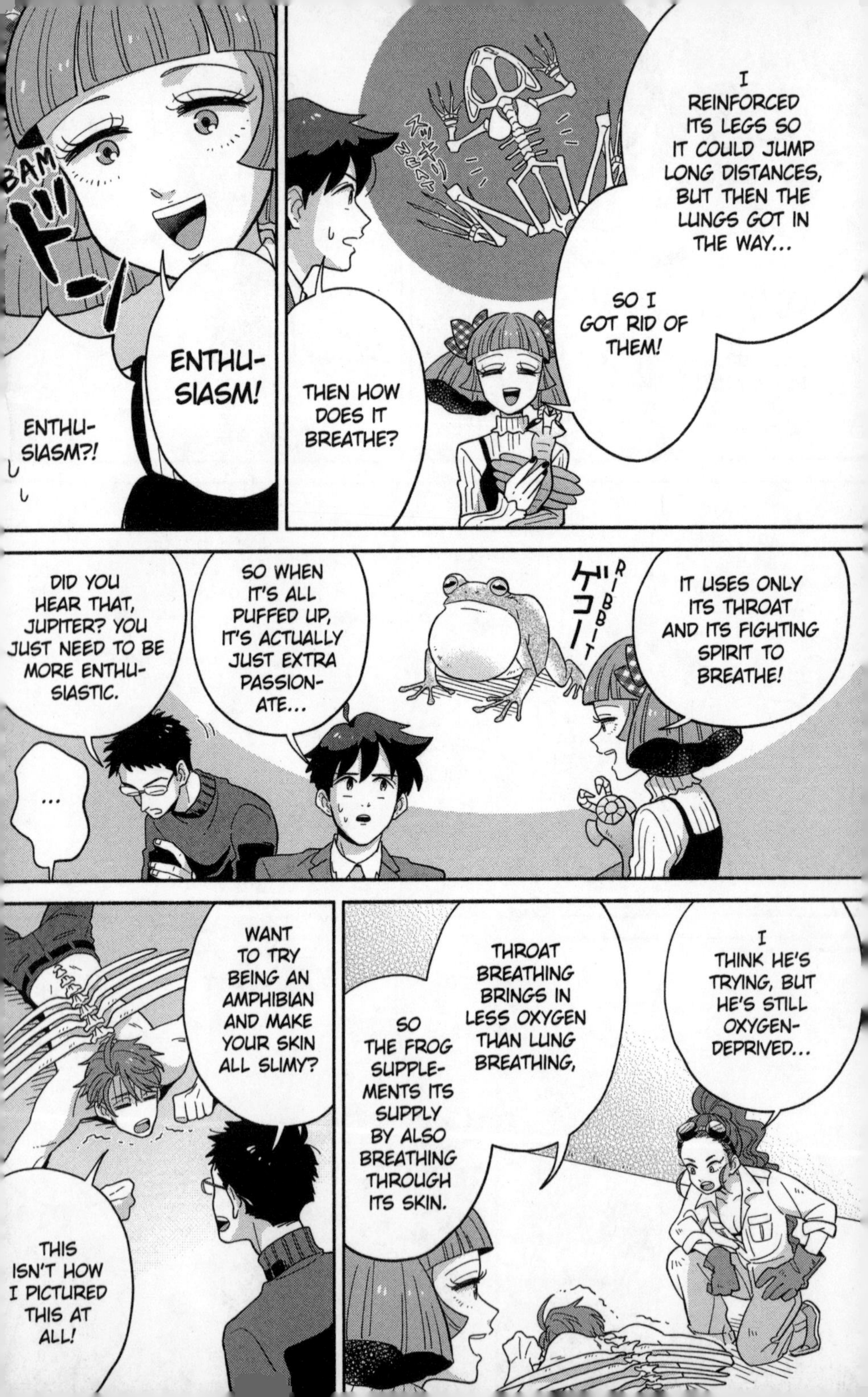
I REINFORCED ITS LEGS SO IT COULD JUMP LONG DISTANCES, BUT THEN THE LUNGS GOT IN THE WAY...
SO I GOT RID OF THEM!
THEN HOW DOES IT BREATHE?
BAM
ドーン
ENTHU-SIASM!
ENTHU-SIASM?!
IT USES ONLY ITS THROAT AND ITS FIGHTING SPIRIT TO BREATHE!
RIBBIT
ゲコー
SO WHEN IT'S ALL PUFFED UP, IT'S ACTUALLY JUST EXTRA PASSION-ATE...
DID YOU HEAR THAT, JUPITER? YOU JUST NEED TO BE MORE ENTHU-SIASTIC.
...
I THINK HE'S TRYING, BUT HE'S STILL OXYGEN-DEPRIVED...
THROAT BREATHING BRINGS IN LESS OXYGEN THAN LUNG BREATHING,
SO THE FROG SUPPLE-MENTS ITS SUPPLY BY ALSO BREATHING THROUGH ITS SKIN.
WANT TO TRY BEING AN AMPHIBIAN AND MAKE YOUR SKIN ALL SLIMY?
THIS ISN'T HOW I PICTURED THIS AT ALL!

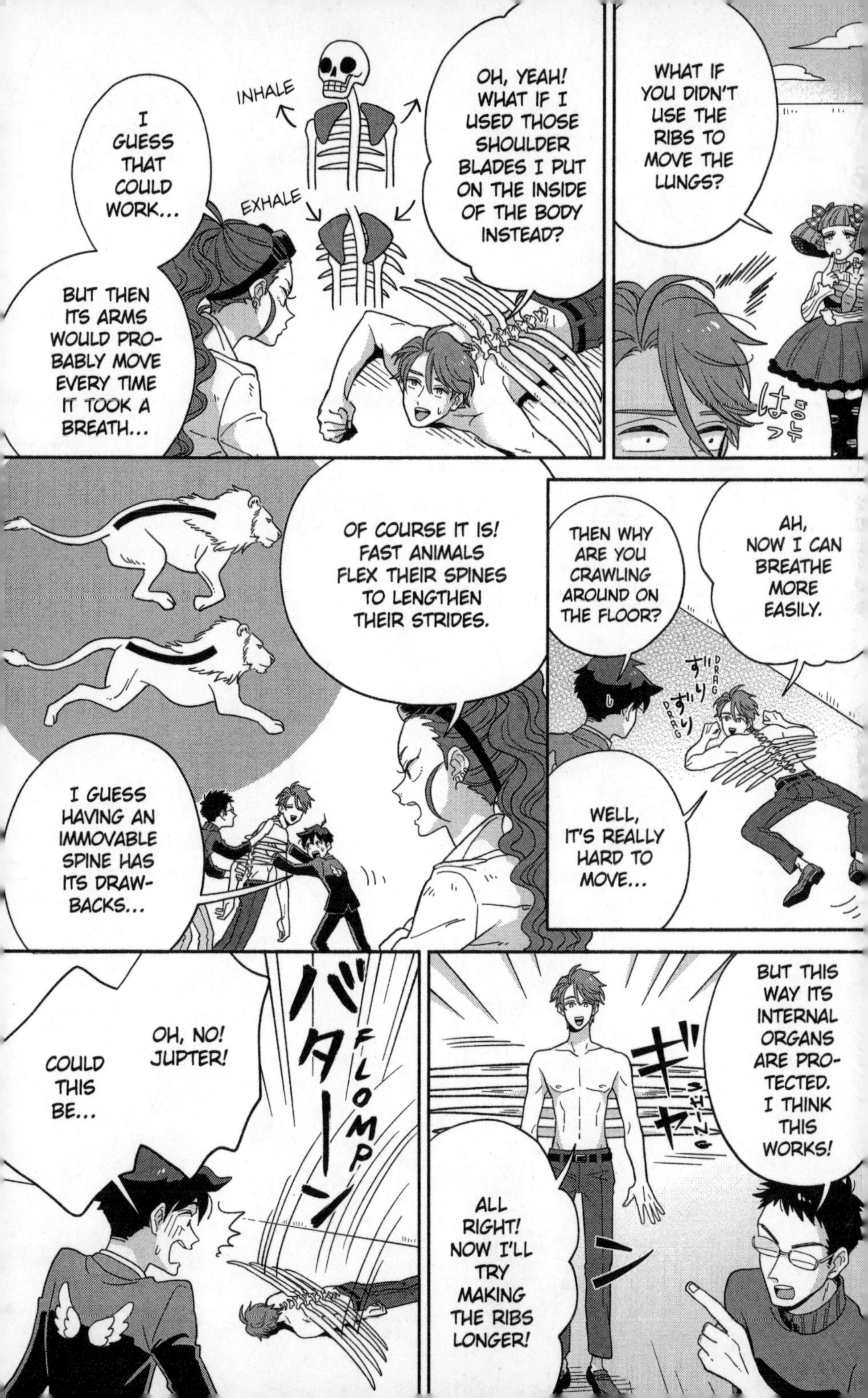
WHAT IF YOU DIDN'T USE THE RIBS TO MOVE THE LUNGS?
は
OH, YEAH! WHAT IF I USED THOSE SHOULDER BLADES I PUT ON THE INSIDE OF THE BODY INSTEAD?
INHALE
EXHALE
I GUESS THAT COULD WORK...
BUT THEN ITS ARMS WOULD PROBABLY MOVE EVERY TIME IT TOOK A BREATH...
AH, NOW I CAN BREATHE MORE EASILY.
THEN WHY ARE YOU CRAWLING AROUND ON THE FLOOR?
ずり DRAG
ずり DRAG
WELL, IT'S REALLY HARD TO MOVE...
OF COURSE IT IS! FAST ANIMALS FLEX THEIR SPINES TO LENGTHEN THEIR STRIDES.
I GUESS HAVING AN IMMOVABLE SPINE HAS ITS DRAWBACKS...
BUT THIS WAY ITS INTERNAL ORGANS ARE PROTECTED. I THINK THIS WORKS!
ギャ SHING
ALL RIGHT! NOW I'LL TRY MAKING THE RIBS LONGER!
バターン FLOMP
OH, NO! JUPTER!
COULD THIS BE...

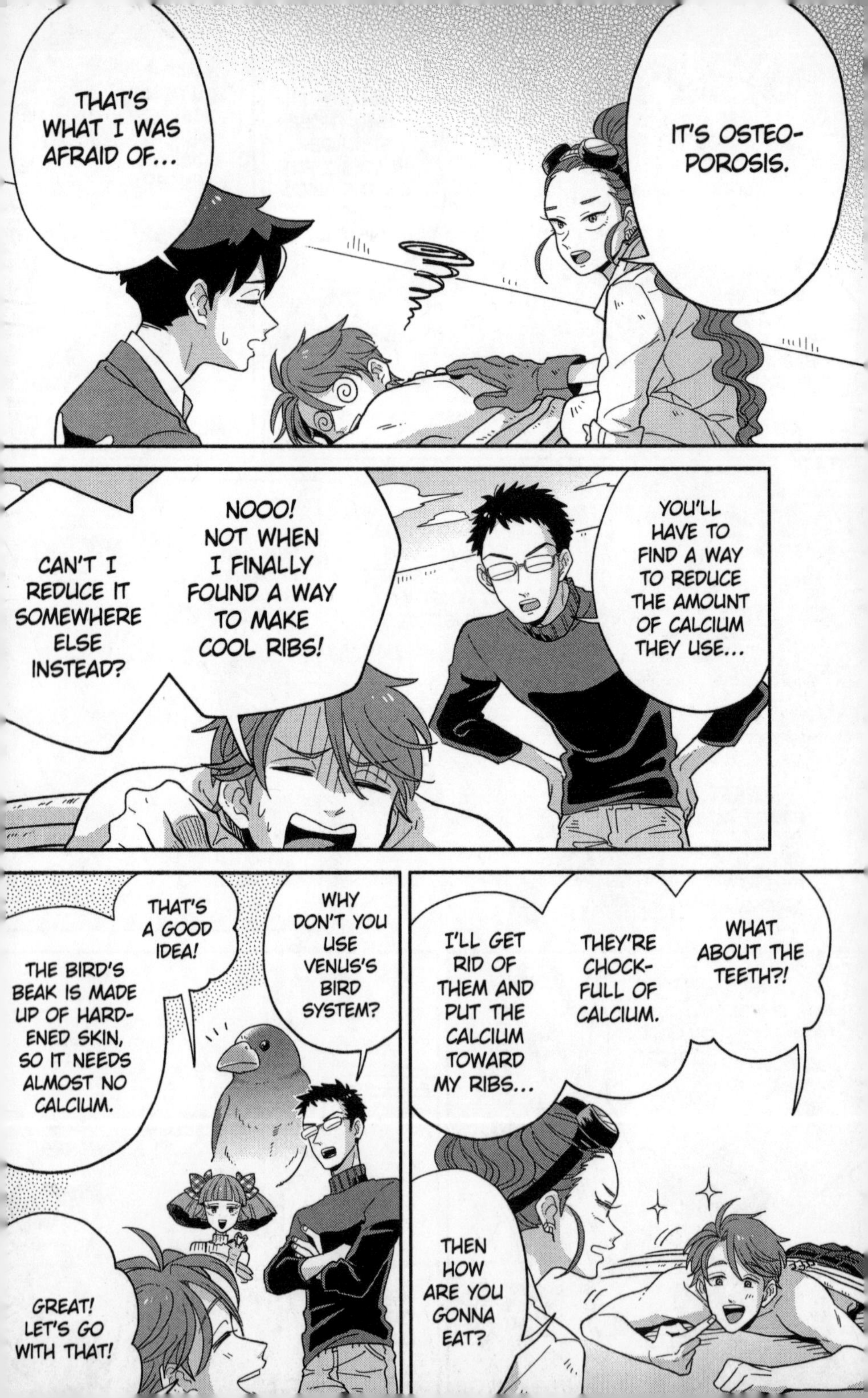
IT'S OSTEO-POROSIS.
THAT'S WHAT I WAS AFRAID OF...
YOU'LL HAVE TO FIND A WAY TO REDUCE THE AMOUNT OF CALCIUM THEY USE...
NOOO! NOT WHEN I FINALLY FOUND A WAY TO MAKE COOL RIBS!
CAN'T I REDUCE IT SOMEWHERE ELSE INSTEAD?
WHAT ABOUT THE TEETH?!
THEY'RE CHOCK-FULL OF CALCIUM.
I'LL GET RID OF THEM AND PUT THE CALCIUM TOWARD MY RIBS...
THEN HOW ARE YOU GONNA EAT?
WHY DON'T YOU USE VENUS'S BIRD SYSTEM?
THAT'S A GOOD IDEA!
THE BIRD'S BEAK IS MADE UP OF HARD-ENED SKIN, SO IT NEEDS ALMOST NO CALCIUM.
GREAT! LET'S GO WITH THAT!

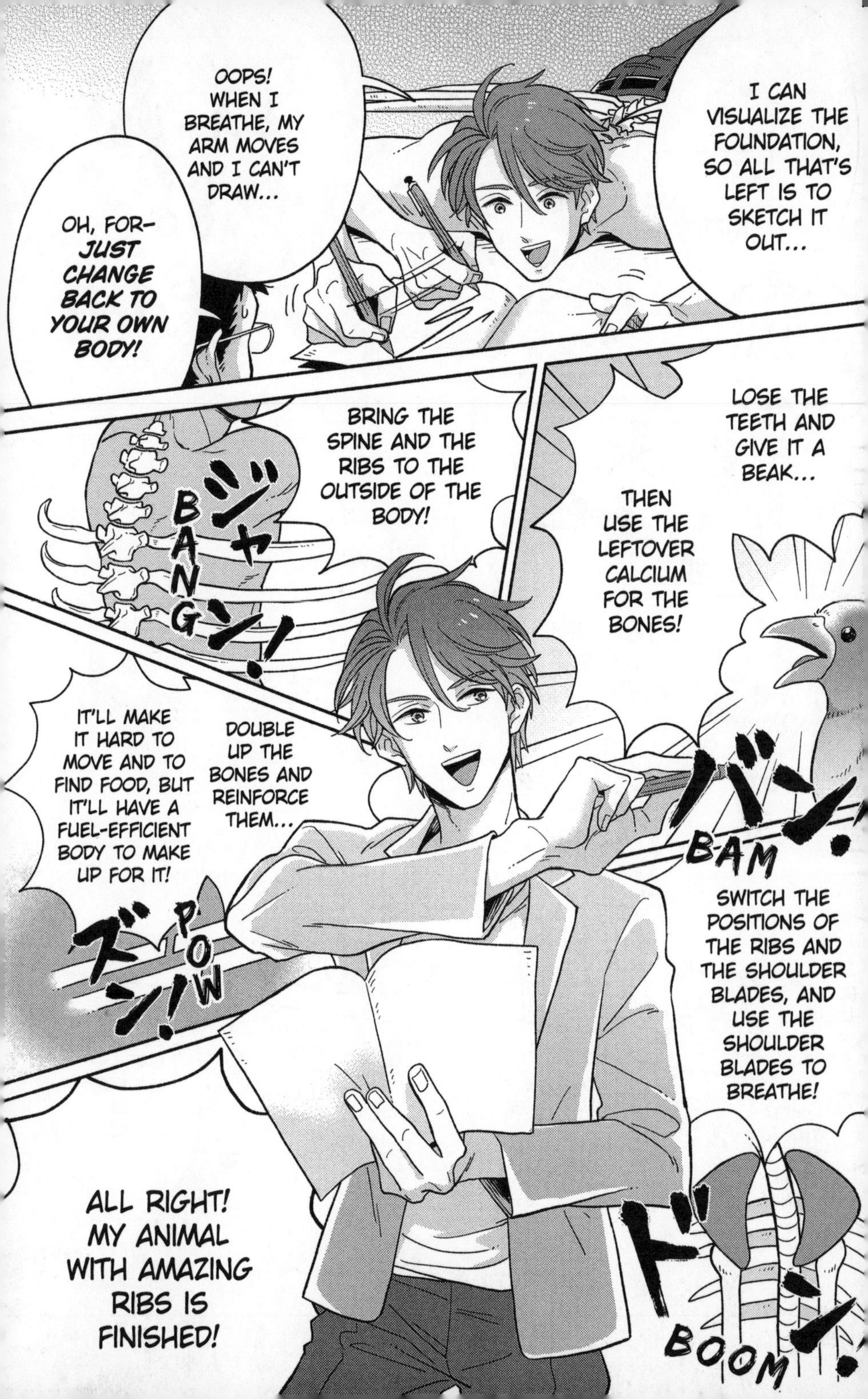
I CAN VISUALIZE THE FOUNDATION, SO ALL THAT'S LEFT IS TO SKETCH IT OUT...
OOPS! WHEN I BREATHE, MY ARM MOVES AND I CAN'T DRAW...
OH, FOR– *JUST CHANGE BACK TO YOUR OWN BODY!*
LOSE THE TEETH AND GIVE IT A BEAK...
THEN USE THE LEFTOVER CALCIUM FOR THE BONES!
BRING THE SPINE AND THE RIBS TO THE OUTSIDE OF THE BODY!
ジャン！
BANG
バン！
BAM
SWITCH THE POSITIONS OF THE RIBS AND THE SHOULDER BLADES, AND USE THE SHOULDER BLADES TO BREATHE!
DOUBLE UP THE BONES AND REINFORCE THEM...
IT'LL MAKE IT HARD TO MOVE AND TO FIND FOOD, BUT IT'LL HAVE A FUEL-EFFICIENT BODY TO MAKE UP FOR IT!
ズン！
POW
ド
BOOM
ALL RIGHT! MY ANIMAL WITH AMAZING RIBS IS FINISHED!

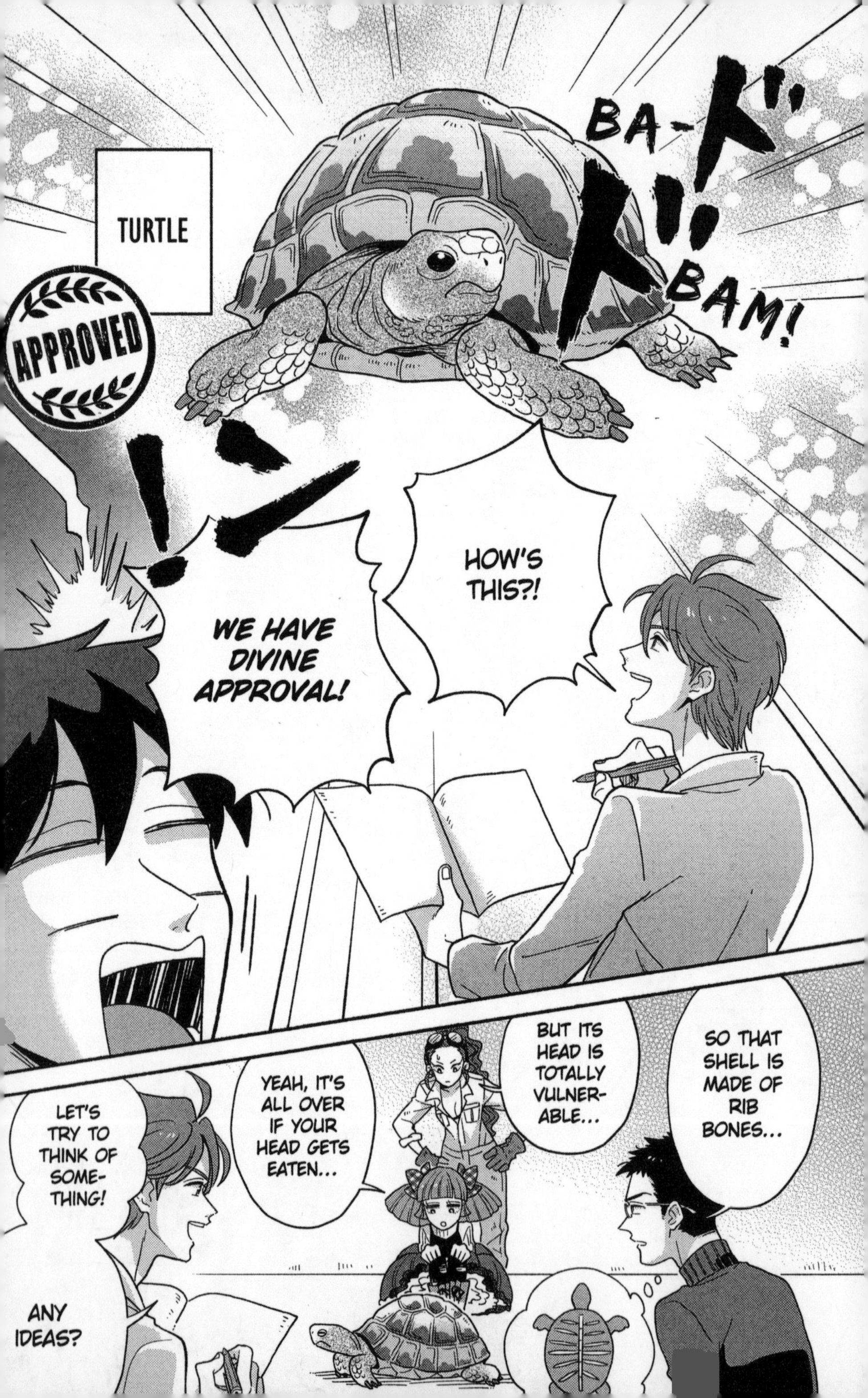
BA-
ド
ド
BAM!
TURTLE
APPROVED
HOW'S THIS?!
!
WE HAVE DIVINE APPROVAL!
SO THAT SHELL IS MADE OF RIB BONES...
BUT ITS HEAD IS TOTALLY VULNER-ABLE...
YEAH, IT'S ALL OVER IF YOUR HEAD GETS EATEN...
LET'S TRY TO THINK OF SOME-THING!
ANY IDEAS?

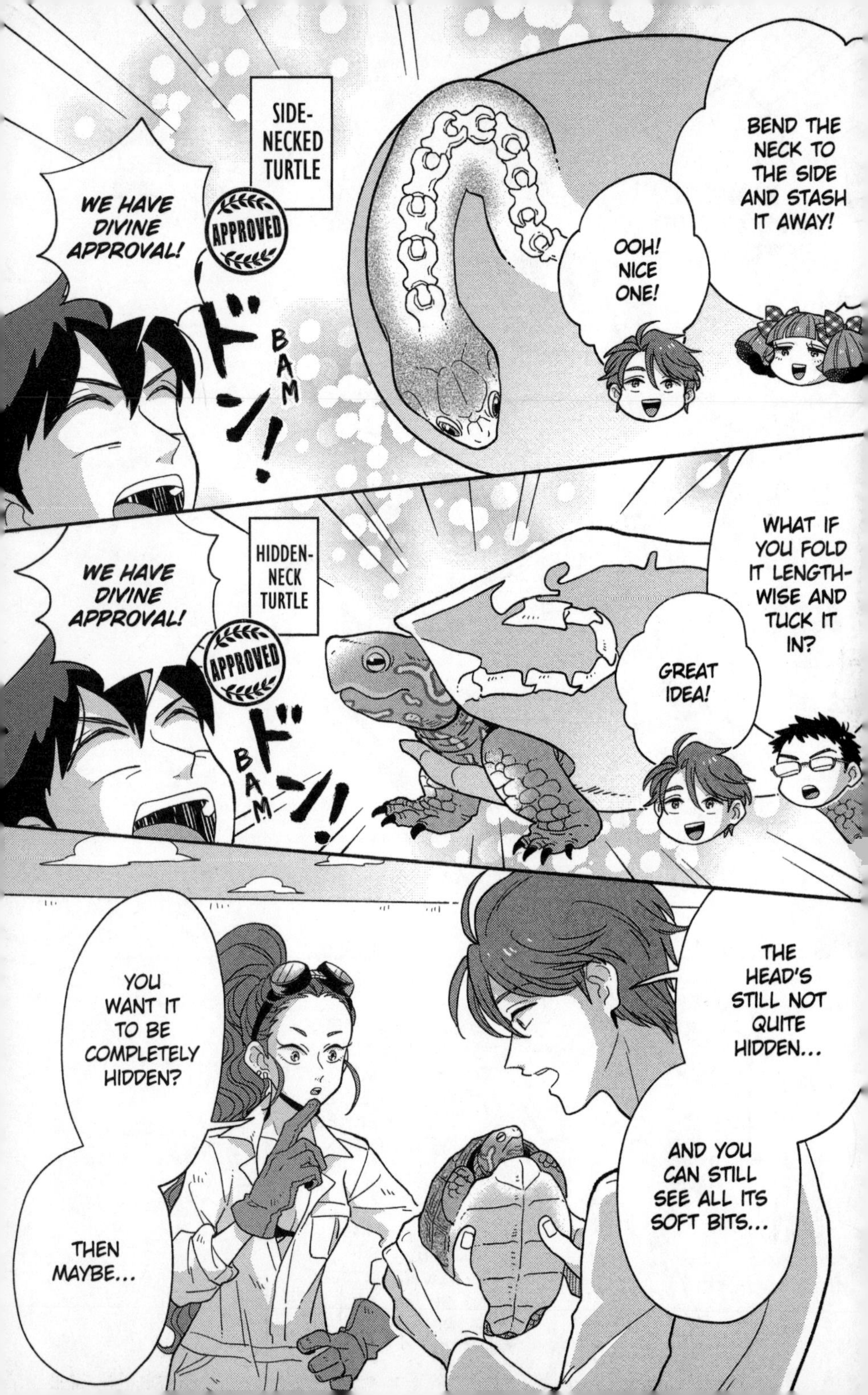
BEND THE NECK TO THE SIDE AND STASH IT AWAY!
OOH! NICE ONE!
SIDE-NECKED TURTLE
APPROVED
ドン!!
BAM
WE HAVE DIVINE APPROVAL!
WHAT IF YOU FOLD IT LENGTH-WISE AND TUCK IT IN?
GREAT IDEA!
HIDDEN-NECK TURTLE
APPROVED
ドン!!
BAM
WE HAVE DIVINE APPROVAL!
THE HEAD'S STILL NOT QUITE HIDDEN...
AND YOU CAN STILL SEE ALL ITS SOFT BITS...
YOU WANT IT TO BE COMPLETELY HIDDEN?
THEN MAYBE...

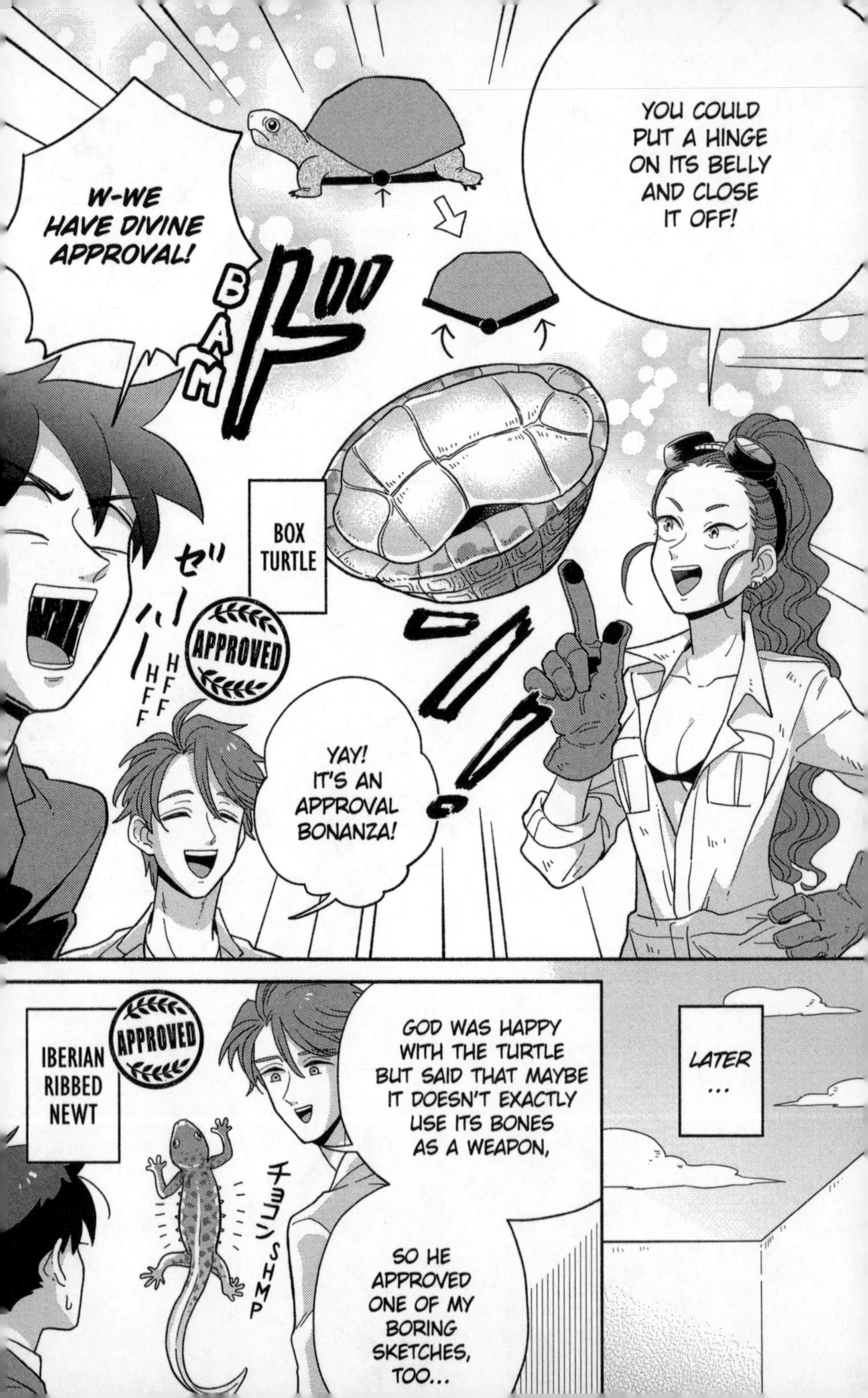
YOU COULD PUT A HINGE ON ITS BELLY AND CLOSE IT OFF!
W-WE HAVE DIVINE APPROVAL!
BAM
BOX TURTLE
APPROVED
HFFF HFFF
YAY! IT'S AN APPROVAL BONANZA!
LATER ...
GOD WAS HAPPY WITH THE TURTLE BUT SAID THAT MAYBE IT DOESN'T EXACTLY USE ITS BONES AS A WEAPON,
SO HE APPROVED ONE OF MY BORING SKETCHES, TOO...
IBERIAN RIBBED NEWT
APPROVED
チョコン
SHMP

THE ENCYCLOPEDIA OF REAL ANIMALS 23

ANIMAL 59 TURTLE

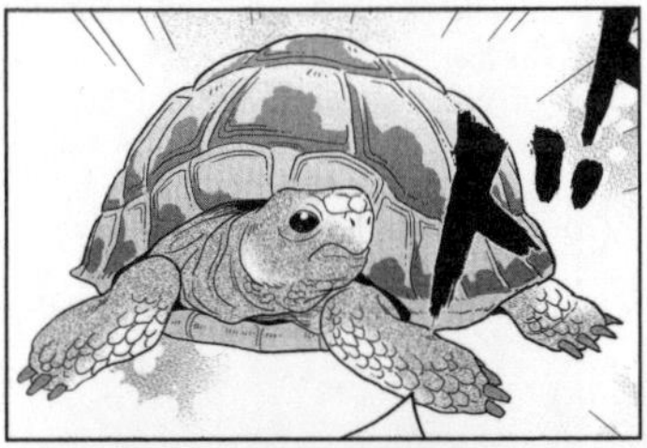

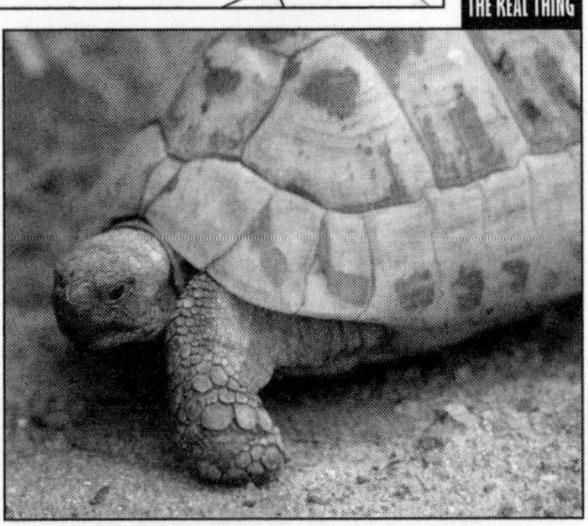
THE REAL THING

A Hermann's tortoise photographed in Germany. Though the spine is fixed, the neck is flexible.

Photo: Aflo

All of the ideas suggested by the designers in this chapter are present in real turtles, including "the spine and the ribs on the outside of the body," "breathing using the shoulder blades," "using a beak instead of teeth," and "a strong, two-layered shell." Defense mechanisms vary among the different species, with some turtles tucking their necks in sideways and others using a hinge on their bellies to seal themselves off. Due in part to these ingenious protective designs, turtles thrive in many environments around the globe. They rarely have a reason to flee, which conserves their energy and allows them to go without food for long periods and enjoy very long lifespans. Accordingly, one specimen of Galápagos tortoise is estimated to have reached 175 years, while a specimen of Aldabra giant tortoise is reputed to have lived to 255 years of age.

[Name]	Turtle
[Classification]	Class: Reptilia Order: Testudines
[Habitat]	Worldwide, but concentrated in tropical and warm environments
[Length]	8 cm (3 in) (Speckled cape tortoise) 190 cm (6.2 ft) (Leatherback sea turtle)

| IBERIAN RIBBED NEWT

The Iberian ribbed newt is the largest newt species in the world, and can reach up to about 30 centimeters (12 inches) in length. The ribs, which are longer than the width of its abdomen, are normally folded within the body much like a half-folded umbrella, but when the animal is under attack, they can be unfurled like an open umbrella and pushed out on either side of the body. The tips of the ribs are sharp, allowing them to puncture the skin with ease but also leaving the newt full of holes. Fortunately, because of the animal's ability to regenerate body parts from its legs to its heart and even its brain, the skin heals quickly. Despite the amount of effort involved in shooting the ribs out, the end result is underwhelming, with the bones sticking out only slightly.

THE REAL THING

The Iberian ribbed newt's ribs stick out on either side of its body. They are sometimes kept as pets, but only with extreme caution, as they can sustain burns from excessive human touch.

Photo: Alamy/Aflo

[Name]	*Pleurodeles waltl*
[Classification]	Class: Amphibia
	Order: Urodela
	Family: Salamandridae
	Genus: *Pleurodeles*
[Habitat]	Iberian Peninsula, Morocco
[Length]	20-31 cm (8-12 in)

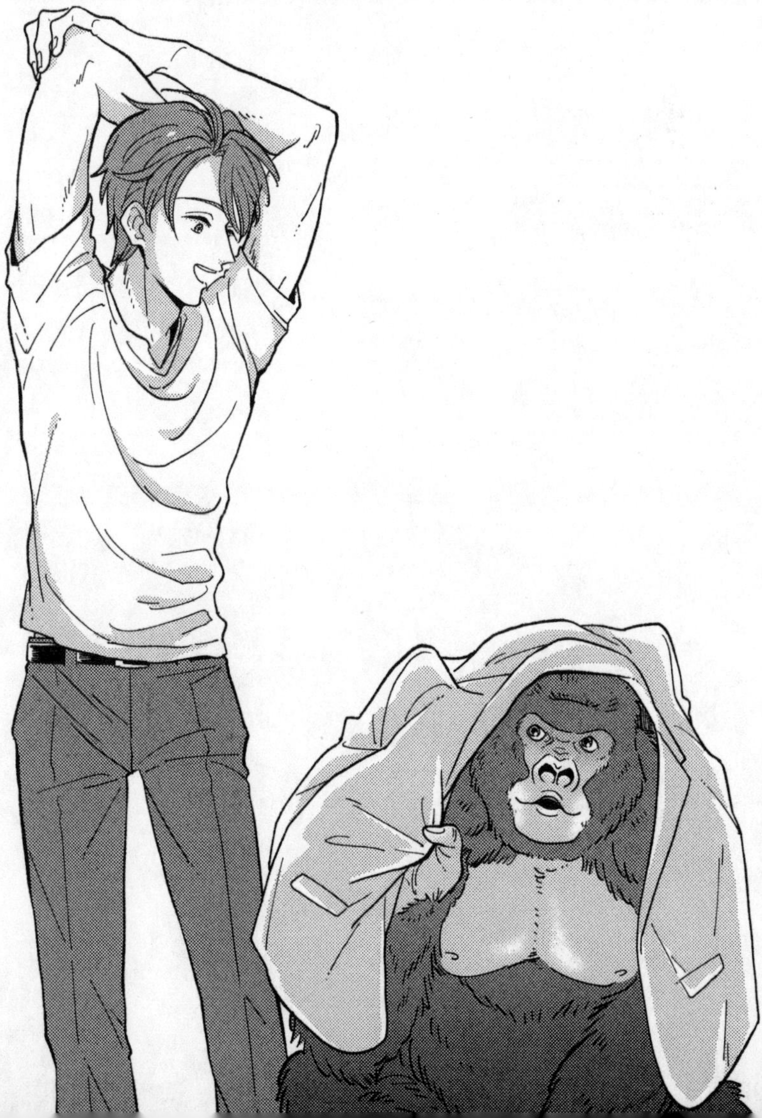

HEAVEN'S DESIGN TEAM

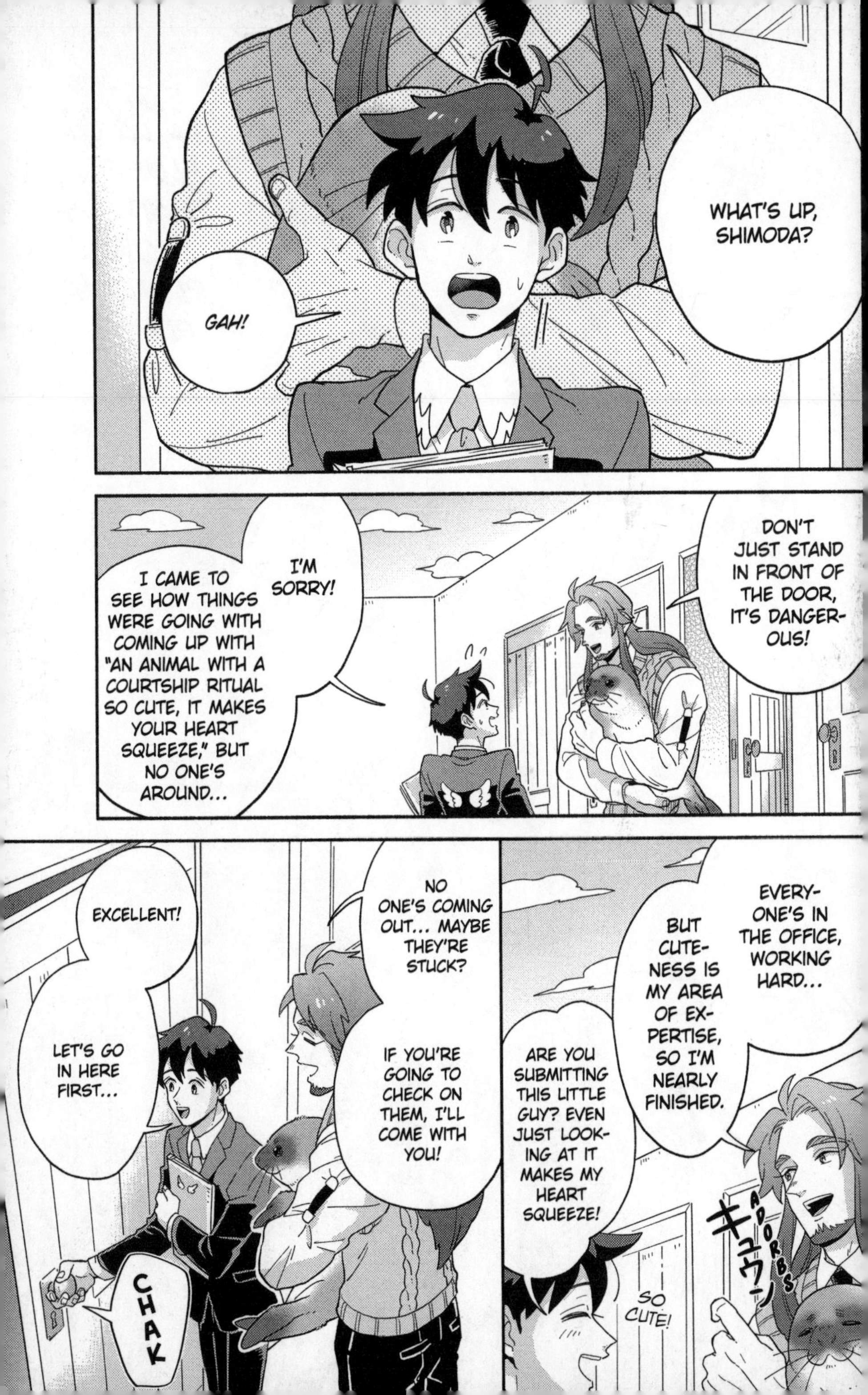
WHAT'S UP, SHIMODA?
GAH!
DON'T JUST STAND IN FRONT OF THE DOOR, IT'S DANGEROUS!
I'M SORRY!
I CAME TO SEE HOW THINGS WERE GOING WITH COMING UP WITH "AN ANIMAL WITH A COURTSHIP RITUAL SO CUTE, IT MAKES YOUR HEART SQUEEZE," BUT NO ONE'S AROUND...
EVERYONE'S IN THE OFFICE, WORKING HARD...
BUT CUTENESS IS MY AREA OF EXPERTISE, SO I'M NEARLY FINISHED.
ARE YOU SUBMITTING THIS LITTLE GUY? EVEN JUST LOOKING AT IT MAKES MY HEART SQUEEZE!
キュウ～ノ ADORBS
SO CUTE!
NO ONE'S COMING OUT... MAYBE THEY'RE STUCK?
EXCELLENT!
IF YOU'RE GOING TO CHECK ON THEM, I'LL COME WITH YOU!
LET'S GO IN HERE FIRST...
CHAK

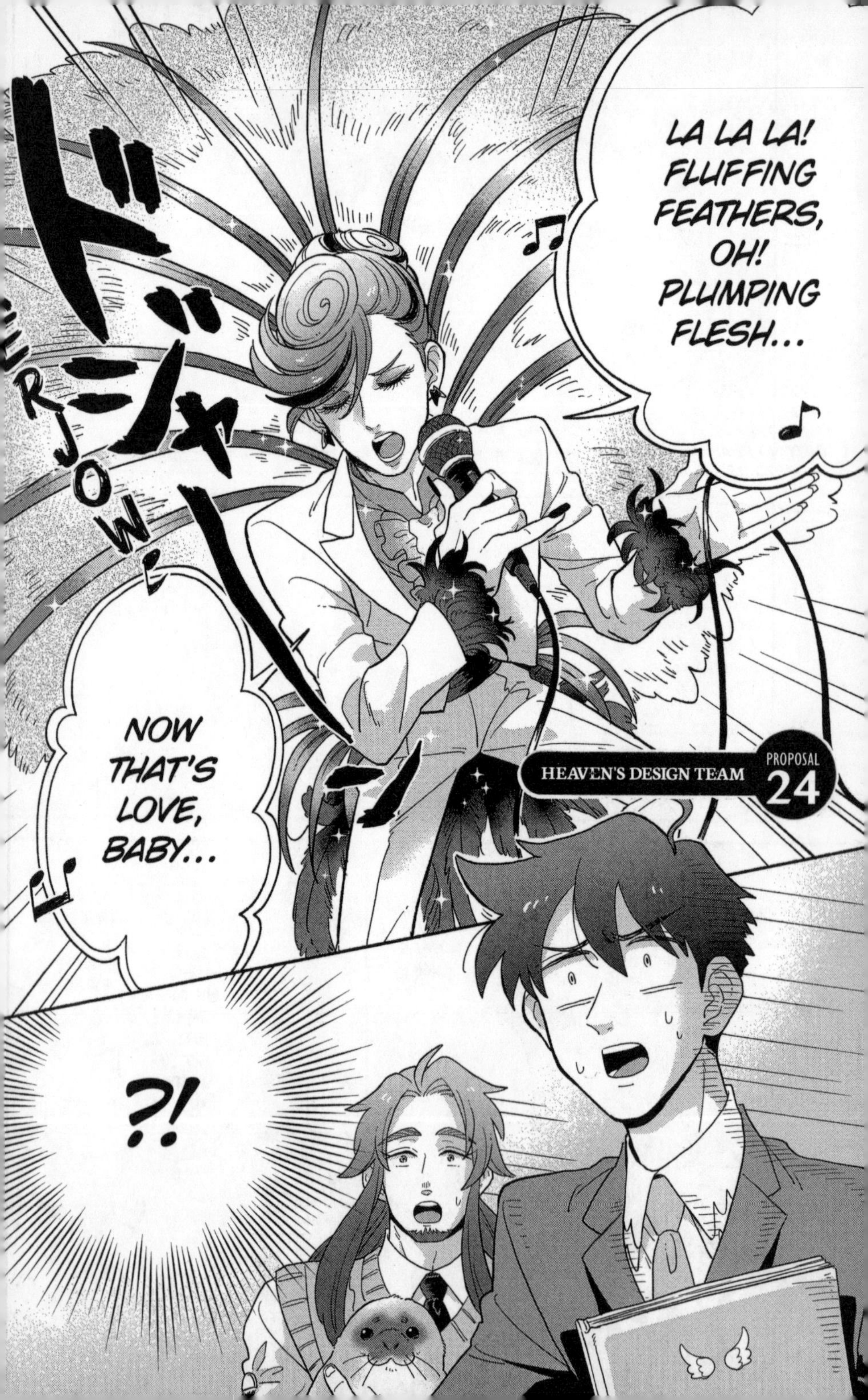
LA LA LA! FLUFFING FEATHERS, OH! PLUMPING FLESH...
NOW THAT'S LOVE, BABY...
RJOWN
HEAVEN'S DESIGN TEAM
PROPOSAL 24
?!

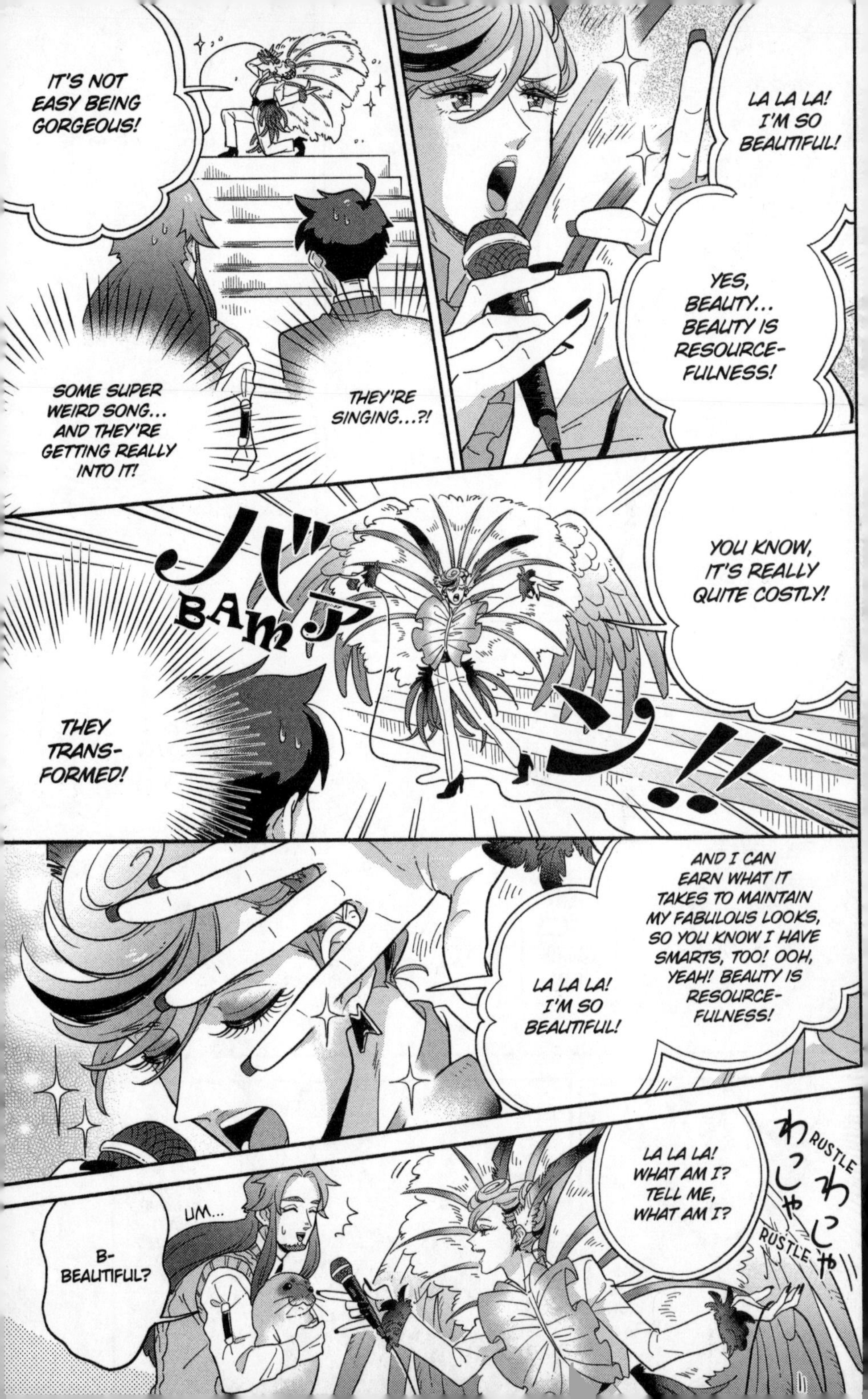
LA LA LA! I'M SO BEAUTIFUL!
YES, BEAUTY... BEAUTY IS RESOURCE-FULNESS!
IT'S NOT EASY BEING GORGEOUS!
THEY'RE SINGING...?!
SOME SUPER WEIRD SONG... AND THEY'RE GETTING REALLY INTO IT!
YOU KNOW, IT'S REALLY QUITE COSTLY!
バーン!!
BAM
THEY TRANS-FORMED!
AND I CAN EARN WHAT IT TAKES TO MAINTAIN MY FABULOUS LOOKS, SO YOU KNOW I HAVE SMARTS, TOO! OOH, YEAH! BEAUTY IS RESOURCE-FULNESS!
LA LA LA! I'M SO BEAUTIFUL!
わっしゃ
RUSTLE
わっしゃ
RUSTLE
LA LA LA! WHAT AM I? TELL ME, WHAT AM I?
UM...
B-BEAUTIFUL?

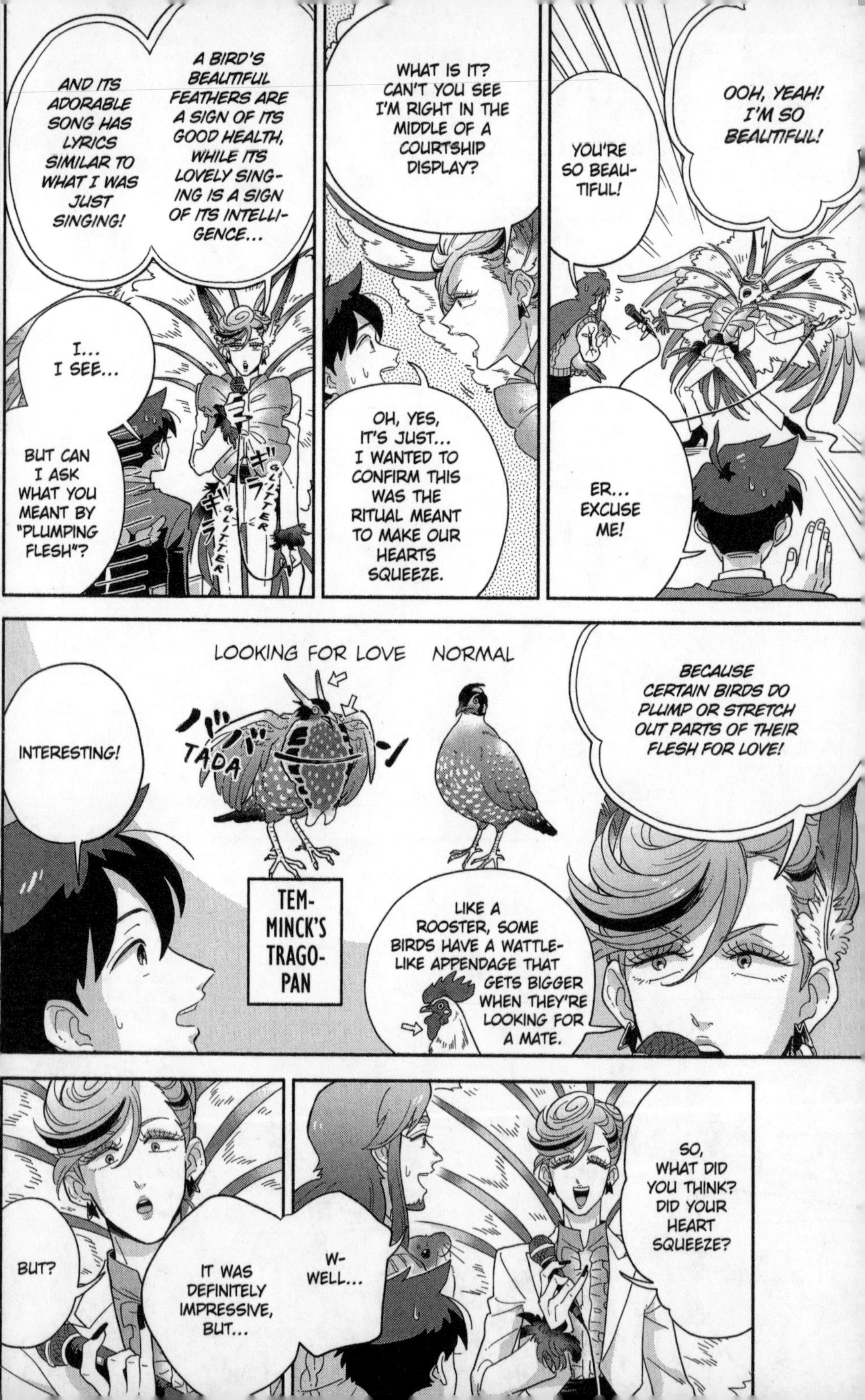
OOH, YEAH! I'M SO BEAUTIFUL!
YOU'RE SO BEAU-TIFUL!
ER... EXCUSE ME!
WHAT IS IT? CAN'T YOU SEE I'M RIGHT IN THE MIDDLE OF A COURTSHIP DISPLAY?
OH, YES, IT'S JUST... I WANTED TO CONFIRM THIS WAS THE RITUAL MEANT TO MAKE OUR HEARTS SQUEEZE.
A BIRD'S BEAUTIFUL FEATHERS ARE A SIGN OF ITS GOOD HEALTH, WHILE ITS LOVELY SING-ING IS A SIGN OF ITS INTELLI-GENCE...
AND ITS ADORABLE SONG HAS LYRICS SIMILAR TO WHAT I WAS JUST SINGING!
I... I SEE...
GLITTER
GLITTER
BUT CAN I ASK WHAT YOU MEANT BY "PLUMPING FLESH"?
BECAUSE CERTAIN BIRDS DO PLUMP OR STRETCH OUT PARTS OF THEIR FLESH FOR LOVE!
LOOKING FOR LOVE
NORMAL
TADA
TEM-MINCK'S TRAGO-PAN
LIKE A ROOSTER, SOME BIRDS HAVE A WATTLE-LIKE APPENDAGE THAT GETS BIGGER WHEN THEY'RE LOOKING FOR A MATE.
INTERESTING!
SO, WHAT DID YOU THINK? DID YOUR HEART SQUEEZE?
W-WELL...
IT WAS DEFINITELY IMPRESSIVE, BUT...
BUT?

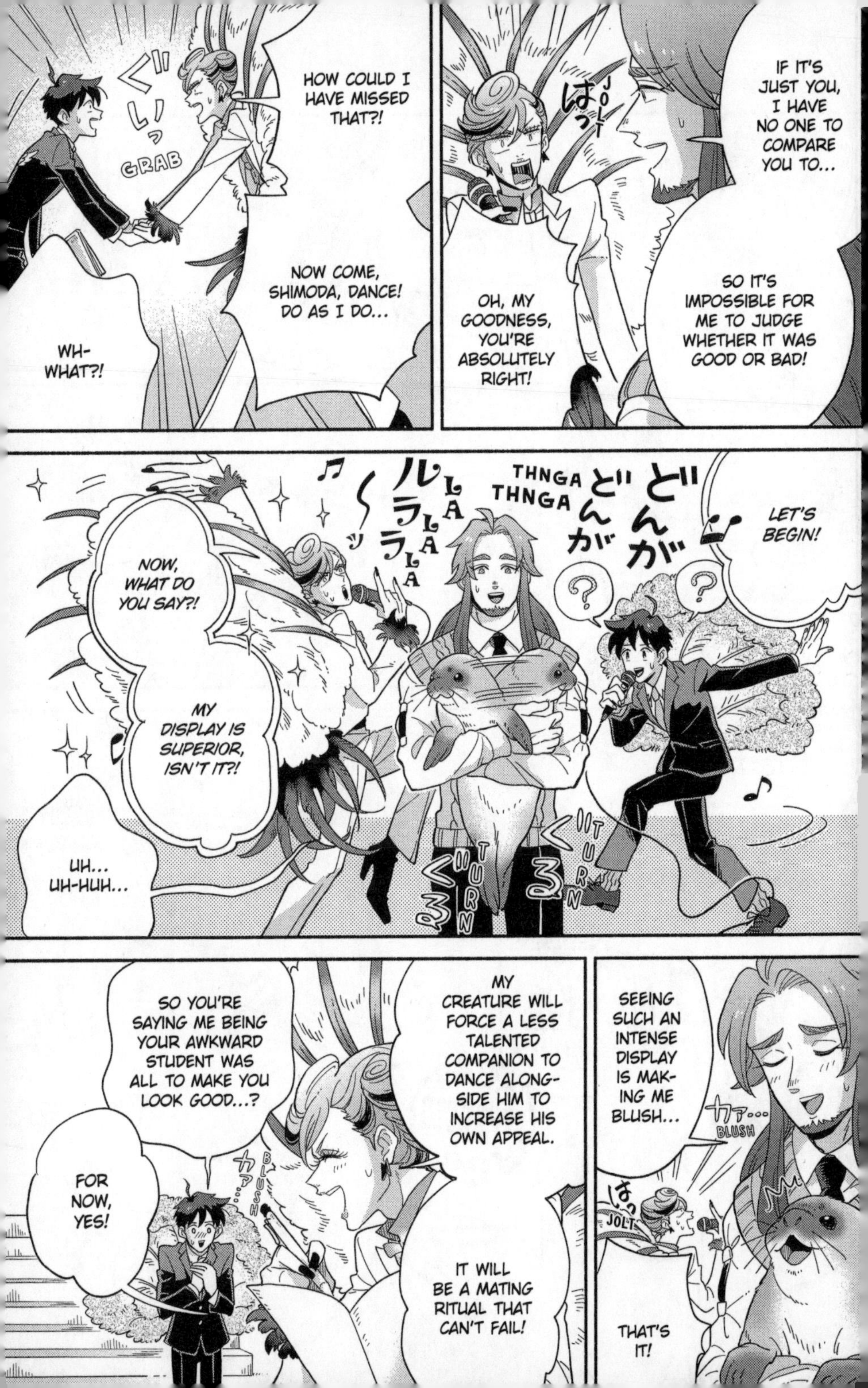
IF IT'S JUST YOU, I HAVE NO ONE TO COMPARE YOU TO...
SO IT'S IMPOSSIBLE FOR ME TO JUDGE WHETHER IT WAS GOOD OR BAD!
はっ JOLT
OH, MY GOODNESS, YOU'RE ABSOLUTELY RIGHT!
HOW COULD I HAVE MISSED THAT?!
NOW COME, SHIMODA, DANCE! DO AS I DO...
ぐいっ GRAB
WH-WHAT?!
LET'S BEGIN!
どんがどんが THNGA THNGA
ルラ〜ラ〜ッ LA LA LA LA
NOW, WHAT DO YOU SAY?!
MY DISPLAY IS SUPERIOR, ISN'T IT?!
くるくる TURN TURN
UH... UH-HUH...
SEEING SUCH AN INTENSE DISPLAY IS MAKING ME BLUSH...
カァ... BLUSH
はっ JOLT
THAT'S IT!
MY CREATURE WILL FORCE A LESS TALENTED COMPANION TO DANCE ALONG-SIDE HIM TO INCREASE HIS OWN APPEAL.
IT WILL BE A MATING RITUAL THAT CAN'T FAIL!
SO YOU'RE SAYING ME BEING YOUR AWKWARD STUDENT WAS ALL TO MAKE YOU LOOK GOOD...?
カァ... BLUSH
FOR NOW, YES!

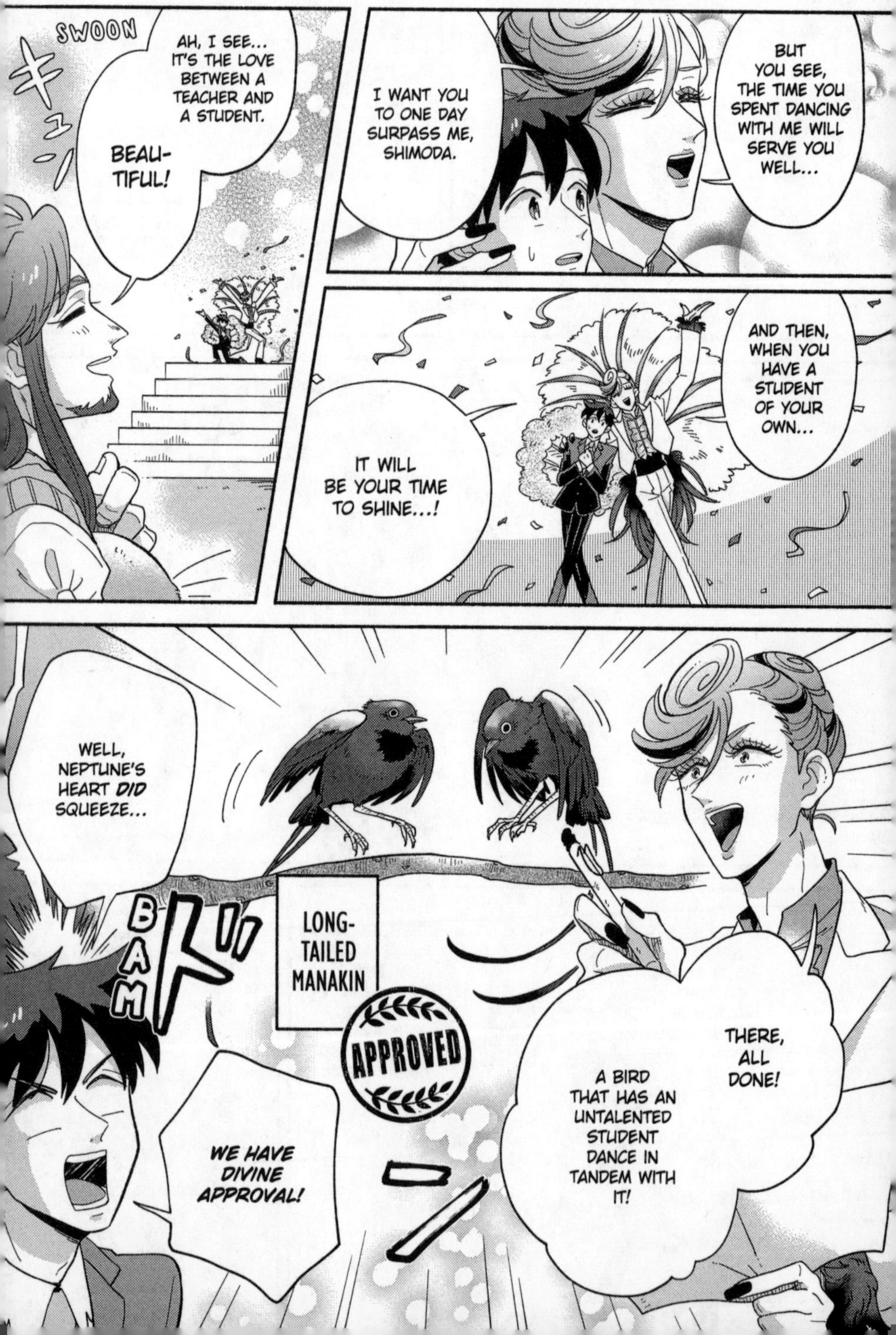
BUT YOU SEE, THE TIME YOU SPENT DANCING WITH ME WILL SERVE YOU WELL...
I WANT YOU TO ONE DAY SURPASS ME, SHIMODA.
AND THEN, WHEN YOU HAVE A STUDENT OF YOUR OWN...
IT WILL BE YOUR TIME TO SHINE...!
SWOON
AH, I SEE... IT'S THE LOVE BETWEEN A TEACHER AND A STUDENT.
BEAUTIFUL!
THERE, ALL DONE!
A BIRD THAT HAS AN UNTALENTED STUDENT DANCE IN TANDEM WITH IT!
LONG-TAILED MANAKIN
APPROVED
WELL, NEPTUNE'S HEART *DID* SQUEEZE...
BAM
WE HAVE DIVINE APPROVAL!

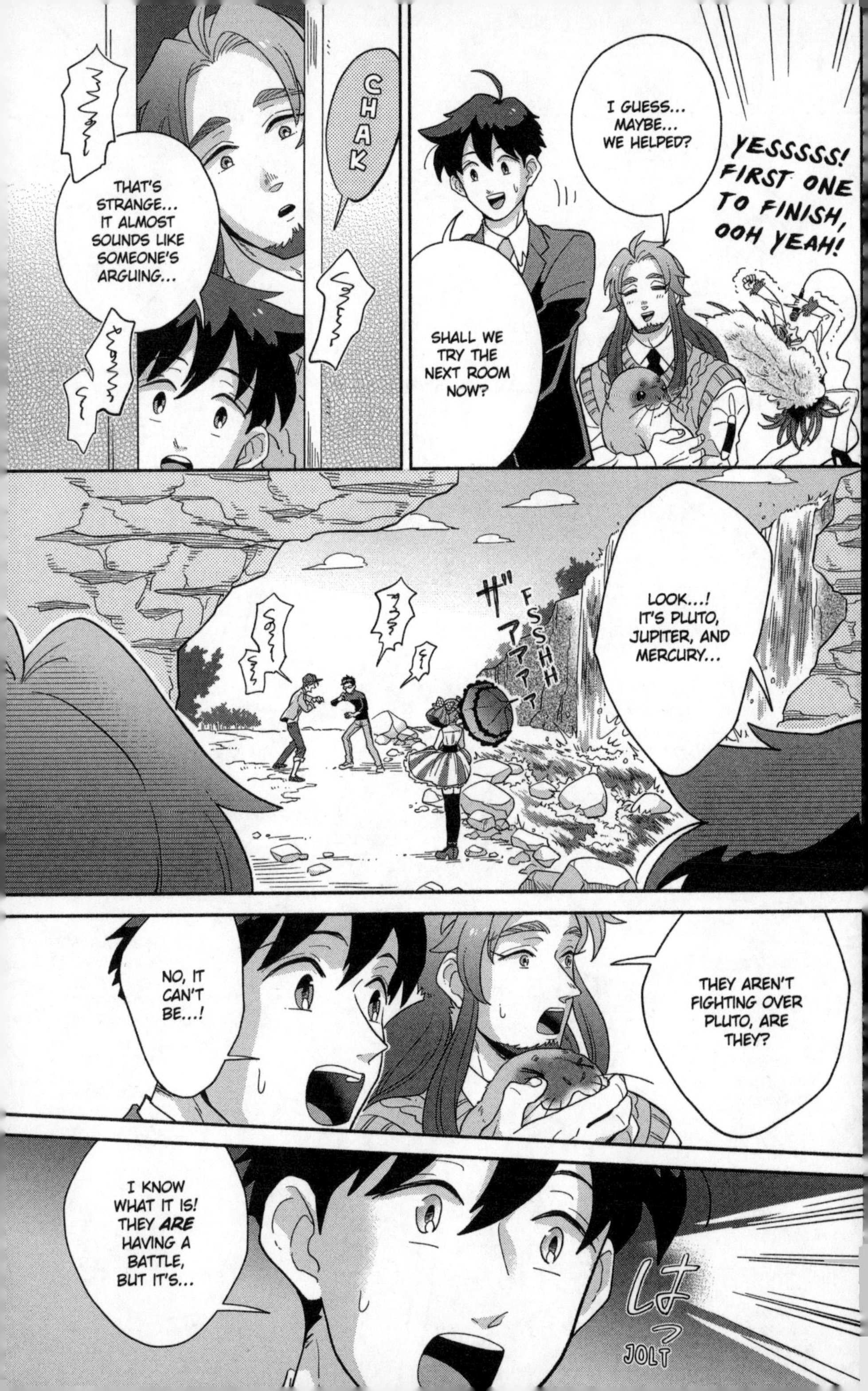
I GUESS... MAYBE... WE HELPED?
YESSSSS! FIRST ONE TO FINISH, OOH YEAH!
SHALL WE TRY THE NEXT ROOM NOW?
CHAK
THAT'S STRANGE... IT ALMOST SOUNDS LIKE SOMEONE'S ARGUING...
LOOK...! IT'S PLUTO, JUPITER, AND MERCURY...
FSSHH
THEY AREN'T FIGHTING OVER PLUTO, ARE THEY?
NO, IT CAN'T BE...!
JOLT
I KNOW WHAT IT IS! THEY **ARE** HAVING A BATTLE, BUT IT'S...

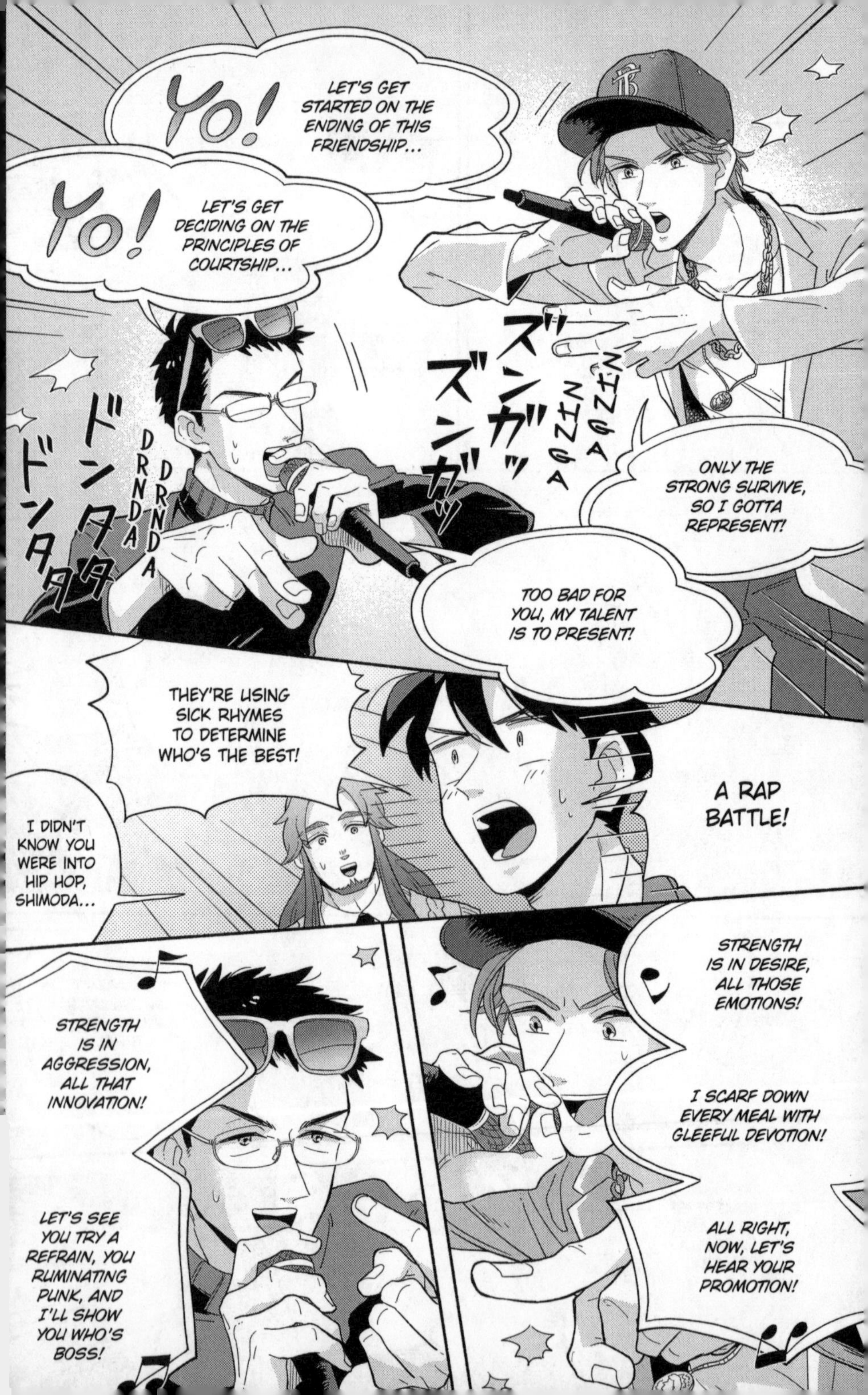
YO! LET'S GET STARTED ON THE ENDING OF THIS FRIENDSHIP…
YO! LET'S GET DECIDING ON THE PRINCIPLES OF COURTSHIP…
ズンガッ ズンガッ
ZNGA ZNGA
ONLY THE STRONG SURVIVE, SO I GOTTA REPRESENT!
ドンタタ ドンタタ
DRNDA DRNDA
TOO BAD FOR YOU, MY TALENT IS TO PRESENT!
THEY'RE USING SICK RHYMES TO DETERMINE WHO'S THE BEST!
A RAP BATTLE!
I DIDN'T KNOW YOU WERE INTO HIP HOP, SHIMODA…
STRENGTH IS IN DESIRE, ALL THOSE EMOTIONS!
I SCARF DOWN EVERY MEAL WITH GLEEFUL DEVOTION!
ALL RIGHT, NOW, LET'S HEAR YOUR PROMOTION!
STRENGTH IS IN AGGRESSION, ALL THAT INNOVATION!
LET'S SEE YOU TRY A REFRAIN, YOU RUMINATING PUNK, AND I'LL SHOW YOU WHO'S BOSS!

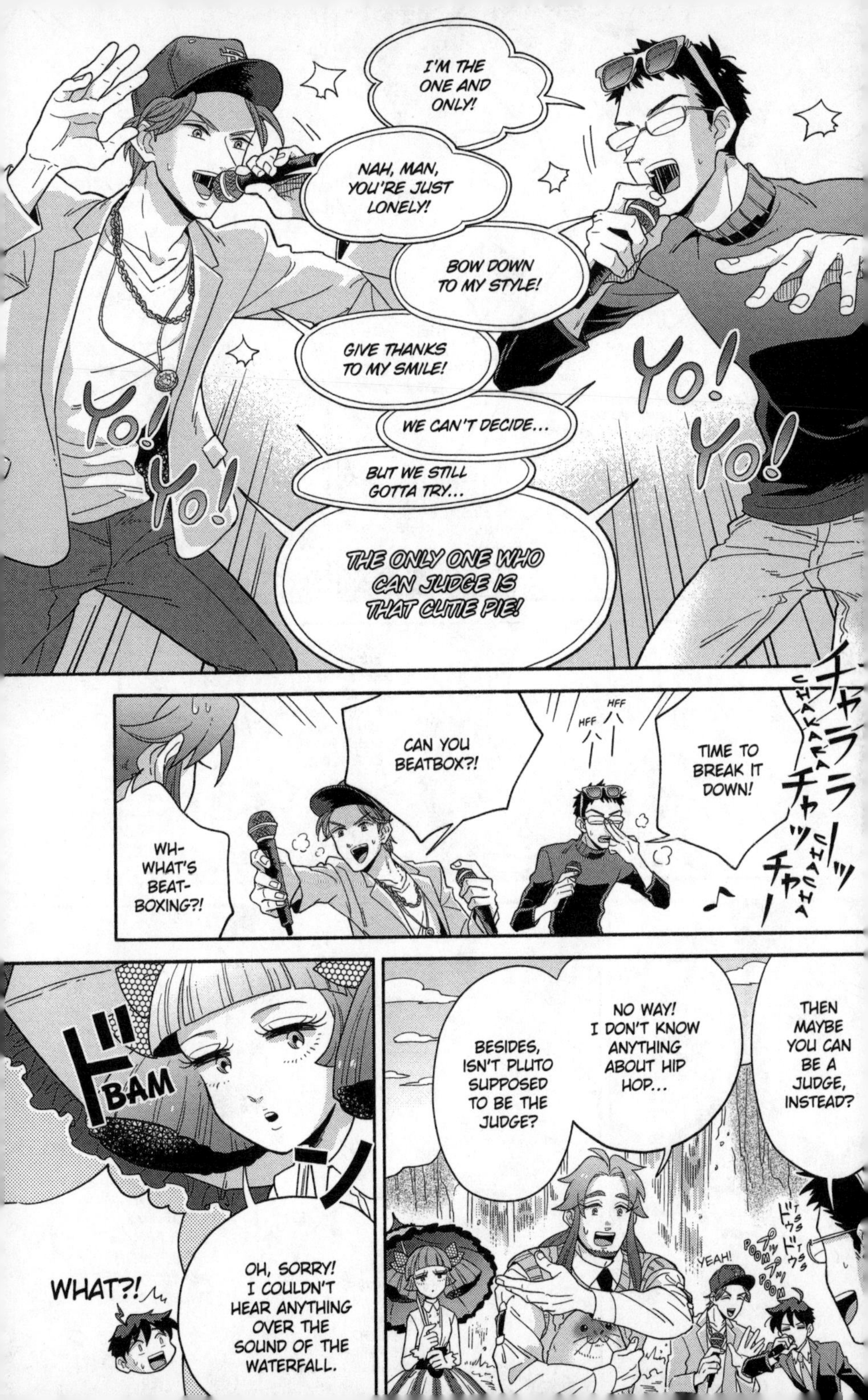
I'M THE ONE AND ONLY!
NAH, MAN, YOU'RE JUST LONELY!
BOW DOWN TO MY STYLE!
GIVE THANKS TO MY SMILE!
WE CAN'T DECIDE...
BUT WE STILL GOTTA TRY...
THE ONLY ONE WHO CAN JUDGE IS THAT CUTIE PIE!
YO! YO!
YO! YO!
チャラララーッ
CHAKAKA
チャッチャッチャー
CHACHA
TIME TO BREAK IT DOWN!
HFF
HFF
CAN YOU BEATBOX?!
WH-WHAT'S BEAT-BOXING?!
THEN MAYBE YOU CAN BE A JUDGE, INSTEAD?
NO WAY! I DON'T KNOW ANYTHING ABOUT HIP HOP...
BESIDES, ISN'T PLUTO SUPPOSED TO BE THE JUDGE?
TSS TSS
POOM POOM
YEAH!
ドーン
BAM
OH, SORRY! I COULDN'T HEAR ANYTHING OVER THE SOUND OF THE WATERFALL.
WHAT?!

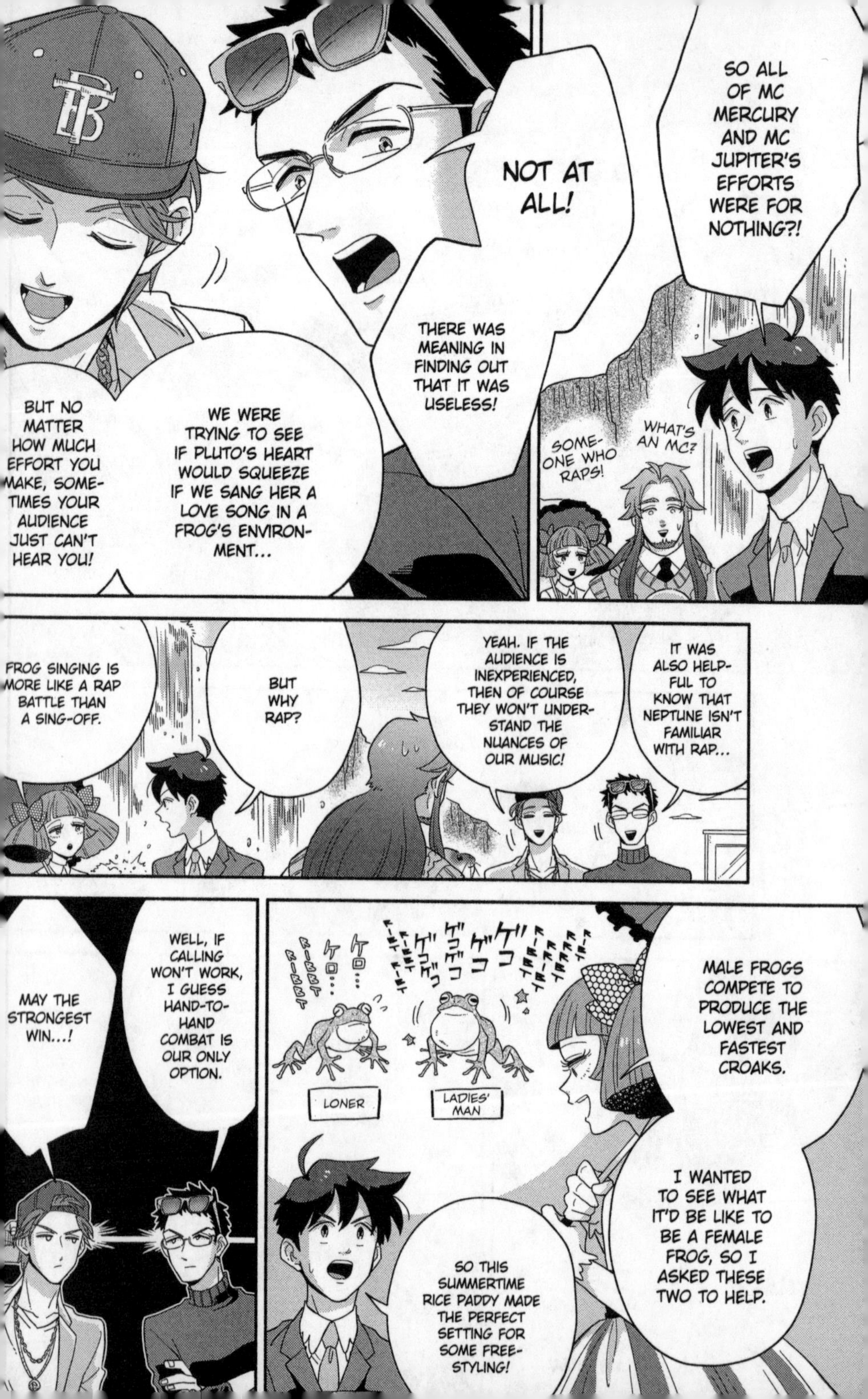
SO ALL OF MC MERCURY AND MC JUPITER'S EFFORTS WERE FOR NOTHING?!
WHAT'S AN MC?
SOME-ONE WHO RAPS!
NOT AT ALL!
THERE WAS MEANING IN FINDING OUT THAT IT WAS USELESS!
WE WERE TRYING TO SEE IF PLUTO'S HEART WOULD SQUEEZE IF WE SANG HER A LOVE SONG IN A FROG'S ENVIRON-MENT...
BUT NO MATTER HOW MUCH EFFORT YOU MAKE, SOME-TIMES YOUR AUDIENCE JUST CAN'T HEAR YOU!
IT WAS ALSO HELP-FUL TO KNOW THAT NEPTUNE ISN'T FAMILIAR WITH RAP...
YEAH. IF THE AUDIENCE IS INEXPERIENCED, THEN OF COURSE THEY WON'T UNDER-STAND THE NUANCES OF OUR MUSIC!
BUT WHY RAP?
FROG SINGING IS MORE LIKE A RAP BATTLE THAN A SING-OFF.
MALE FROGS COMPETE TO PRODUCE THE LOWEST AND FASTEST CROAKS.
ゲコゲコ ゲコゲコ
ケロ… ケロ…
RIBBIT RIBBIT
LONER
LADIES' MAN
I WANTED TO SEE WHAT IT'D BE LIKE TO BE A FEMALE FROG, SO I ASKED THESE TWO TO HELP.
SO THIS SUMMERTIME RICE PADDY MADE THE PERFECT SETTING FOR SOME FREE-STYLING!
WELL, IF CALLING WON'T WORK, I GUESS HAND-TO-HAND COMBAT IS OUR ONLY OPTION.
MAY THE STRONGEST WIN...!

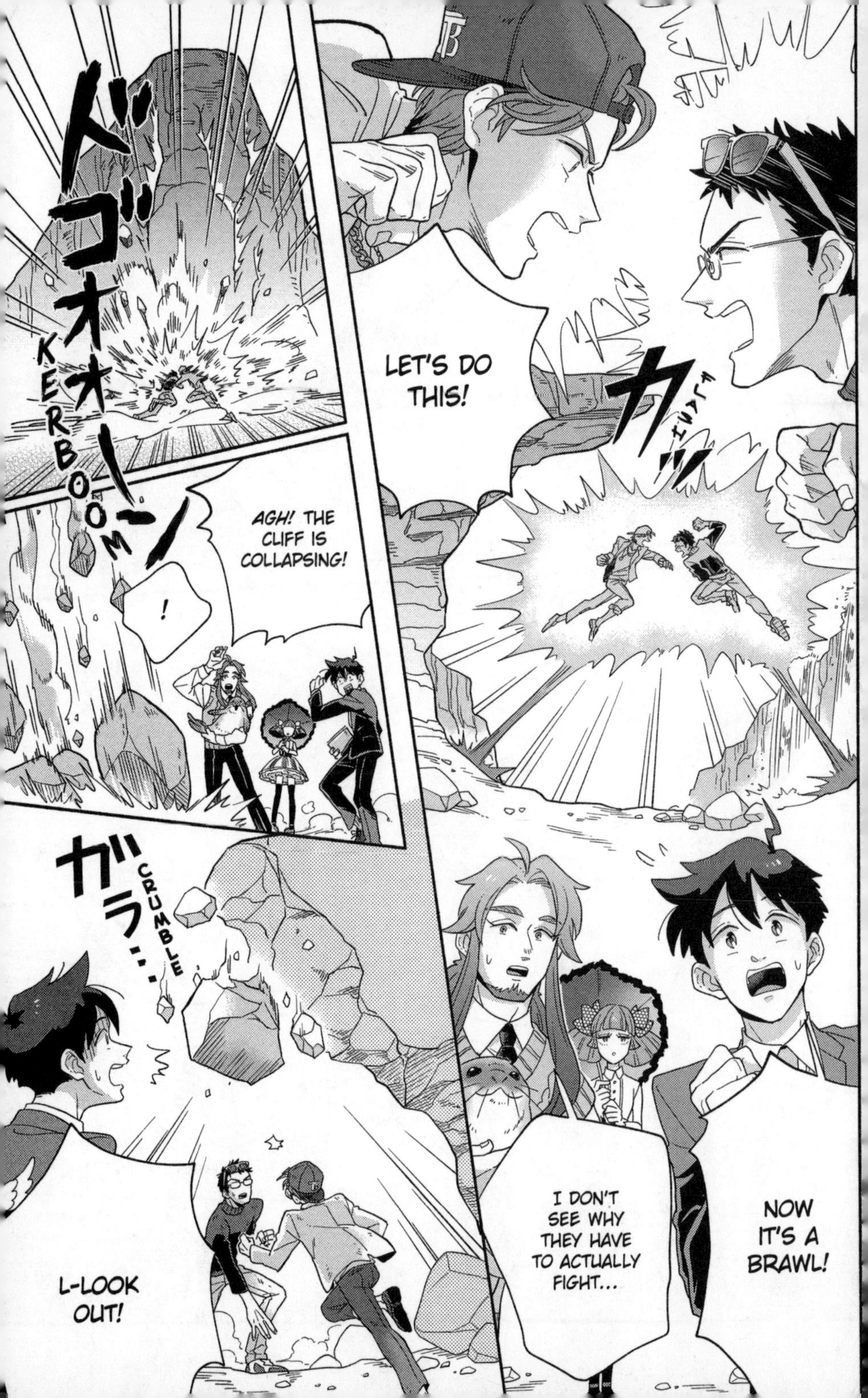
LET'S DO THIS!
カッ
FLASH
ドゴオオーン
KERBOOM
AGH! THE CLIFF IS COLLAPSING!
!
NOW IT'S A BRAWL!
I DON'T SEE WHY THEY HAVE TO ACTUALLY FIGHT...
ガラ…
CRUMBLE
L-LOOK OUT!

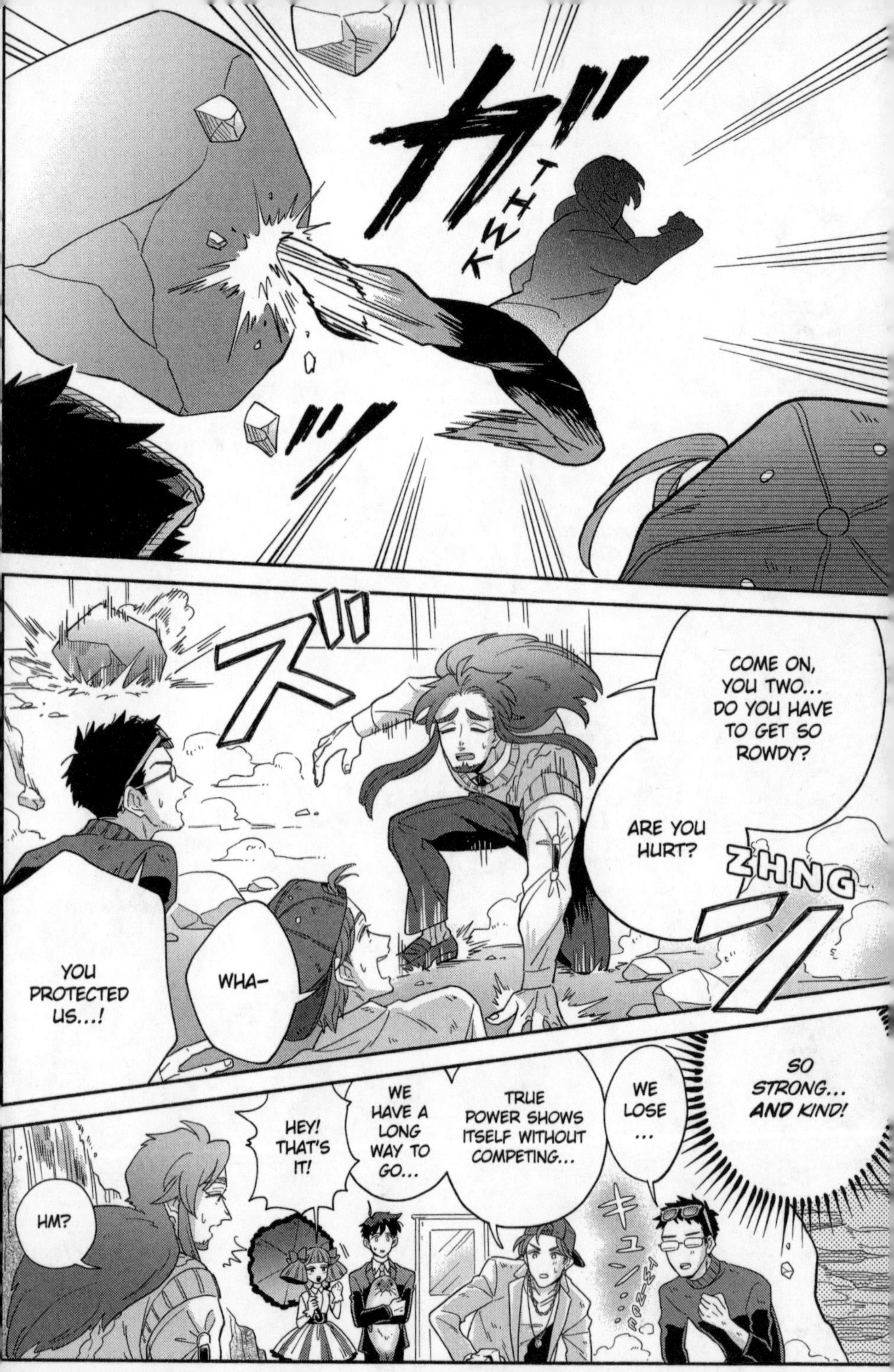
ガ
THWK
ズ
COME ON, YOU TWO... DO YOU HAVE TO GET SO ROWDY?
ARE YOU HURT?
ZHNG
WHA-
YOU PROTECTED US...!
SO STRONG... AND KIND!
WE LOSE ...
キュン
TWINGE
TRUE POWER SHOWS ITSELF WITHOUT COMPETING...
WE HAVE A LONG WAY TO GO...
HEY! THAT'S IT!
HM?

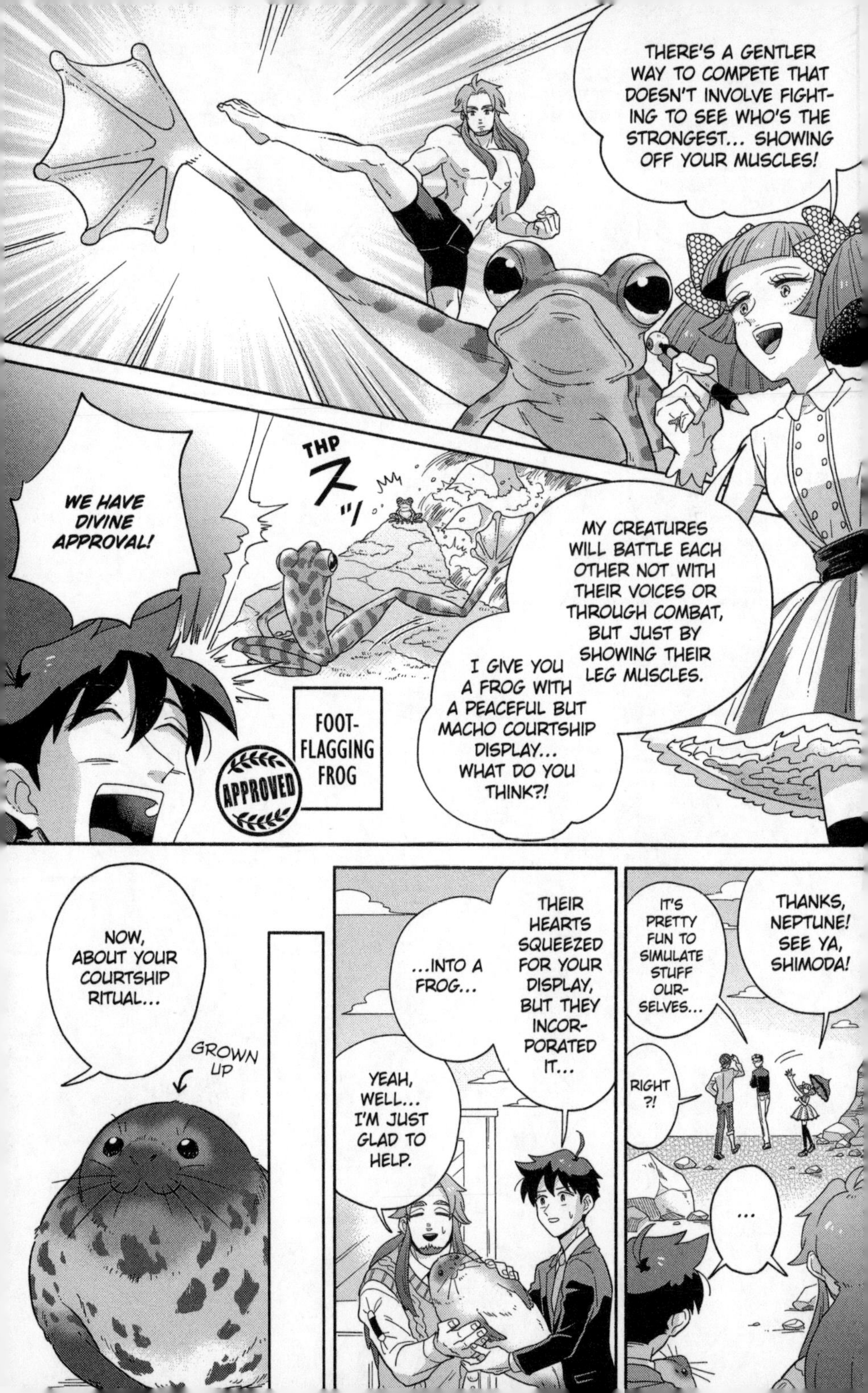
THERE'S A GENTLER WAY TO COMPETE THAT DOESN'T INVOLVE FIGHTING TO SEE WHO'S THE STRONGEST... SHOWING OFF YOUR MUSCLES!
MY CREATURES WILL BATTLE EACH OTHER NOT WITH THEIR VOICES OR THROUGH COMBAT, BUT JUST BY SHOWING THEIR LEG MUSCLES.
I GIVE YOU A FROG WITH A PEACEFUL BUT MACHO COURTSHIP DISPLAY... WHAT DO YOU THINK?!
THP
FOOT-FLAGGING FROG
WE HAVE DIVINE APPROVAL!
APPROVED
THANKS, NEPTUNE! SEE YA, SHIMODA!
IT'S PRETTY FUN TO SIMULATE STUFF OURSELVES...
RIGHT?!
...
THEIR HEARTS SQUEEZED FOR YOUR DISPLAY, BUT THEY INCORPORATED IT...
...INTO A FROG...
YEAH, WELL... I'M JUST GLAD TO HELP.
NOW, ABOUT YOUR COURTSHIP RITUAL...
GROWN UP

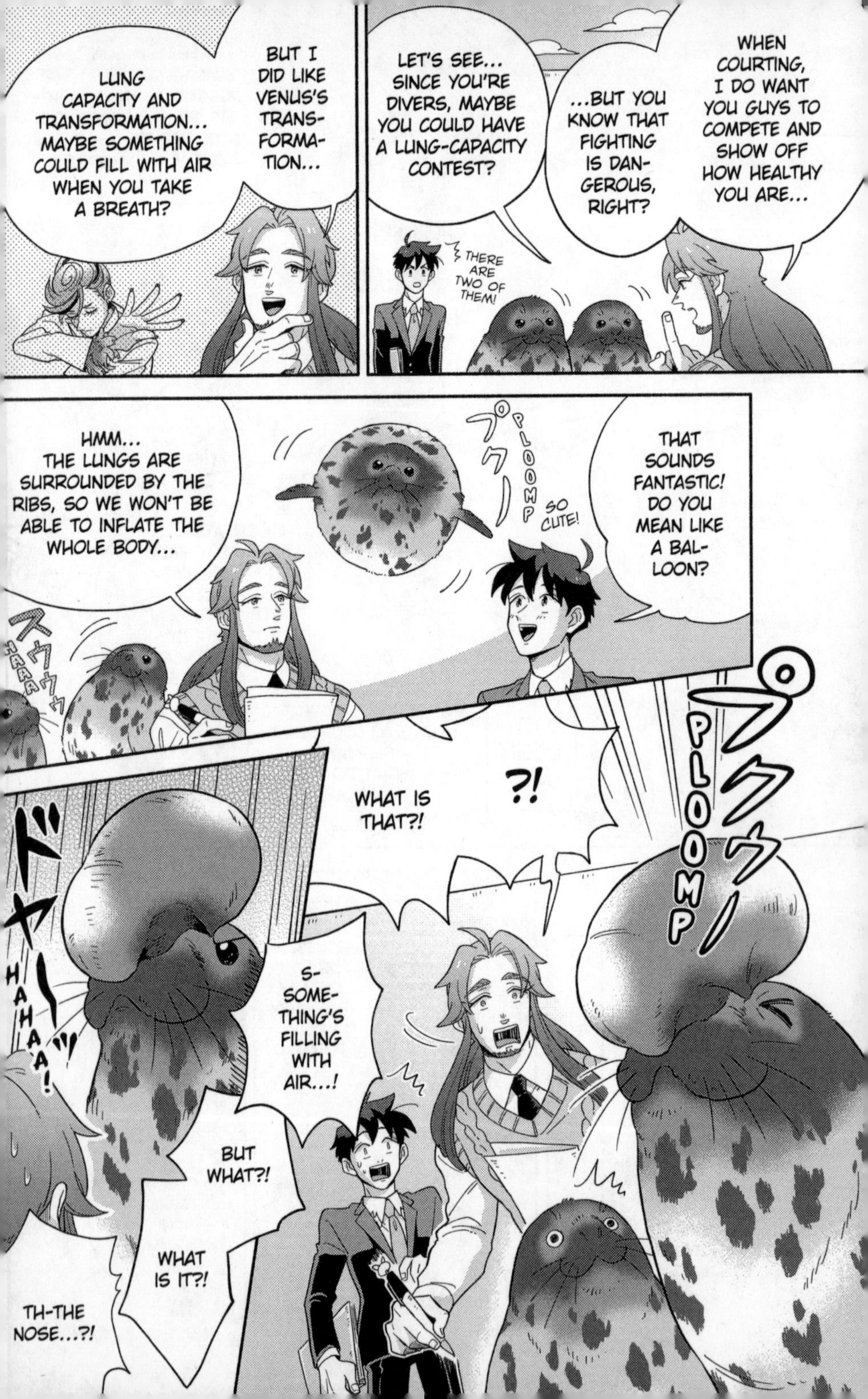
WHEN COURTING, I DO WANT YOU GUYS TO COMPETE AND SHOW OFF HOW HEALTHY YOU ARE…
…BUT YOU KNOW THAT FIGHTING IS DANGEROUS, RIGHT?
LET'S SEE… SINCE YOU'RE DIVERS, MAYBE YOU COULD HAVE A LUNG-CAPACITY CONTEST?
THERE ARE TWO OF THEM!
BUT I DID LIKE VENUS'S TRANSFORMATION…
LUNG CAPACITY AND TRANSFORMATION… MAYBE SOMETHING COULD FILL WITH AIR WHEN YOU TAKE A BREATH?
THAT SOUNDS FANTASTIC! DO YOU MEAN LIKE A BALLOON?
SO CUTE!
プクー PLOOMP
HMM… THE LUNGS ARE SURROUNDED BY THE RIBS, SO WE WON'T BE ABLE TO INFLATE THE WHOLE BODY…
スウウウ HAAAA
プクウー PLOOMP
?!
WHAT IS THAT?!
ドヤー HAHAAA!!
S-SOMETHING'S FILLING WITH AIR…!
BUT WHAT?!
WHAT IS IT?!
TH-THE NOSE…?!

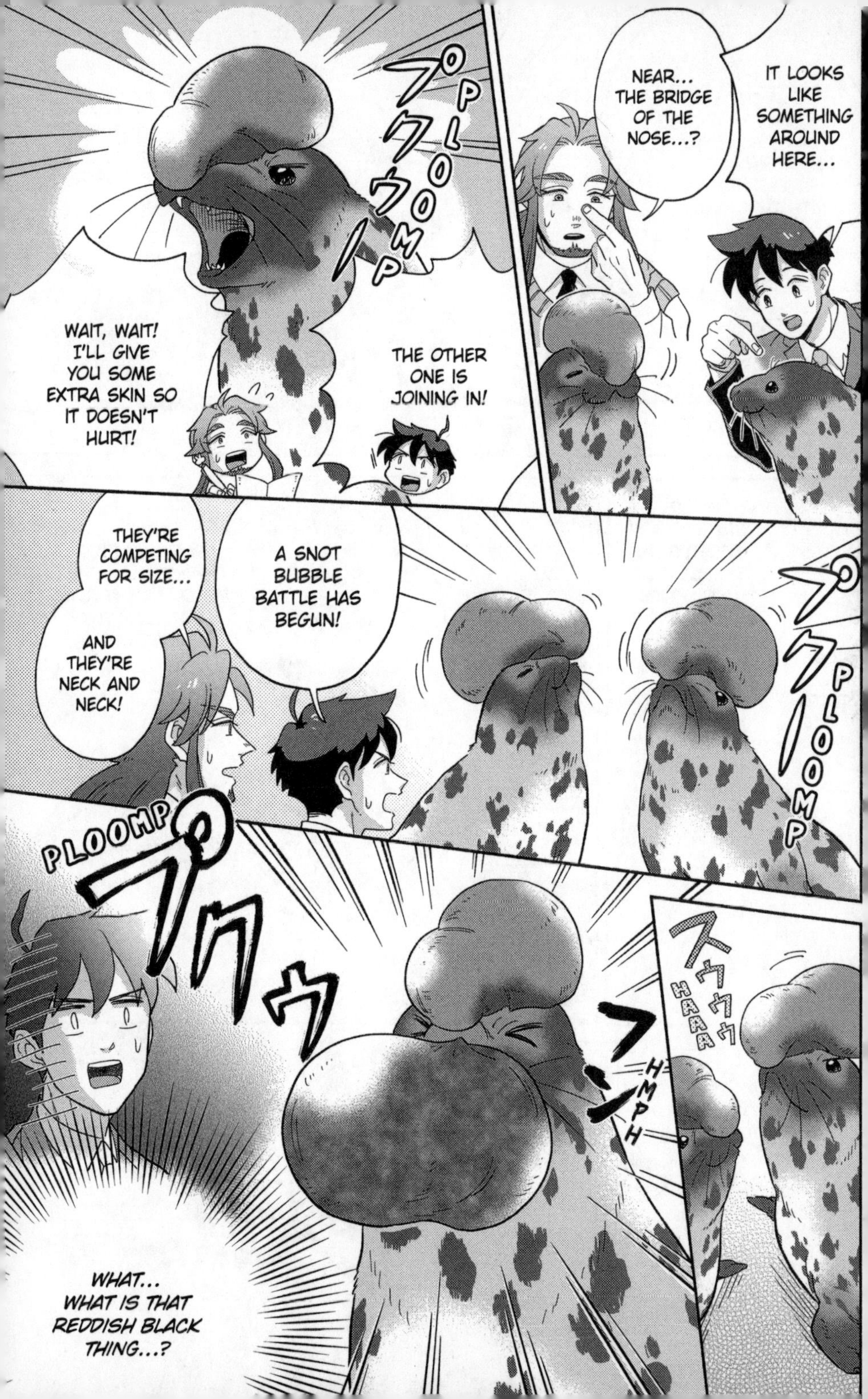

IT LOOKS LIKE SOMETHING AROUND HERE...
NEAR... THE BRIDGE OF THE NOSE...?
PLOOMP
THE OTHER ONE IS JOINING IN!
WAIT, WAIT! I'LL GIVE YOU SOME EXTRA SKIN SO IT DOESN'T HURT!
PLOOMP
A SNOT BUBBLE BATTLE HAS BEGUN!
THEY'RE COMPETING FOR SIZE...
AND THEY'RE NECK AND NECK!
HAAA
HMPH
PLOOMP
WHAT... WHAT IS THAT REDDISH BLACK THING...?

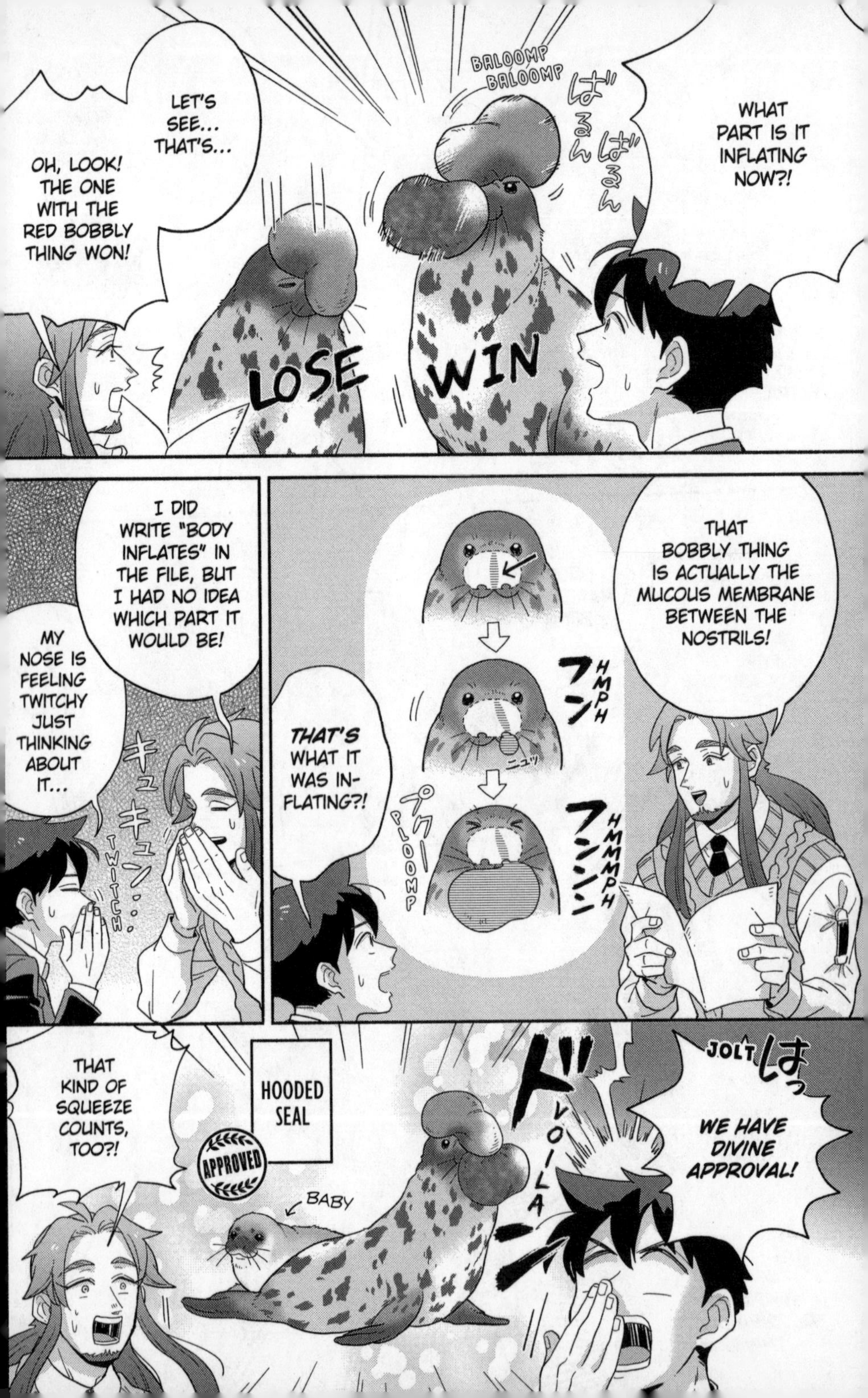
WHAT PART IS IT INFLATING NOW?!
BALOOMP BALOOMP
ばるん ばるん
WIN
LOSE
LET'S SEE... THAT'S...
OH, LOOK! THE ONE WITH THE RED BOBBLY THING WON!
THAT BOBBLY THING IS ACTUALLY THE MUCOUS MEMBRANE BETWEEN THE NOSTRILS!
フン HMPH
ニュッ
フンン HMMMPH
プクー PLOOMP
THAT'S WHAT IT WAS IN-FLATING?!
I DID WRITE "BODY INFLATES" IN THE FILE, BUT I HAD NO IDEA WHICH PART IT WOULD BE!
MY NOSE IS FEELING TWITCHY JUST THINKING ABOUT IT...
キュキューン TWITCH
JOLT はっ
WE HAVE DIVINE APPROVAL!
ド VOILA
HOODED SEAL
APPROVED
BABY
THAT KIND OF SQUEEZE COUNTS, TOO?!

THE ENCYCLOPEDIA OF REAL ANIMALS 24

ANIMAL 61 | HOODED SEAL

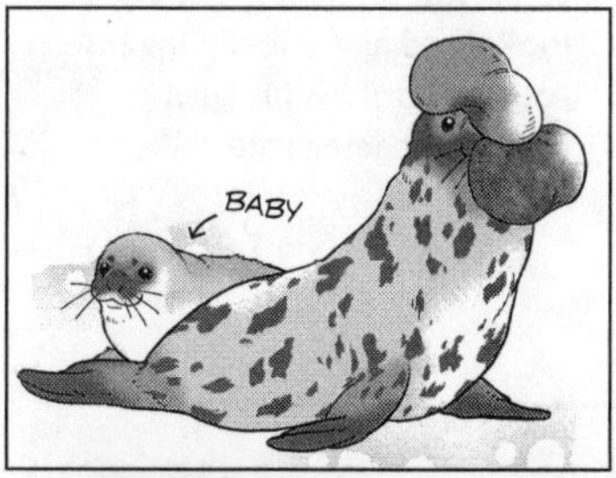
BABY

THE REAL THING

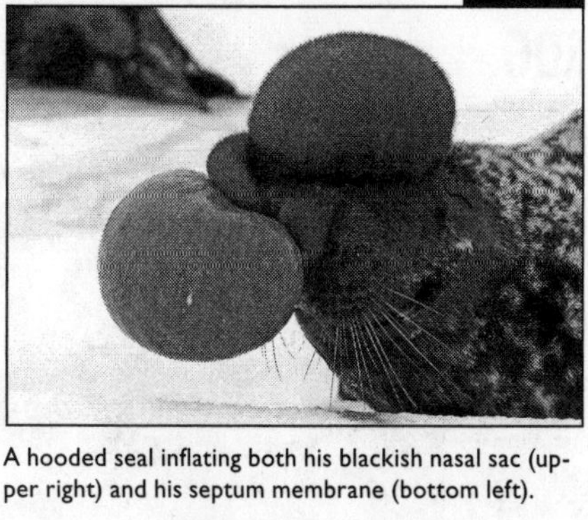

A hooded seal inflating both his blackish nasal sac (upper right) and his septum membrane (bottom left).

Photo: HEMIS/Aflo

Though its young are covered in fluffy grayish-white fur, the adult hooded seal has a mottled black coat. When the males reach around four years of age, they begin inflating their black nasal sacs to intimidate other males and attract females. The animal is named for the hood-like appearance of this sexual ornament.

When inflating the nasal sac is insufficiently impressive, the seal can also inflate its septum membrane from its left nostril, giving it the appearance of having a red balloon attached to its face. The animal is able to inflate these ornaments due to the flexible, elastic nature of its skin and septum. The hooded seal only nurses its pups for four days, giving it the record for the shortest lactation period of any mammal.

[Name]	*Cystophora cristata*
[Classification]	Class: Mammalia Order: Carnivora Family: Phodicae Genus: *Cystophora*
[Habitat]	Arctic and North Atlantic oceans
[Length]	220-250 cm (7-8 ft)

| # LONG-TAILED MANAKIN

THE REAL THING

As its name implies, the long-tailed manakin has beautiful, long tail feathers.
Photo: Photoshot/Aflo

Though many bird species attract mates with a courtship dance, the display of some members of the manakin family is unusual in that two males will cooperate to woo one female. If the dance is successful, only the alpha, or the "teacher," will mate with the female, while the companion, or "student," is relegated to his job of making the alpha look good and fine-tuning his routine until it's his turn to take the leading role.

[Name]   *Chiroxiphia linearis*
[Classification]   Class: Aves
Order: Passeriformes
Family: Pipridae
Genus: *Chiroxiphia*
[Habitat]   North and Central America
[Length]   10 cm (4 in)

| # FOOT-FLAGGING FROG

In the same way that a cello produces a lower tone than a violin, larger objects can create sounds with lower frequencies. This is why many frog species use calls and croaks in their mating display. The foot-flagging frog, however, lives primarily near the rapids of the rivers of Borneo, and therefore adapted to avoid its calls being drowned out by the sound of rushing water. The species instead raises and waves its hind legs and feet, the latter of which turn bluish white to better attract attention.

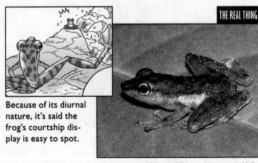

THE REAL THING

Because of its diurnal nature, it's said the frog's courtship display is easy to spot.

Photo: Hiroya Mizuguchi/Aflo

[Name]   Foot-flagging frog
[Classification]   Class: Amphibia
Order: Anura
Family: Ranidae
Genus: *Staurois*
[Habitat]   Primarily Borneo
[Length]   12-17 cm (4.7-6.7 in)

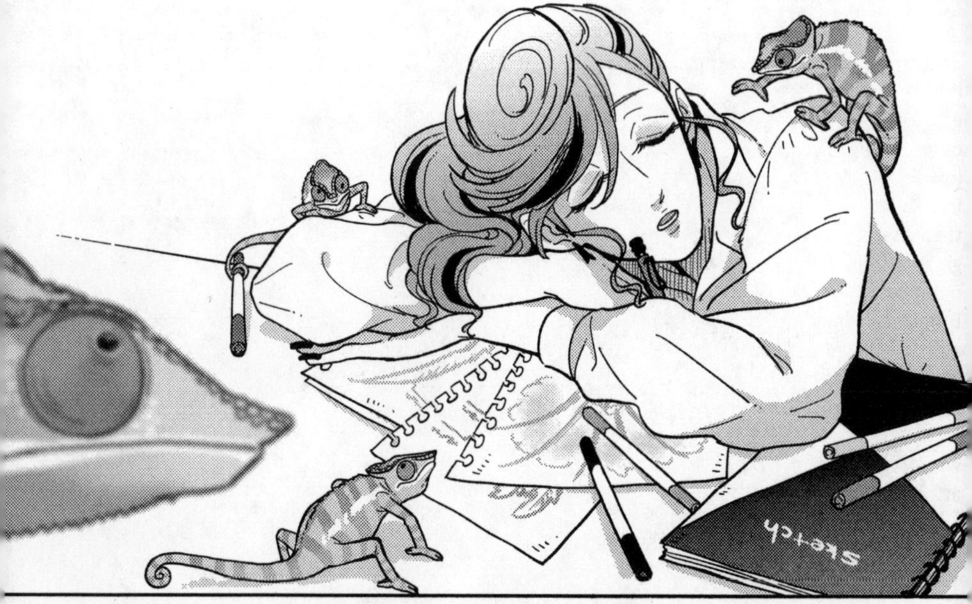
sketch

HEAVEN'S DESIGN TEAM

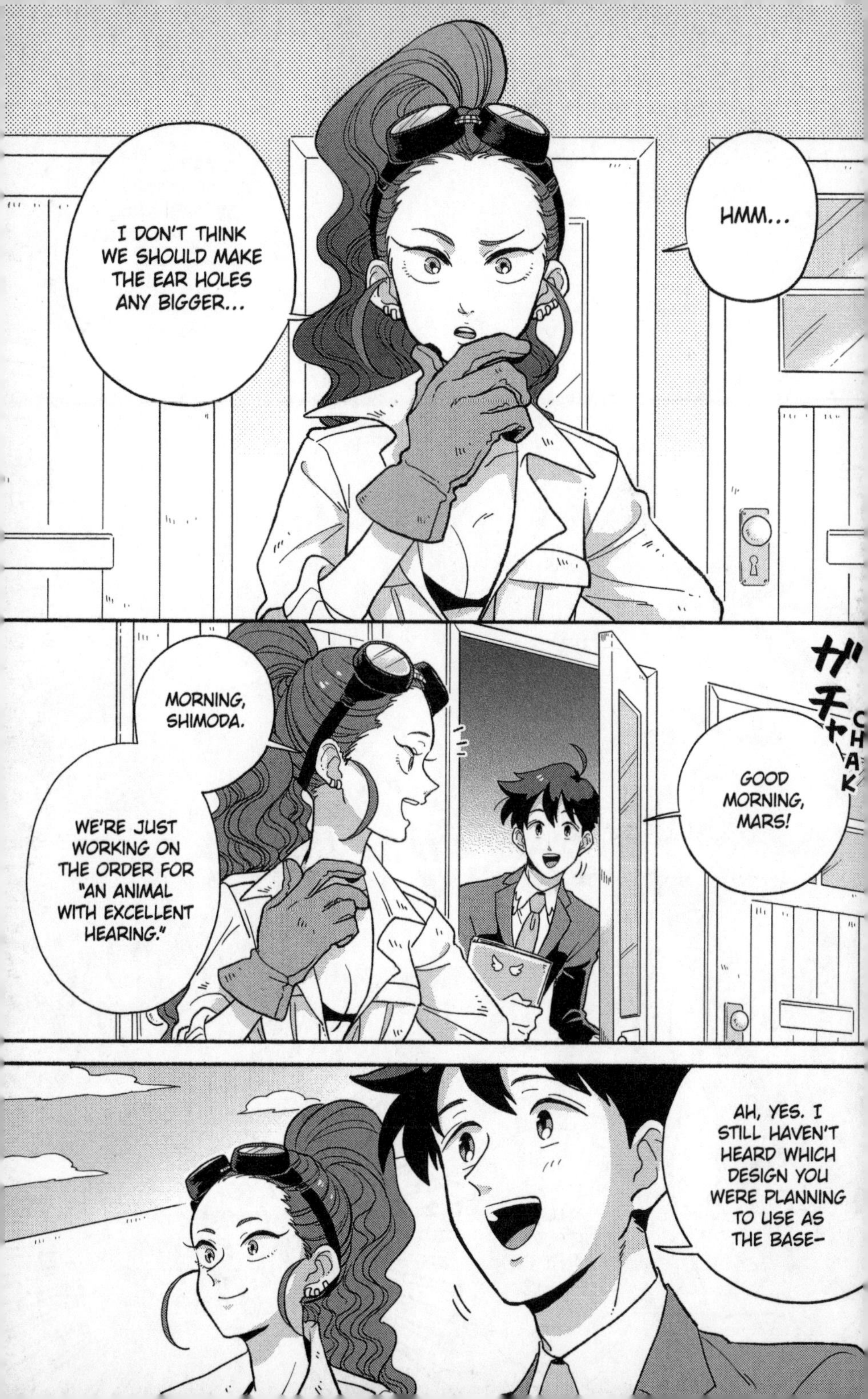
HMM...
I DON'T THINK WE SHOULD MAKE THE EAR HOLES ANY BIGGER...
ガチャ CHAK
GOOD MORNING, MARS!
MORNING, SHIMODA.
WE'RE JUST WORKING ON THE ORDER FOR "AN ANIMAL WITH EXCELLENT HEARING."
AH, YES. I STILL HAVEN'T HEARD WHICH DESIGN YOU WERE PLANNING TO USE AS THE BASE-

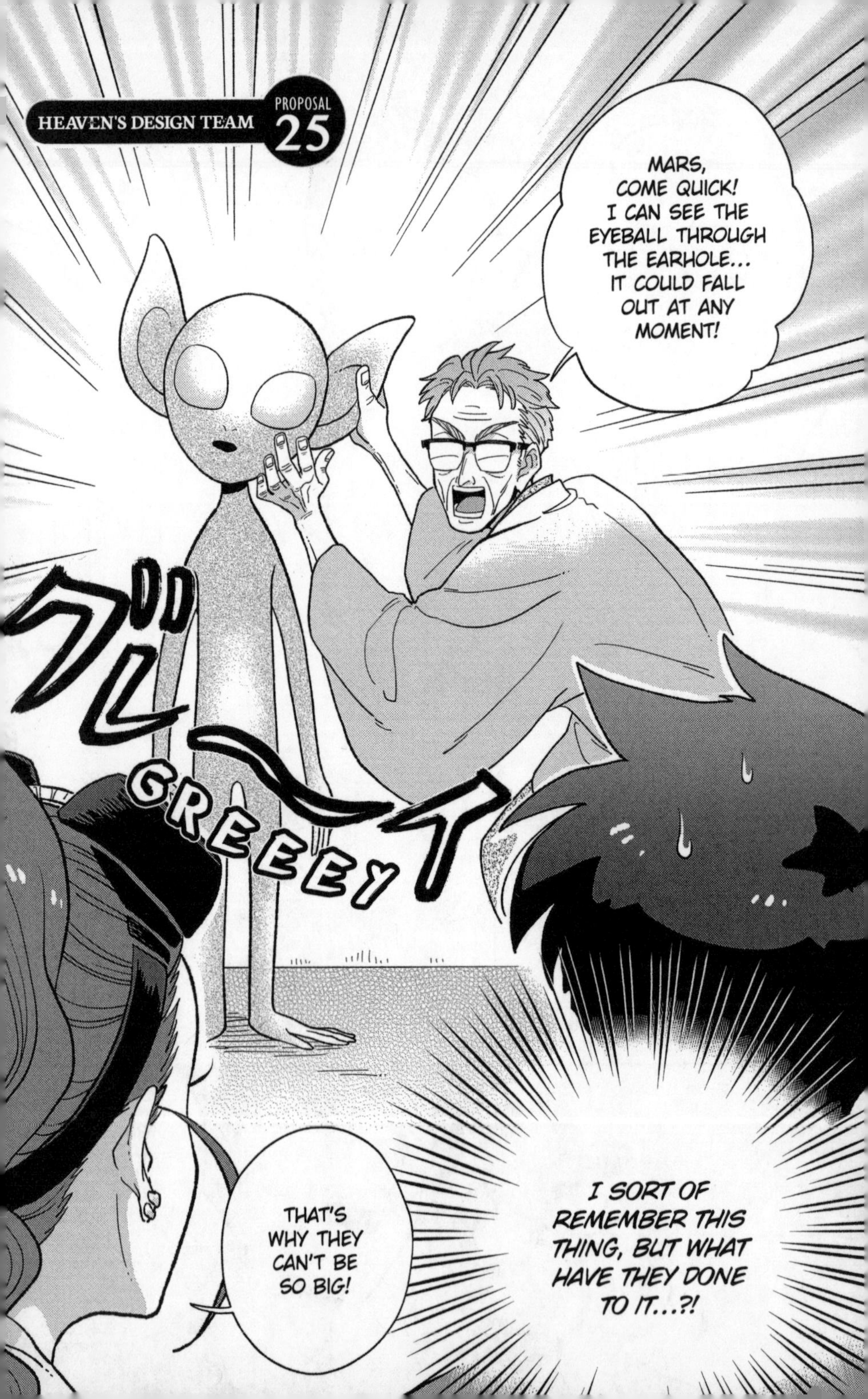
HEAVEN'S DESIGN TEAM
PROPOSAL 25
MARS, COME QUICK! I CAN SEE THE EYEBALL THROUGH THE EARHOLE... IT COULD FALL OUT AT ANY MOMENT!
グレ〜イ
GREEEY
I SORT OF REMEMBER THIS THING, BUT WHAT HAVE THEY DONE TO IT...?!
THAT'S WHY THEY CAN'T BE SO BIG!

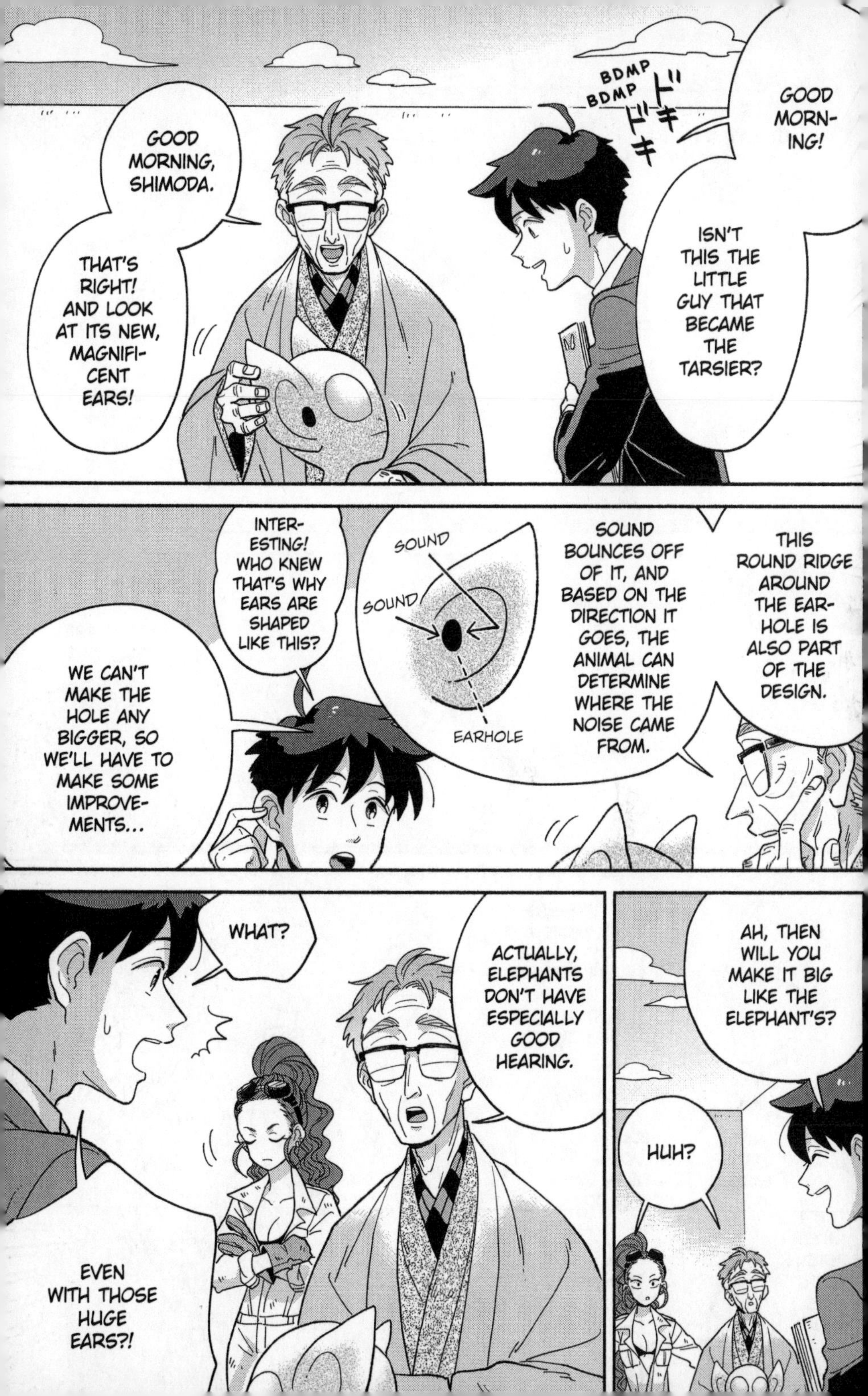

GOOD MORNING!
BDMP BDMP ドキドキ
GOOD MORNING, SHIMODA.
ISN'T THIS THE LITTLE GUY THAT BECAME THE TARSIER?
THAT'S RIGHT! AND LOOK AT ITS NEW, MAGNIFICENT EARS!
THIS ROUND RIDGE AROUND THE EAR-HOLE IS ALSO PART OF THE DESIGN.
SOUND BOUNCES OFF OF IT, AND BASED ON THE DIRECTION IT GOES, THE ANIMAL CAN DETERMINE WHERE THE NOISE CAME FROM.
SOUND
SOUND
EARHOLE
INTER-ESTING! WHO KNEW THAT'S WHY EARS ARE SHAPED LIKE THIS?
WE CAN'T MAKE THE HOLE ANY BIGGER, SO WE'LL HAVE TO MAKE SOME IMPROVE-MENTS...
AH, THEN WILL YOU MAKE IT BIG LIKE THE ELEPHANT'S?
HUH?
ACTUALLY, ELEPHANTS DON'T HAVE ESPECIALLY GOOD HEARING.
WHAT?
EVEN WITH THOSE HUGE EARS?!

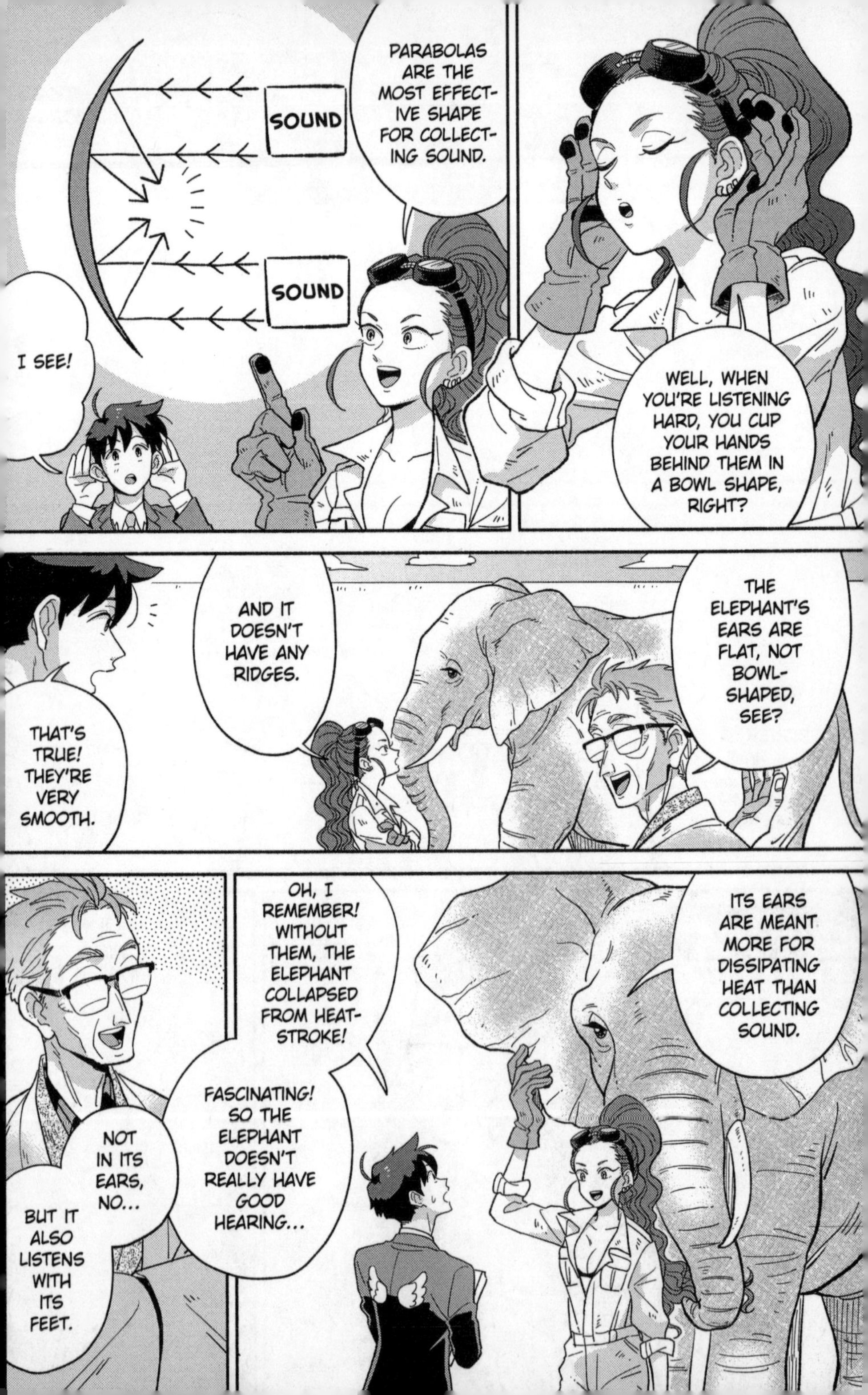
WELL, WHEN YOU'RE LISTENING HARD, YOU CUP YOUR HANDS BEHIND THEM IN A BOWL SHAPE, RIGHT?
PARABOLAS ARE THE MOST EFFECTIVE SHAPE FOR COLLECTING SOUND.
SOUND
SOUND
I SEE!
THE ELEPHANT'S EARS ARE FLAT, NOT BOWL-SHAPED, SEE?
AND IT DOESN'T HAVE ANY RIDGES.
THAT'S TRUE! THEY'RE VERY SMOOTH.
ITS EARS ARE MEANT MORE FOR DISSIPATING HEAT THAN COLLECTING SOUND.
OH, I REMEMBER! WITHOUT THEM, THE ELEPHANT COLLAPSED FROM HEAT-STROKE!
FASCINATING! SO THE ELEPHANT DOESN'T REALLY HAVE GOOD HEARING...
NOT IN ITS EARS, NO...
BUT IT ALSO LISTENS WITH ITS FEET.

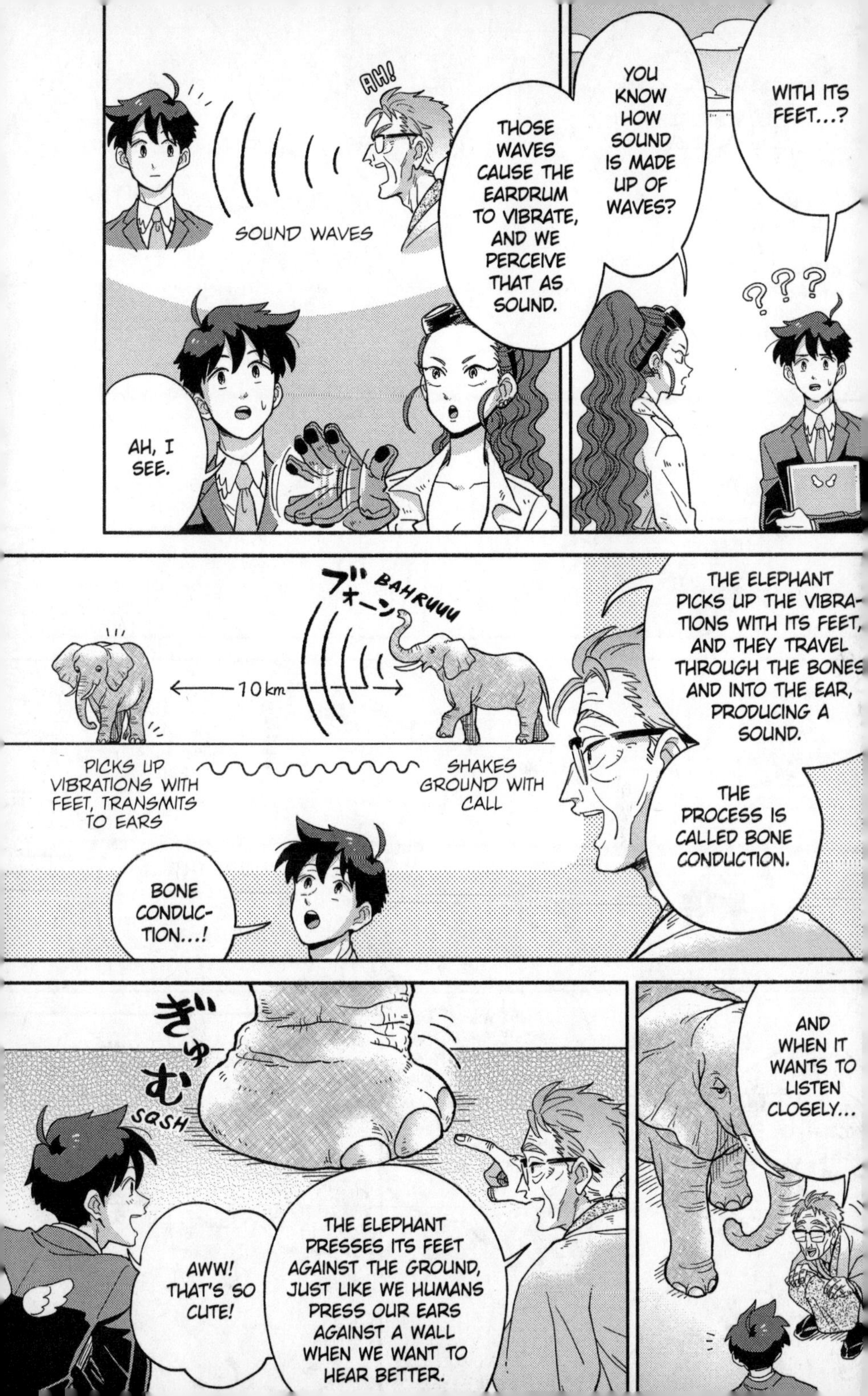
WITH ITS FEET...?
YOU KNOW HOW SOUND IS MADE UP OF WAVES?
???
AH!
SOUND WAVES
THOSE WAVES CAUSE THE EARDRUM TO VIBRATE, AND WE PERCEIVE THAT AS SOUND.
AH, I SEE.
THE ELEPHANT PICKS UP THE VIBRATIONS WITH ITS FEET, AND THEY TRAVEL THROUGH THE BONES AND INTO THE EAR, PRODUCING A SOUND.
THE PROCESS IS CALLED BONE CONDUCTION.
ブォーン BAHRUUU
10 km
SHAKES GROUND WITH CALL
PICKS UP VIBRATIONS WITH FEET, TRANSMITS TO EARS
BONE CONDUCTION...!
AND WHEN IT WANTS TO LISTEN CLOSELY...
ぎゅむ SQSH
THE ELEPHANT PRESSES ITS FEET AGAINST THE GROUND, JUST LIKE WE HUMANS PRESS OUR EARS AGAINST A WALL WHEN WE WANT TO HEAR BETTER.
AWW! THAT'S SO CUTE!

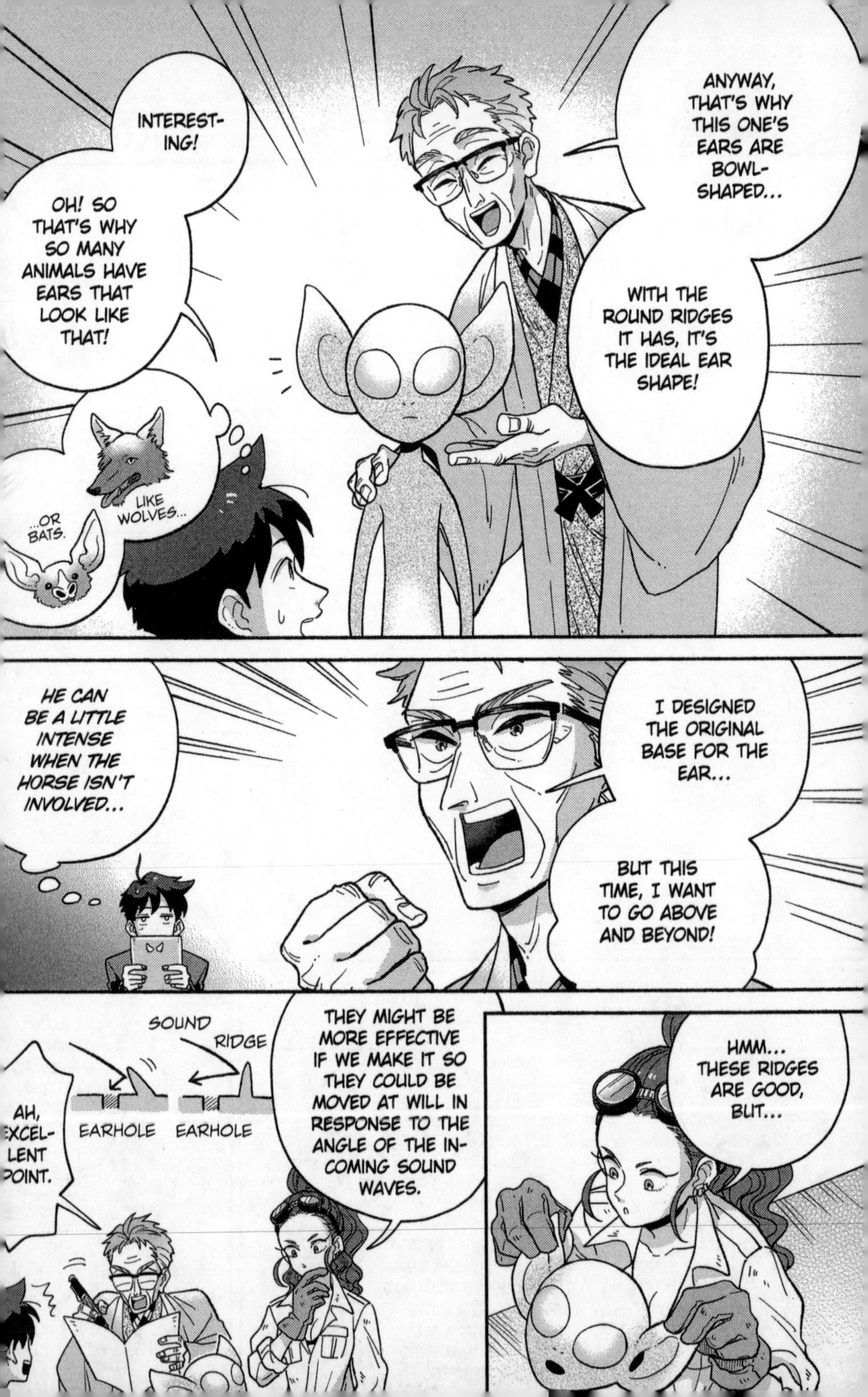

ANYWAY, THAT'S WHY THIS ONE'S EARS ARE BOWL-SHAPED...
WITH THE ROUND RIDGES IT HAS, IT'S THE IDEAL EAR SHAPE!
INTERESTING!
OH! SO THAT'S WHY SO MANY ANIMALS HAVE EARS THAT LOOK LIKE THAT!
LIKE WOLVES...
...OR BATS.
I DESIGNED THE ORIGINAL BASE FOR THE EAR...
BUT THIS TIME, I WANT TO GO ABOVE AND BEYOND!
HE CAN BE A LITTLE INTENSE WHEN THE HORSE ISN'T INVOLVED...
HMM... THESE RIDGES ARE GOOD, BUT...
THEY MIGHT BE MORE EFFECTIVE IF WE MAKE IT SO THEY COULD BE MOVED AT WILL IN RESPONSE TO THE ANGLE OF THE INCOMING SOUND WAVES.
SOUND
RIDGE
EARHOLE
EARHOLE
AH, EXCELLENT POINT.

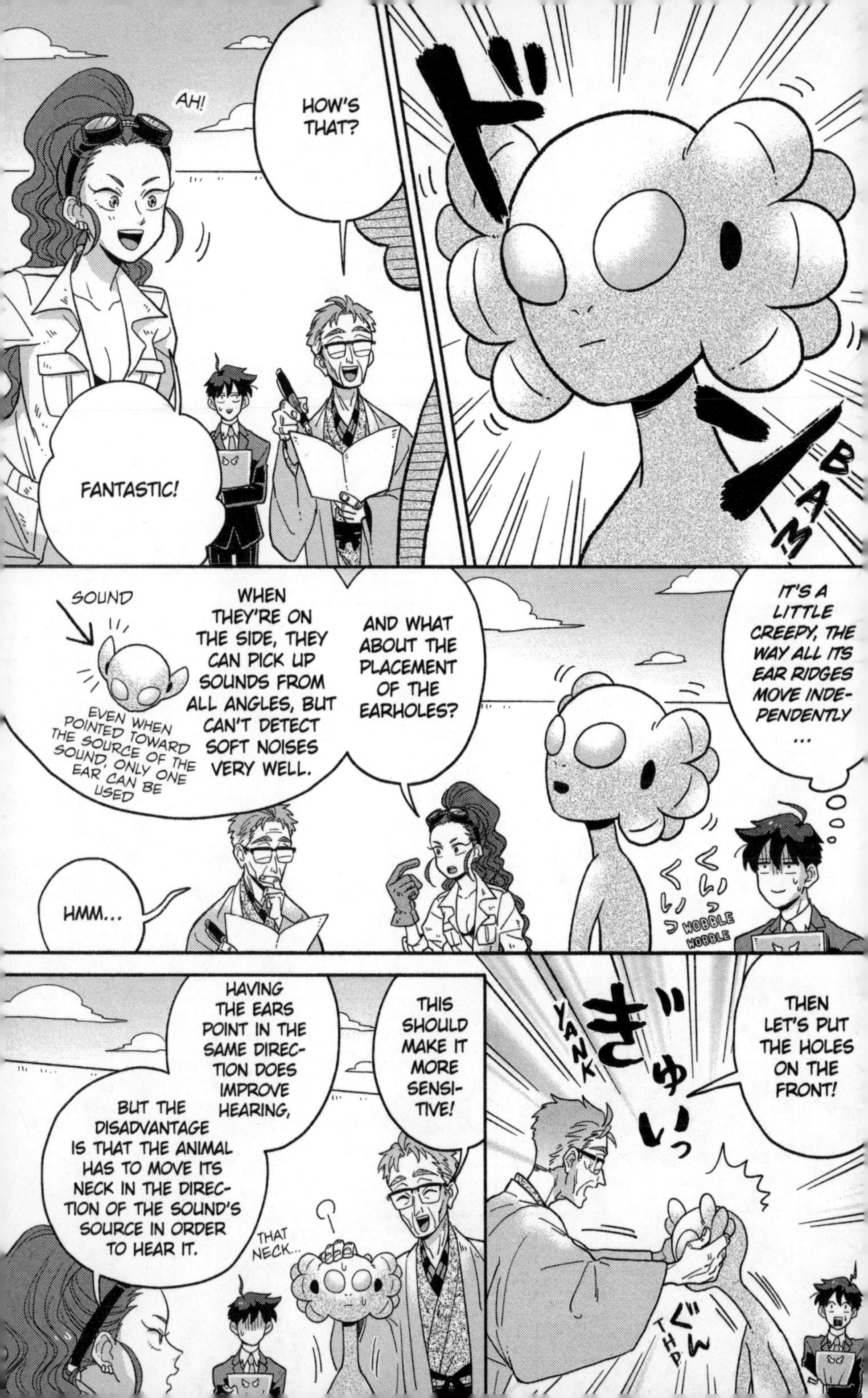
ドー
BAM
HOW'S THAT?
AH!
FANTASTIC!
IT'S A LITTLE CREEPY, THE WAY ALL ITS EAR RIDGES MOVE INDEPENDENTLY...
くんっ くんっ
WOBBLE WOBBLE
AND WHAT ABOUT THE PLACEMENT OF THE EARHOLES?
WHEN THEY'RE ON THE SIDE, THEY CAN PICK UP SOUNDS FROM ALL ANGLES, BUT CAN'T DETECT SOFT NOISES VERY WELL.
SOUND
EVEN WHEN POINTED TOWARD THE SOURCE OF THE SOUND, ONLY ONE EAR CAN BE USED
HMM...
THEN LET'S PUT THE HOLES ON THE FRONT!
きゅいっ
YANK
ぐん
THP
THIS SHOULD MAKE IT MORE SENSITIVE!
HAVING THE EARS POINT IN THE SAME DIRECTION DOES IMPROVE HEARING,
BUT THE DISADVANTAGE IS THAT THE ANIMAL HAS TO MOVE ITS NECK IN THE DIRECTION OF THE SOUND'S SOURCE IN ORDER TO HEAR IT.
THAT NECK...

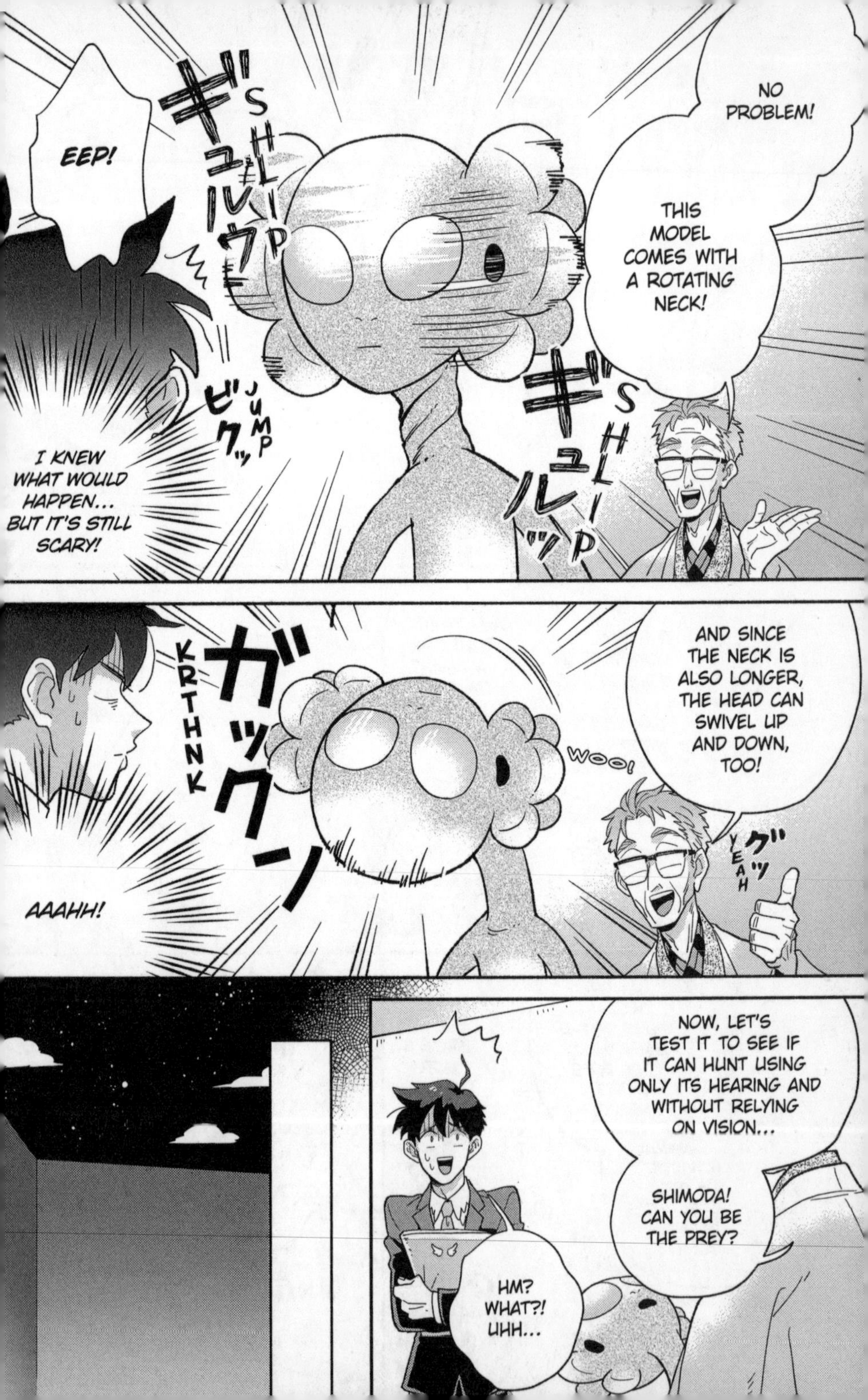
NO PROBLEM!
THIS MODEL COMES WITH A ROTATING NECK!
ギュルッ
SHLIP
ギュルウ
SHLIP
EEP!
ビクッ
JUMP
I KNEW WHAT WOULD HAPPEN... BUT IT'S STILL SCARY!
AND SINCE THE NECK IS ALSO LONGER, THE HEAD CAN SWIVEL UP AND DOWN, TOO!
WOO!
グッ
YEAH
ガックーン
KRTHNK
AAAHH!
NOW, LET'S TEST IT TO SEE IF IT CAN HUNT USING ONLY ITS HEARING AND WITHOUT RELYING ON VISION...
SHIMODA! CAN YOU BE THE PREY?
HM? WHAT?! UHH...

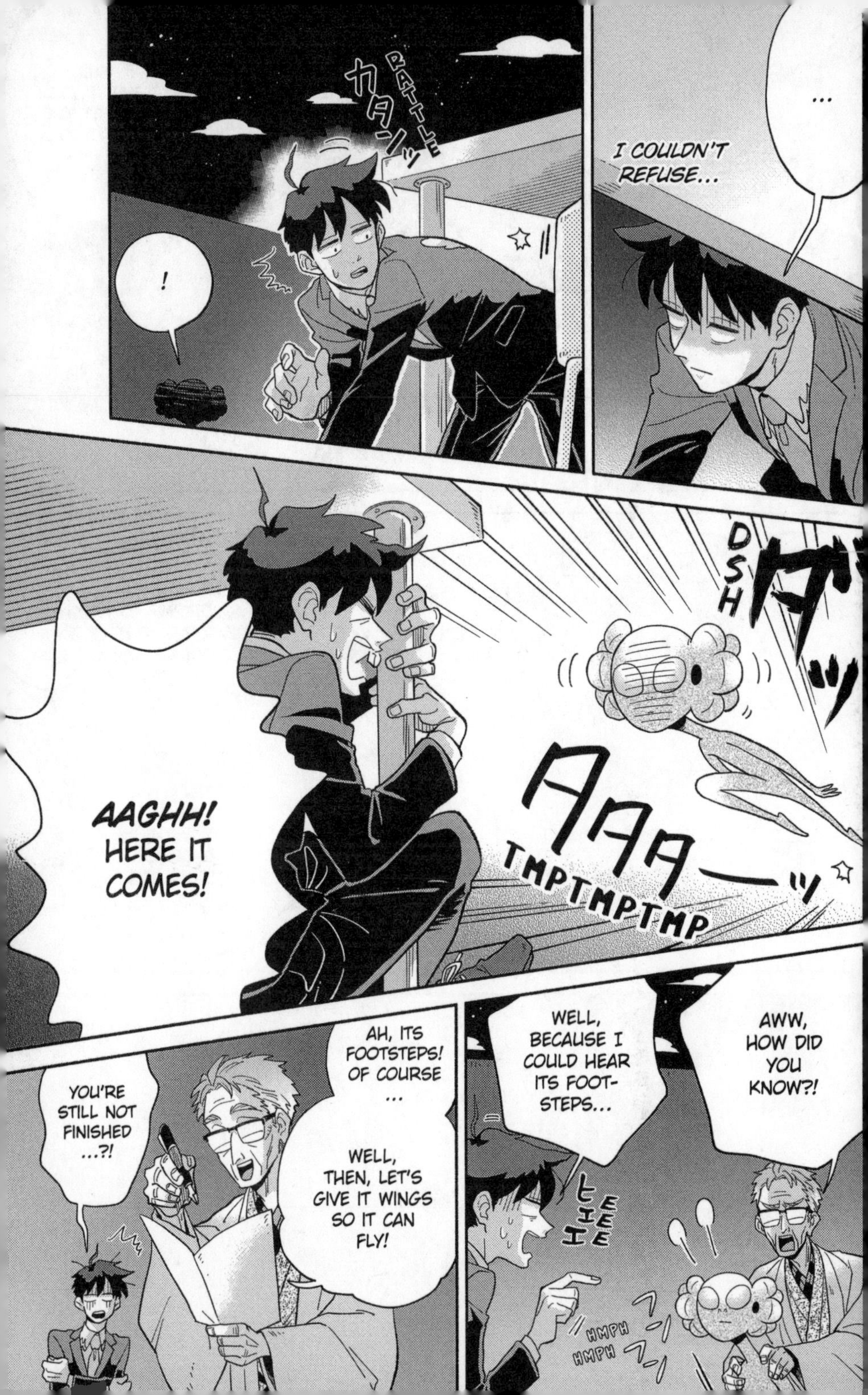
...
I COULDN'T REFUSE...
RATTLE
!
DSH
AAGHH! HERE IT COMES!
TMPTMPTMP
AWW, HOW DID YOU KNOW?!
WELL, BECAUSE I COULD HEAR ITS FOOT-STEPS...
EEEE
HMPH HMPH
AH, ITS FOOTSTEPS! OF COURSE ...
WELL, THEN, LET'S GIVE IT WINGS SO IT CAN FLY!
YOU'RE STILL NOT FINISHED ...?!

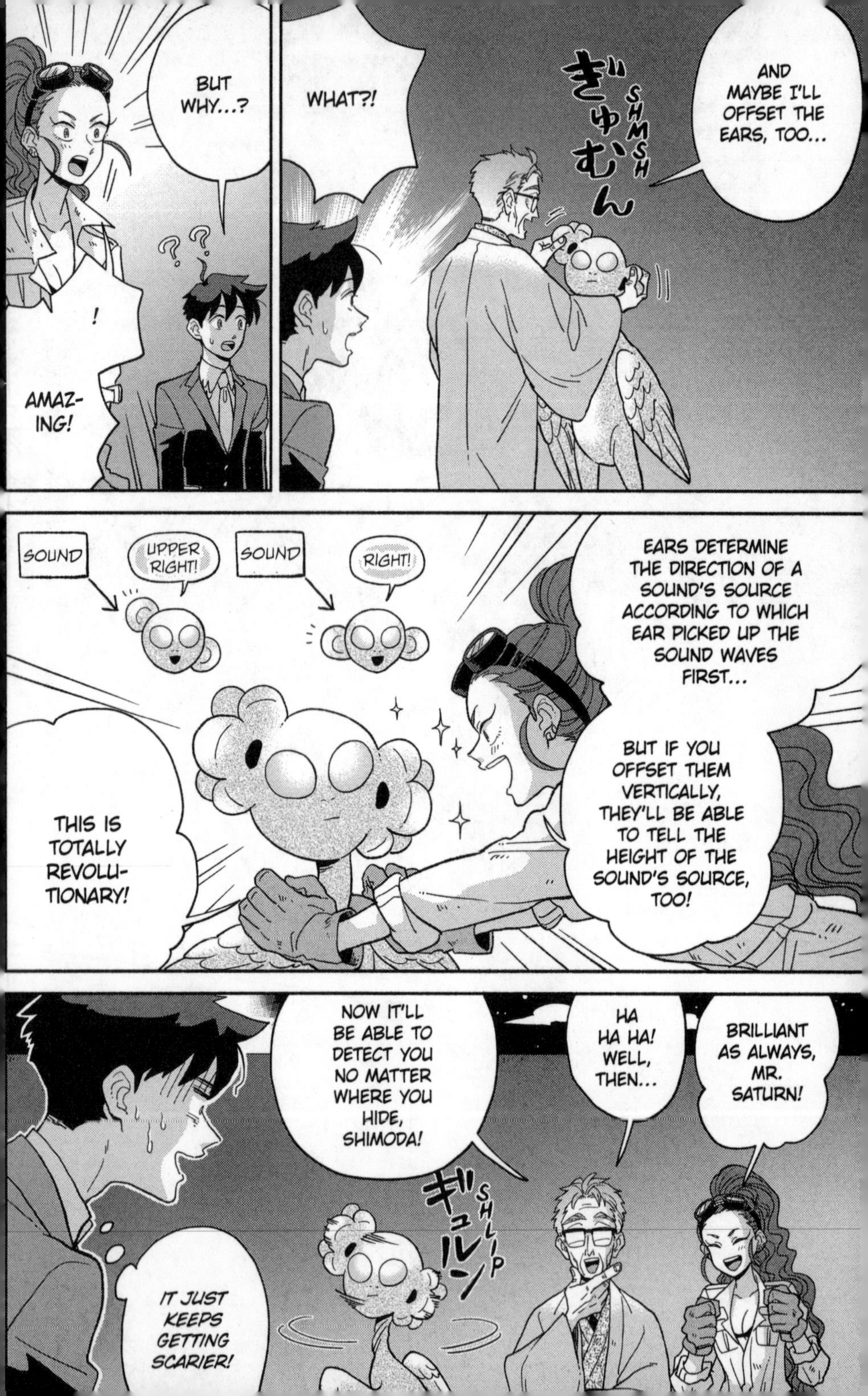
AND MAYBE I'LL OFFSET THE EARS, TOO...
ぎゅむん
SHMSH
WHAT?!
BUT WHY...?
!
AMAZ-ING!
EARS DETERMINE THE DIRECTION OF A SOUND'S SOURCE ACCORDING TO WHICH EAR PICKED UP THE SOUND WAVES FIRST...
SOUND
UPPER RIGHT!
SOUND
RIGHT!
BUT IF YOU OFFSET THEM VERTICALLY, THEY'LL BE ABLE TO TELL THE HEIGHT OF THE SOUND'S SOURCE, TOO!
THIS IS TOTALLY REVOLU-TIONARY!
BRILLIANT AS ALWAYS, MR. SATURN!
HA HA HA! WELL, THEN...
NOW IT'LL BE ABLE TO DETECT YOU NO MATTER WHERE YOU HIDE, SHIMODA!
ギュルン
SHLIP
IT JUST KEEPS GETTING SCARIER!

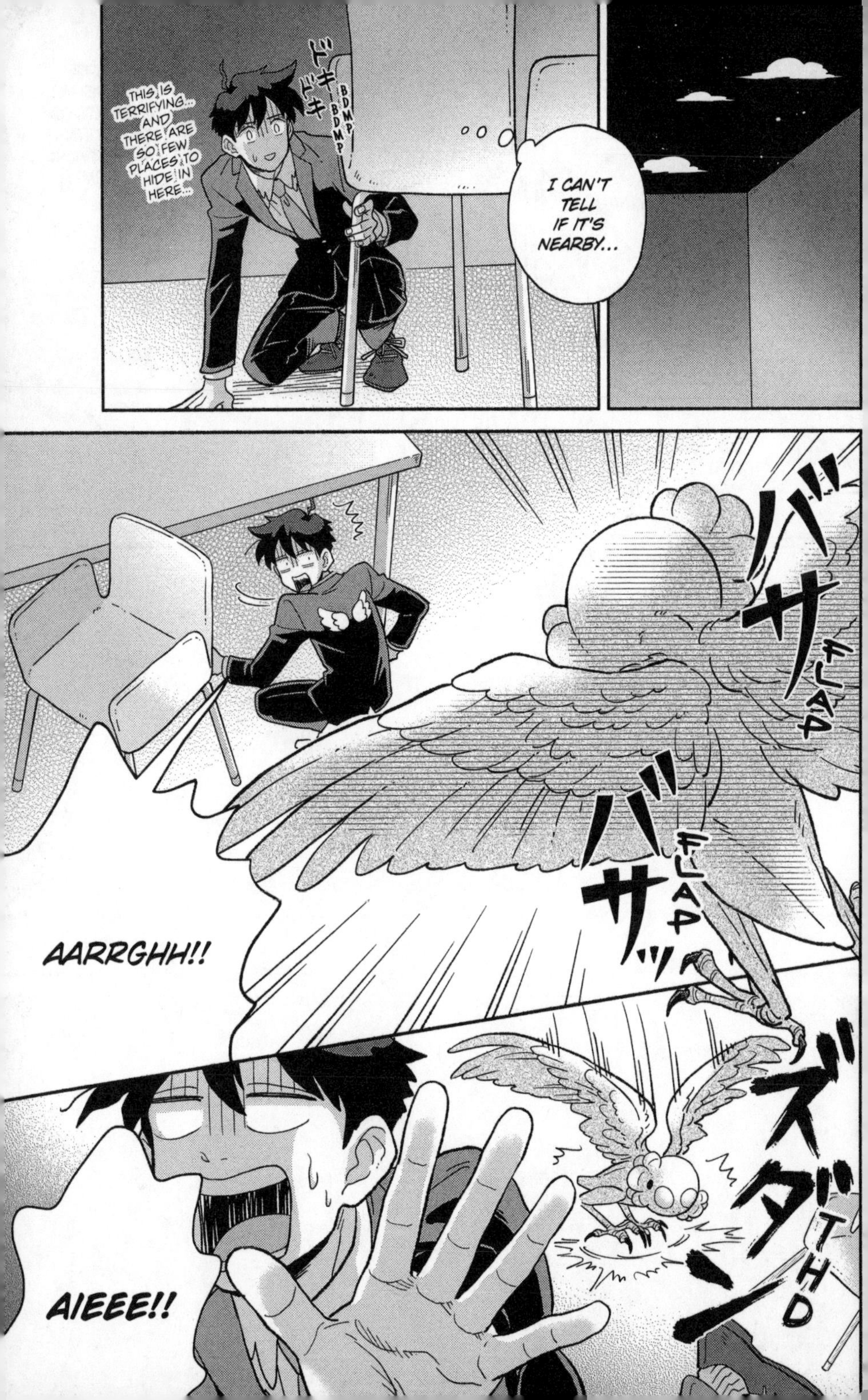
I CAN'T TELL IF IT'S NEARBY...
ドキドキ
BDMP BDMP
THIS IS TERRIFYING... AND THERE ARE SO FEW PLACES TO HIDE IN HERE...
バサ
FLAP
バサッ
FLAP
AARRGHH!!
ズダーン
THD
AIEEE!!

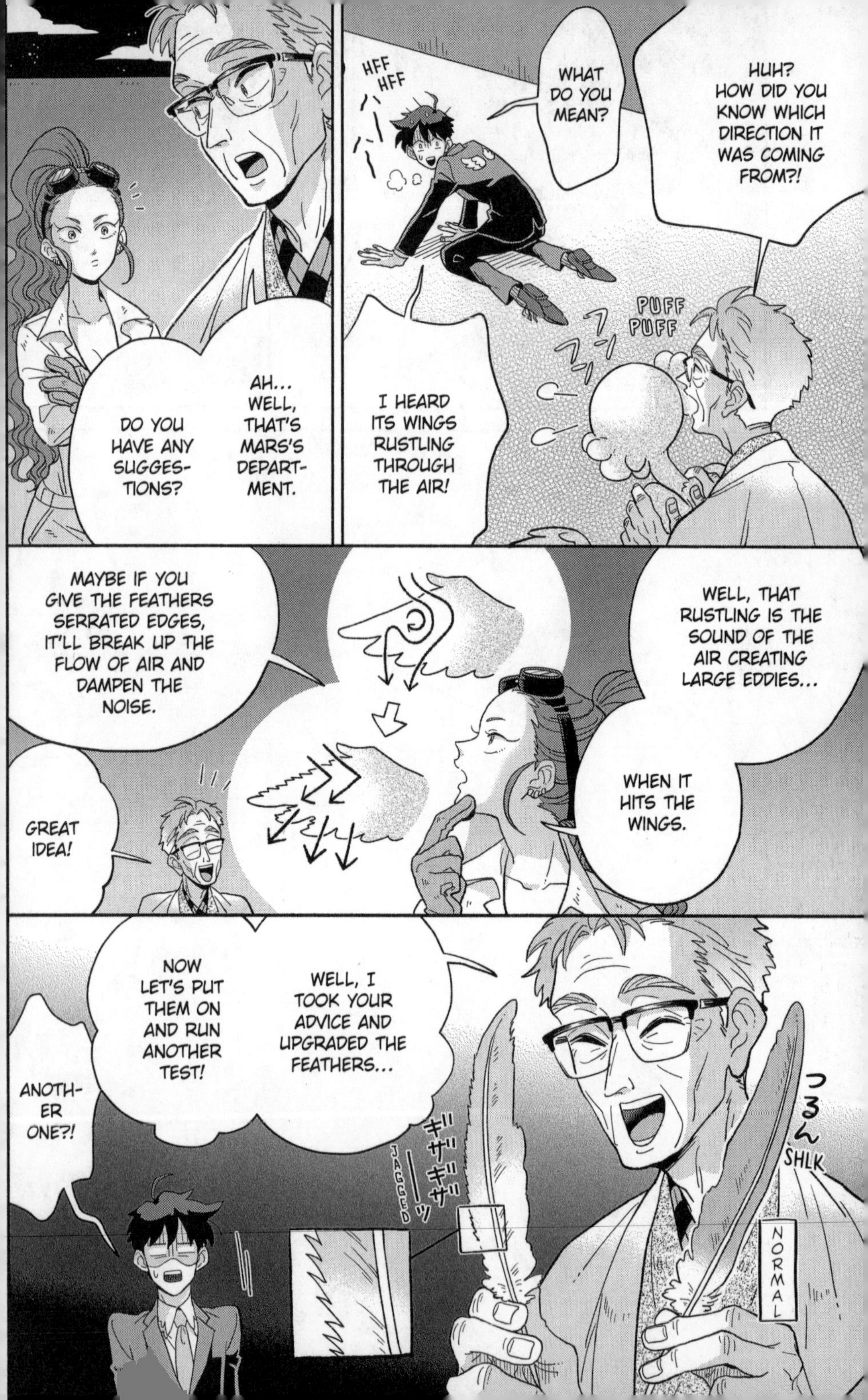
HUH? HOW DID YOU KNOW WHICH DIRECTION IT WAS COMING FROM?!
WHAT DO YOU MEAN?
HFF HFF
PUFF PUFF
I HEARD ITS WINGS RUSTLING THROUGH THE AIR!
AH... WELL, THAT'S MARS'S DEPART-MENT.
DO YOU HAVE ANY SUGGES-TIONS?
WELL, THAT RUSTLING IS THE SOUND OF THE AIR CREATING LARGE EDDIES...
WHEN IT HITS THE WINGS.
MAYBE IF YOU GIVE THE FEATHERS SERRATED EDGES, IT'LL BREAK UP THE FLOW OF AIR AND DAMPEN THE NOISE.
GREAT IDEA!
WELL, I TOOK YOUR ADVICE AND UPGRADED THE FEATHERS...
NOW LET'S PUT THEM ON AND RUN ANOTHER TEST!
つるん
SHLK
NORMAL
ギザギザ
JAGGED
ANOTH-ER ONE?!

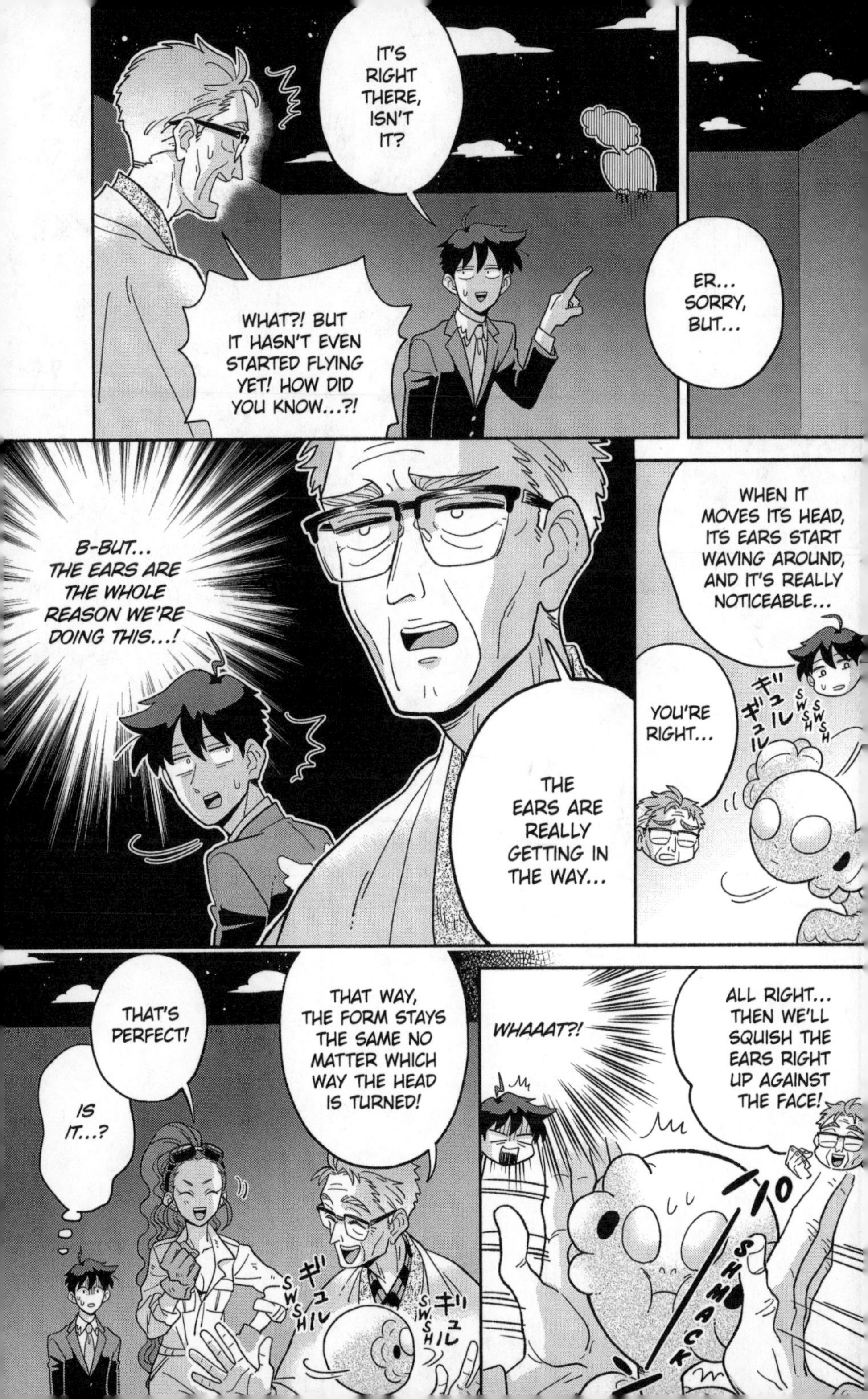
ER... SORRY, BUT...
IT'S RIGHT THERE, ISN'T IT?
WHAT?! BUT IT HASN'T EVEN STARTED FLYING YET! HOW DID YOU KNOW...?!
WHEN IT MOVES ITS HEAD, ITS EARS START WAVING AROUND, AND IT'S REALLY NOTICEABLE...
YOU'RE RIGHT...
ギュル ギュル
SWSH SWSH
THE EARS ARE REALLY GETTING IN THE WAY...
B-BUT... THE EARS ARE THE WHOLE REASON WE'RE DOING THIS...!
ALL RIGHT... THEN WE'LL SQUISH THE EARS RIGHT UP AGAINST THE FACE!
WHAAAT?!
SHMACK
THAT WAY, THE FORM STAYS THE SAME NO MATTER WHICH WAY THE HEAD IS TURNED!
THAT'S PERFECT!
IS IT...?
ギュル SWSH
ギュル SWSH

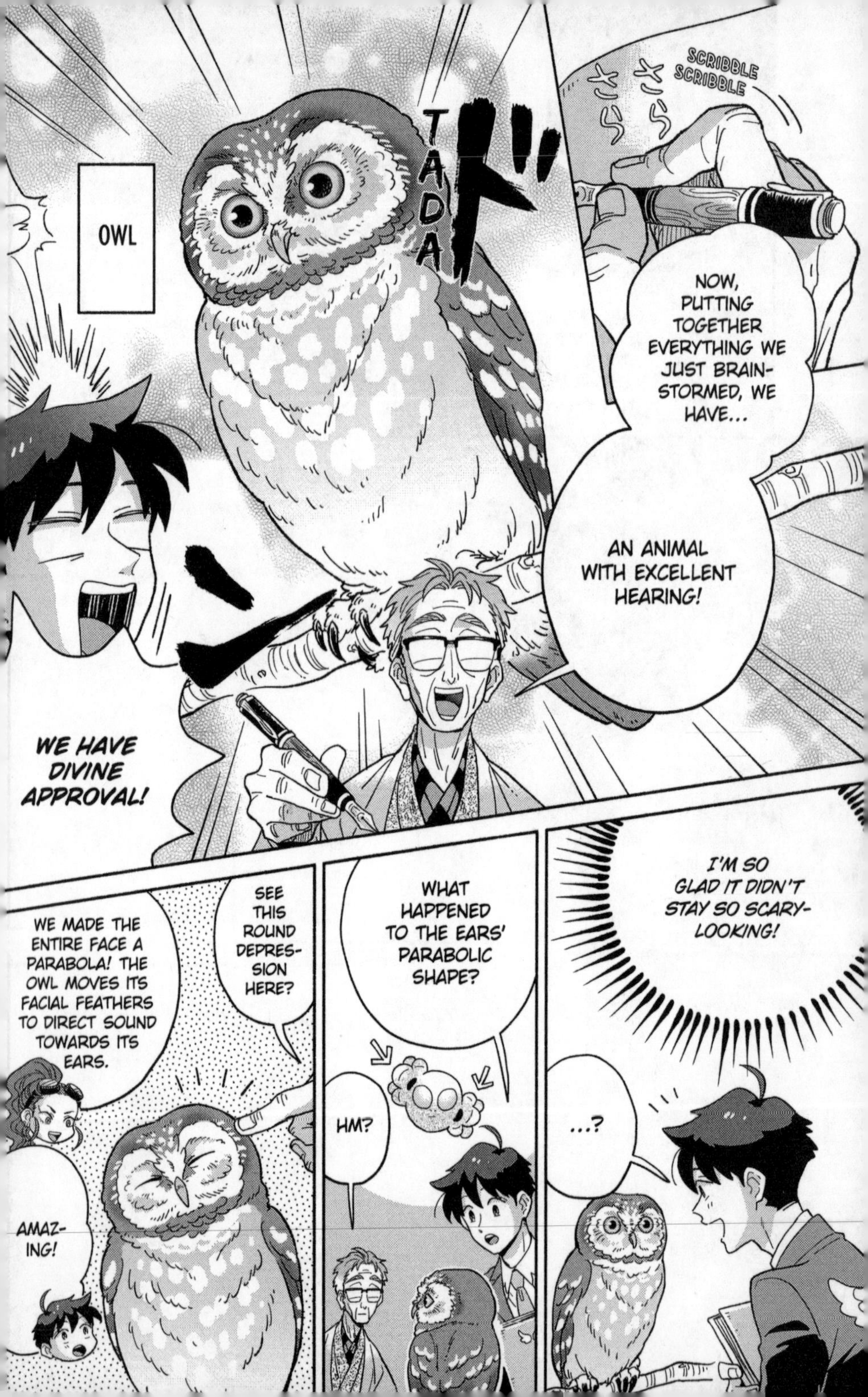
SCRIBBLE SCRIBBLE
NOW, PUTTING TOGETHER EVERYTHING WE JUST BRAIN-STORMED, WE HAVE...
AN ANIMAL WITH EXCELLENT HEARING!
TADA
OWL
WE HAVE DIVINE APPROVAL!
I'M SO GLAD IT DIDN'T STAY SO SCARY-LOOKING!
...?
WHAT HAPPENED TO THE EARS' PARABOLIC SHAPE?
HM?
SEE THIS ROUND DEPRES-SION HERE?
WE MADE THE ENTIRE FACE A PARABOLA! THE OWL MOVES ITS FACIAL FEATHERS TO DIRECT SOUND TOWARDS ITS EARS.
AMAZ-ING!

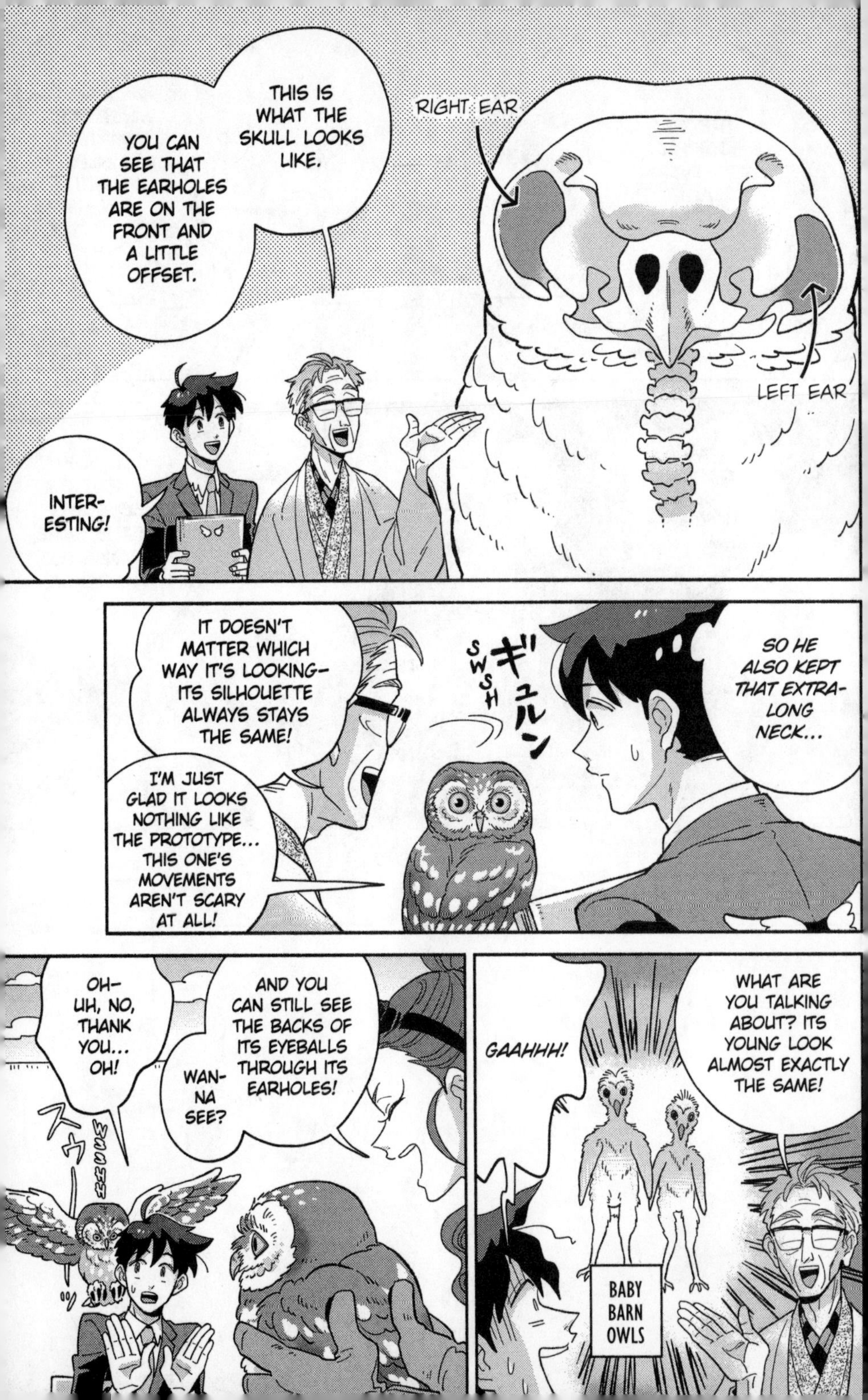
RIGHT EAR
THIS IS WHAT THE SKULL LOOKS LIKE.
YOU CAN SEE THAT THE EARHOLES ARE ON THE FRONT AND A LITTLE OFFSET.
LEFT EAR
INTER-ESTING!
SO HE ALSO KEPT THAT EXTRA-LONG NECK...
ギュルン
SWSH
IT DOESN'T MATTER WHICH WAY IT'S LOOKING–ITS SILHOUETTE ALWAYS STAYS THE SAME!
I'M JUST GLAD IT LOOKS NOTHING LIKE THE PROTOTYPE... THIS ONE'S MOVEMENTS AREN'T SCARY AT ALL!
WHAT ARE YOU TALKING ABOUT? ITS YOUNG LOOK ALMOST EXACTLY THE SAME!
GAAHHH!
BABY BARN OWLS
AND YOU CAN STILL SEE THE BACKS OF ITS EYEBALLS THROUGH ITS EARHOLES!
WAN-NA SEE?
OH– UH, NO, THANK YOU... OH!
スゥー

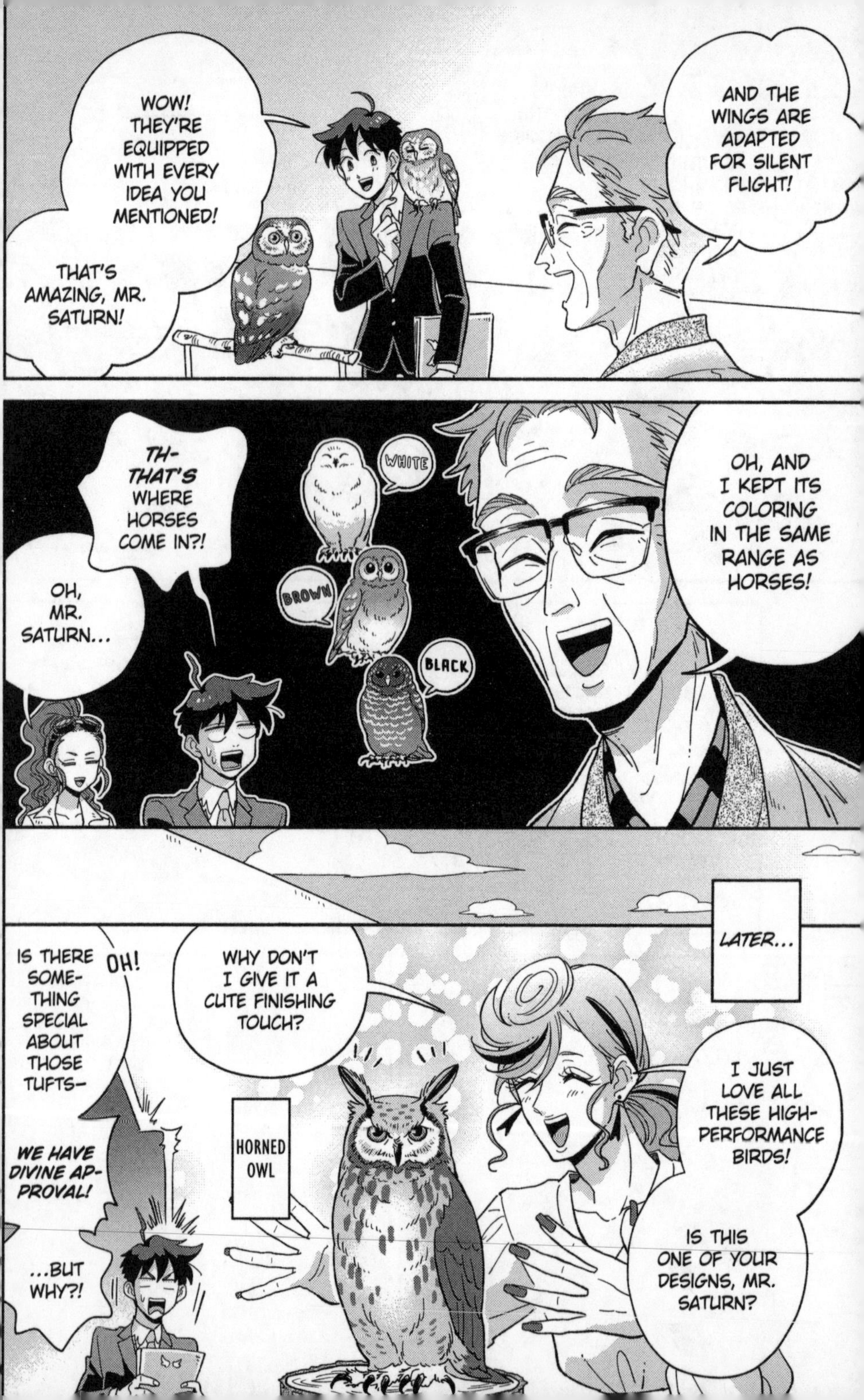
AND THE WINGS ARE ADAPTED FOR SILENT FLIGHT!
WOW! THEY'RE EQUIPPED WITH EVERY IDEA YOU MENTIONED!
THAT'S AMAZING, MR. SATURN!
OH, AND I KEPT ITS COLORING IN THE SAME RANGE AS HORSES!
WHITE
BROWN
BLACK
TH-THAT'S WHERE HORSES COME IN?!
OH, MR. SATURN...
LATER...
I JUST LOVE ALL THESE HIGH-PERFORMANCE BIRDS!
IS THIS ONE OF YOUR DESIGNS, MR. SATURN?
WHY DON'T I GIVE IT A CUTE FINISHING TOUCH?
HORNED OWL
OH!
IS THERE SOMETHING SPECIAL ABOUT THOSE TUFTS—
WE HAVE DIVINE APPROVAL!
...BUT WHY?!

THE ENCYCLOPEDIA OF REAL ANIMALS 25

ANIMAL 64 OWL

THE REAL THING

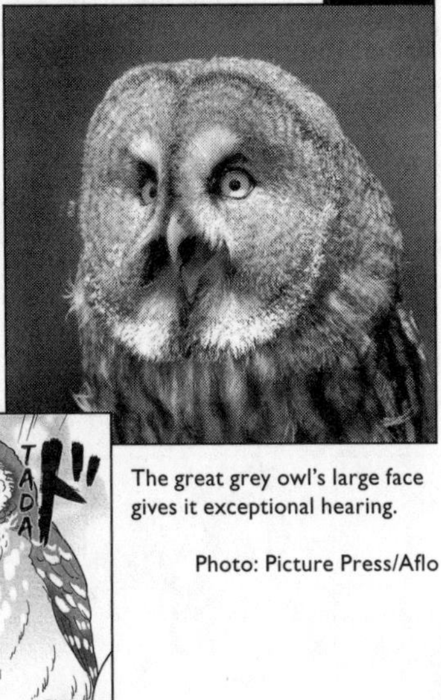

The great grey owl's large face gives it exceptional hearing.

Photo: Picture Press/Aflo

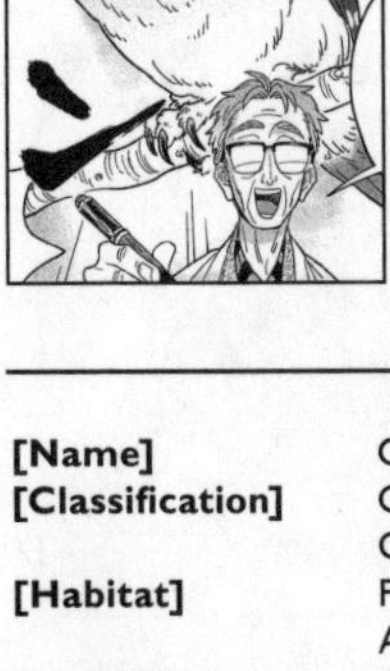
TADA

The owl is a carnivore, and most members of the species do their hunting at night. To help with this, the bird has exceptionally well-developed hearing, due in part to a round, convex facial disc that acts as a parabola to collect sound. The earholes are also positioned at different heights, allowing it to accurately determine the source of noise. The holes' front-facing position helps collect sound more effectively; however, this also forces the owl to turn its head toward the noise in order to hear it better. To overcome this, the owl's neck is adapted to be able to turn the head 360 degrees.

So as to avoid making noise itself, the owl's feathers have serrated edges which reduce aerodynamic disruptions as well as sound. The same noise-dampening design is used in bullet train pantographs.

[Name]	Owl
[Classification]	Class: Aves Order: Stigriformes
[Habitat]	Forests worldwide, excluding Antarctica
[Length]	15-80 cm (6 in - 2.6 ft)

| # HORNED OWL

THE REAL THING

The genus name *Bubo* is Latin for the Eurasian eagle-owl.

Photo: Jeurgen & Christine Sohns/Aflo

The genus *Bubo* includes many owl species with "horns," or ear-tufts, which are unrelated to the birds' hearing and are purely decorative. In fact, the purpose of the ear-tufts is unknown, as the horned owl's ears are located on the front of its head, similar to other owls. Some researchers theorize that they are meant to look like tree leaves; however, since being able to see the owl's head movements gives its hiding place away, it would be more practical not to have them.

[Name]	*Bubo*
[Classification]	Class: Aves
	Order: Strigiformes
[Habitat]	Forests worldwide, excluding Antarctica
[Length]	20-70 cm (8 in - 2.3 ft)

SPECIAL FEATURE | ELEPHANT FEET

Faraway sounds are transmitted to an elephant's ears from its feet through its bones (bone conduction) rather than through air conduction. When it wants to listen closely, it presses its feet against the ground. It can hear the calls of family members from over 10 kilometers (6.2 miles) away, and determines the direction of a sound's source according to which foot the vibrations reached first.

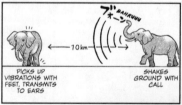

PICKS UP VIBRATIONS WITH FEET, TRANSMITS TO EARS

SHAKES GROUND WITH CALL

BAHRUUU

10 km

THE REAL THING

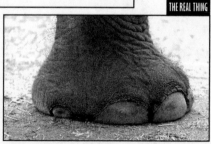

An Asian elephant's foot can reach up to 40 cm (16 in) in diameter.

Photo: Naoki Nishimura/Aflo

HEAVEN'S DESIGN TEAM

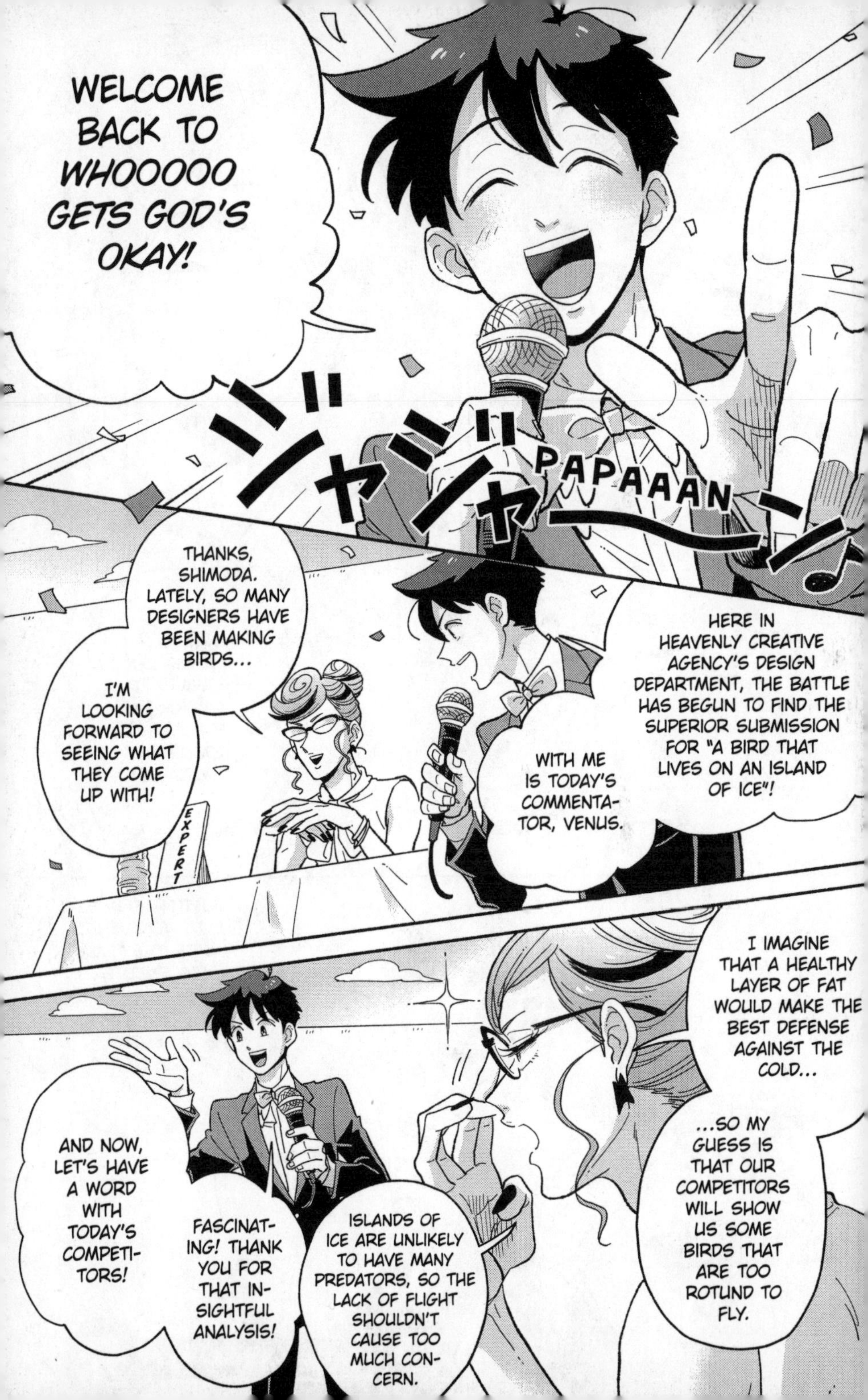

WELCOME BACK TO WHOOOOO GETS GOD'S OKAY!
ジャジャーン
PAPAAAN
HERE IN HEAVENLY CREATIVE AGENCY'S DESIGN DEPARTMENT, THE BATTLE HAS BEGUN TO FIND THE SUPERIOR SUBMISSION FOR "A BIRD THAT LIVES ON AN ISLAND OF ICE"!
WITH ME IS TODAY'S COMMENTATOR, VENUS.
THANKS, SHIMODA. LATELY, SO MANY DESIGNERS HAVE BEEN MAKING BIRDS...
I'M LOOKING FORWARD TO SEEING WHAT THEY COME UP WITH!
EXPERT
I IMAGINE THAT A HEALTHY LAYER OF FAT WOULD MAKE THE BEST DEFENSE AGAINST THE COLD...
...SO MY GUESS IS THAT OUR COMPETITORS WILL SHOW US SOME BIRDS THAT ARE TOO ROTUND TO FLY.
ISLANDS OF ICE ARE UNLIKELY TO HAVE MANY PREDATORS, SO THE LACK OF FLIGHT SHOULDN'T CAUSE TOO MUCH CONCERN.
FASCINATING! THANK YOU FOR THAT INSIGHTFUL ANALYSIS!
AND NOW, LET'S HAVE A WORD WITH TODAY'S COMPETITORS!

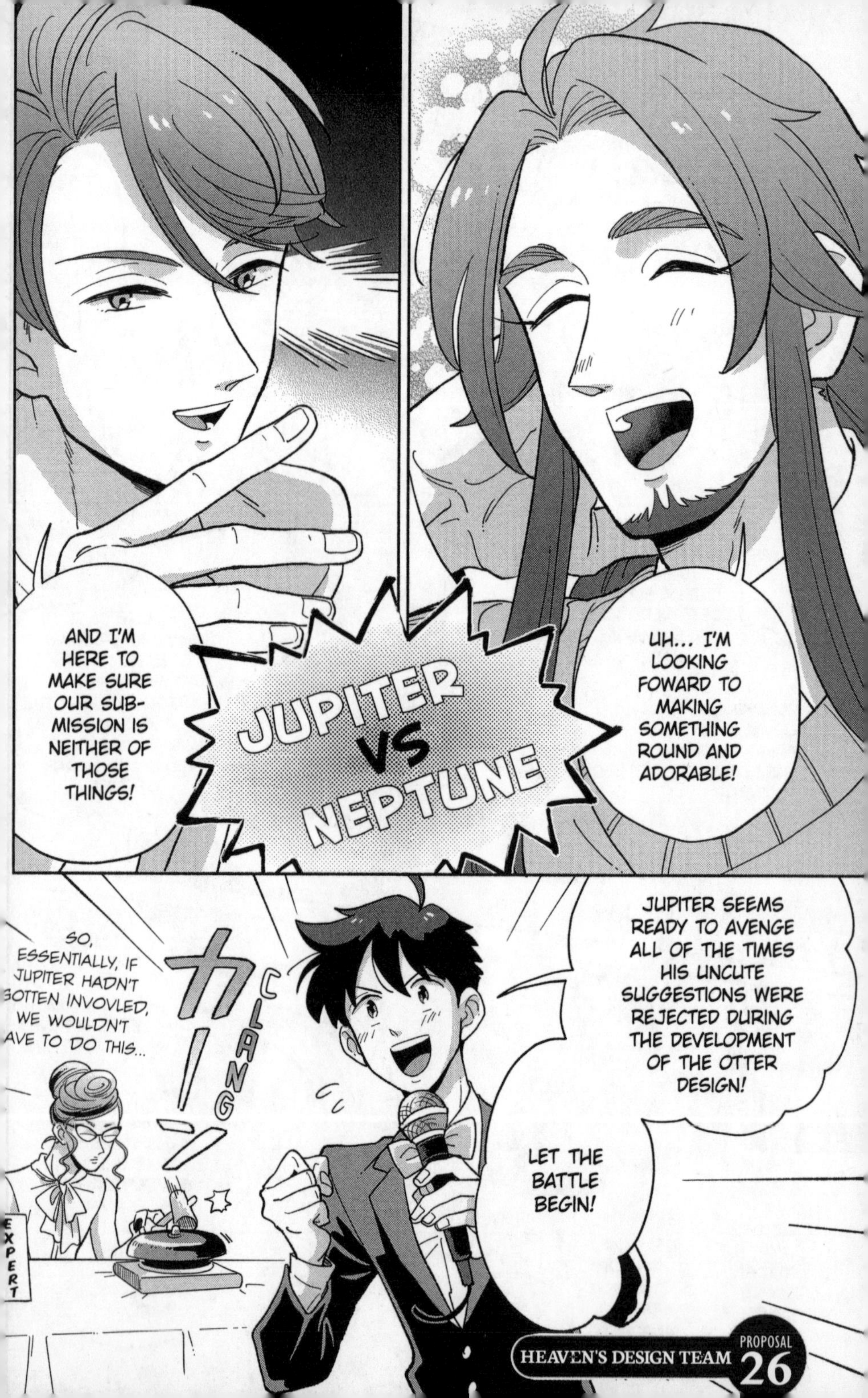
UH... I'M LOOKING FOWARD TO MAKING SOMETHING ROUND AND ADORABLE!
JUPITER VS NEPTUNE
AND I'M HERE TO MAKE SURE OUR SUB-MISSION IS NEITHER OF THOSE THINGS!
JUPITER SEEMS READY TO AVENGE ALL OF THE TIMES HIS UNCUTE SUGGESTIONS WERE REJECTED DURING THE DEVELOPMENT OF THE OTTER DESIGN!
LET THE BATTLE BEGIN!
CLANG
SO, ESSENTIALLY, IF JUPITER HADN'T GOTTEN INVOVLED, WE WOULDN'T AVE TO DO THIS...
EXPERT

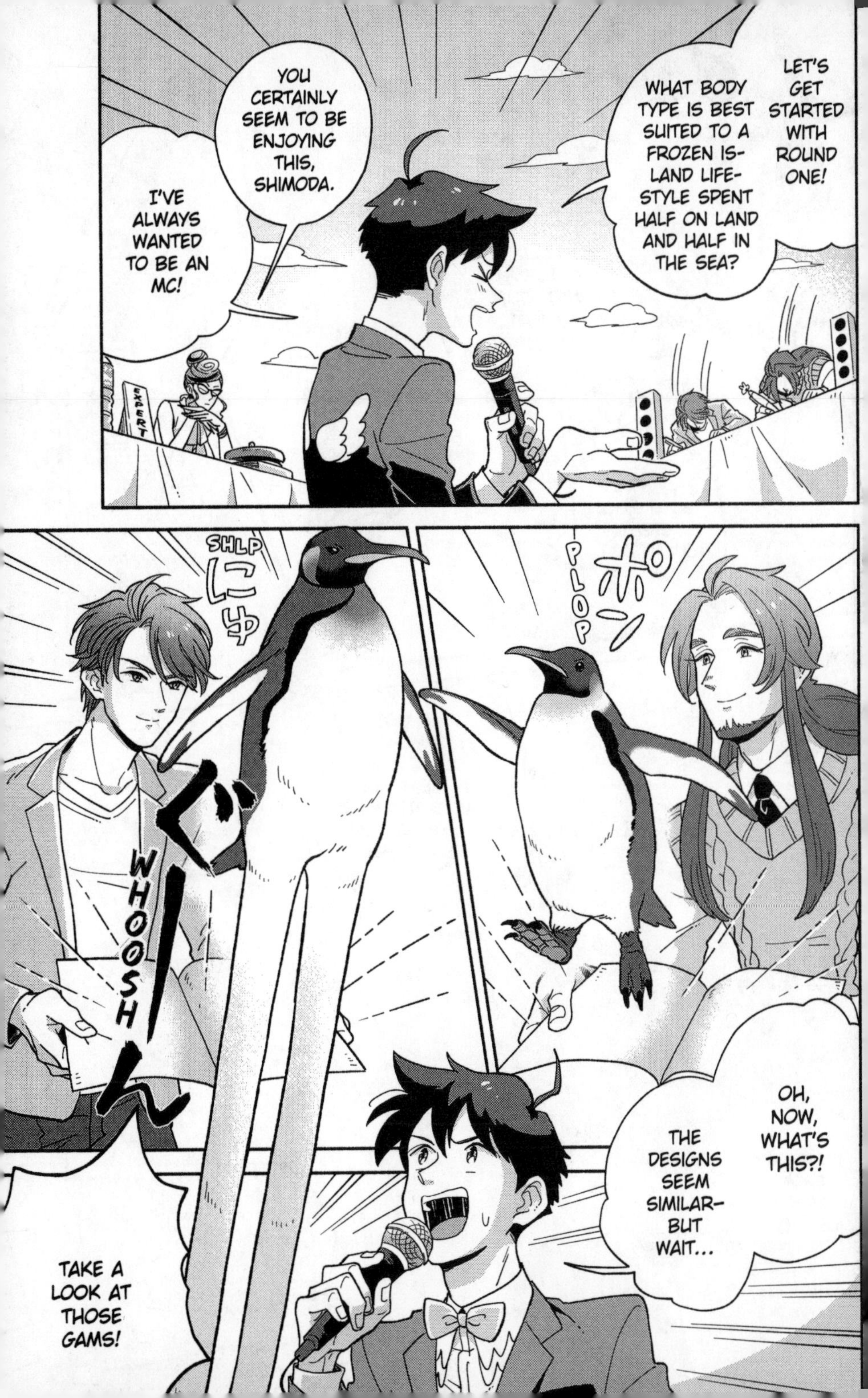
LET'S GET STARTED WITH ROUND ONE!
WHAT BODY TYPE IS BEST SUITED TO A FROZEN IS-LAND LIFE-STYLE SPENT HALF ON LAND AND HALF IN THE SEA?
YOU CERTAINLY SEEM TO BE ENJOYING THIS, SHIMODA.
I'VE ALWAYS WANTED TO BE AN MC!
EXPERT
PLOP
ポーン
SHLP
にゅ
WHOOSH
OH, NOW, WHAT'S THIS?!
THE DESIGNS SEEM SIMILAR-BUT WAIT...
TAKE A LOOK AT THOSE GAMS!

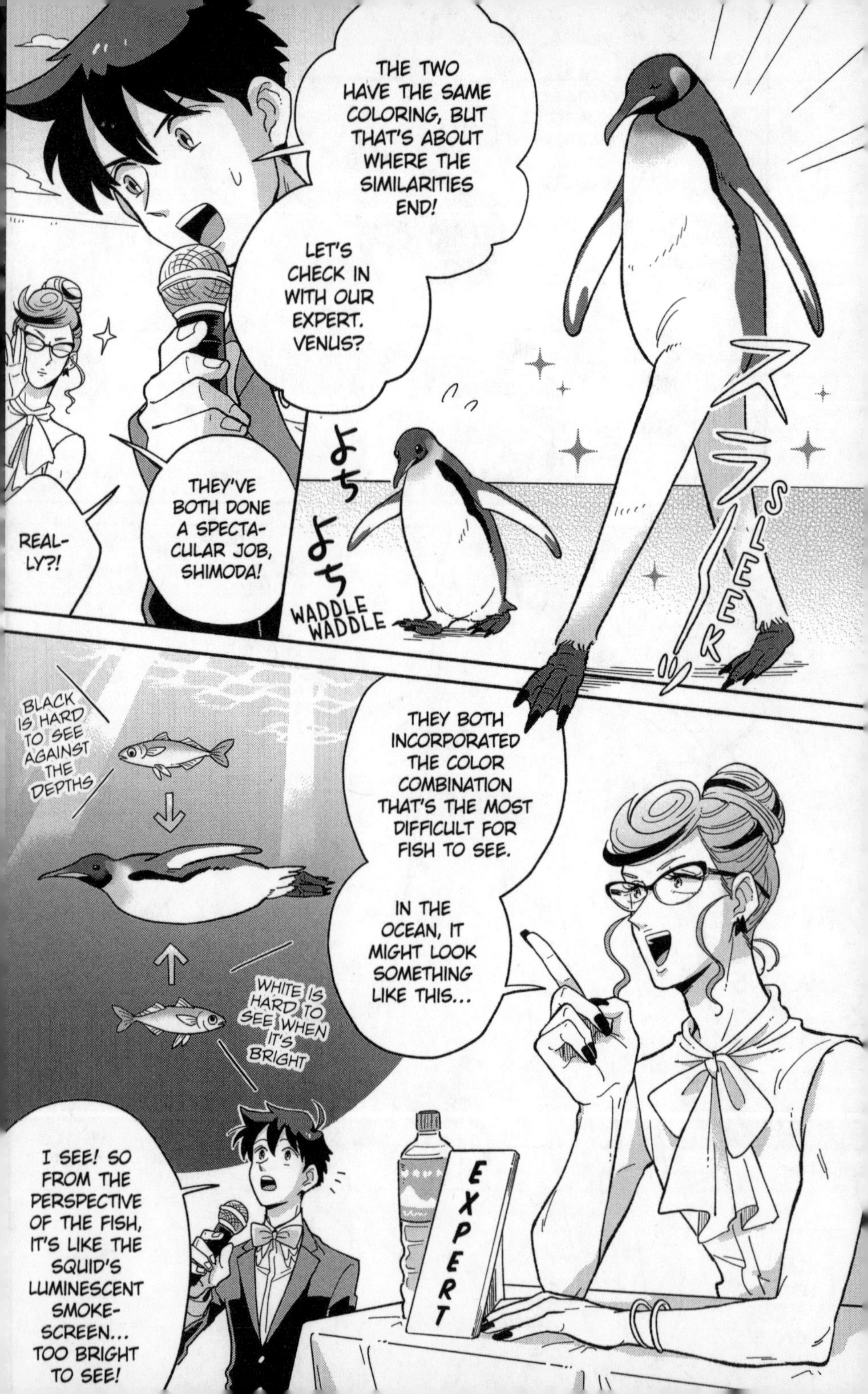
THE TWO HAVE THE SAME COLORING, BUT THAT'S ABOUT WHERE THE SIMILARITIES END!
LET'S CHECK IN WITH OUR EXPERT. VENUS?
SLEEK
よちよち
WADDLE WADDLE
THEY'VE BOTH DONE A SPECTACULAR JOB, SHIMODA!
REALLY?!
THEY BOTH INCORPORATED THE COLOR COMBINATION THAT'S THE MOST DIFFICULT FOR FISH TO SEE.
IN THE OCEAN, IT MIGHT LOOK SOMETHING LIKE THIS...
BLACK IS HARD TO SEE AGAINST THE DEPTHS
WHITE IS HARD TO SEE WHEN IT'S BRIGHT
EXPERT
I SEE! SO FROM THE PERSPECTIVE OF THE FISH, IT'S LIKE THE SQUID'S LUMINESCENT SMOKE-SCREEN... TOO BRIGHT TO SEE!

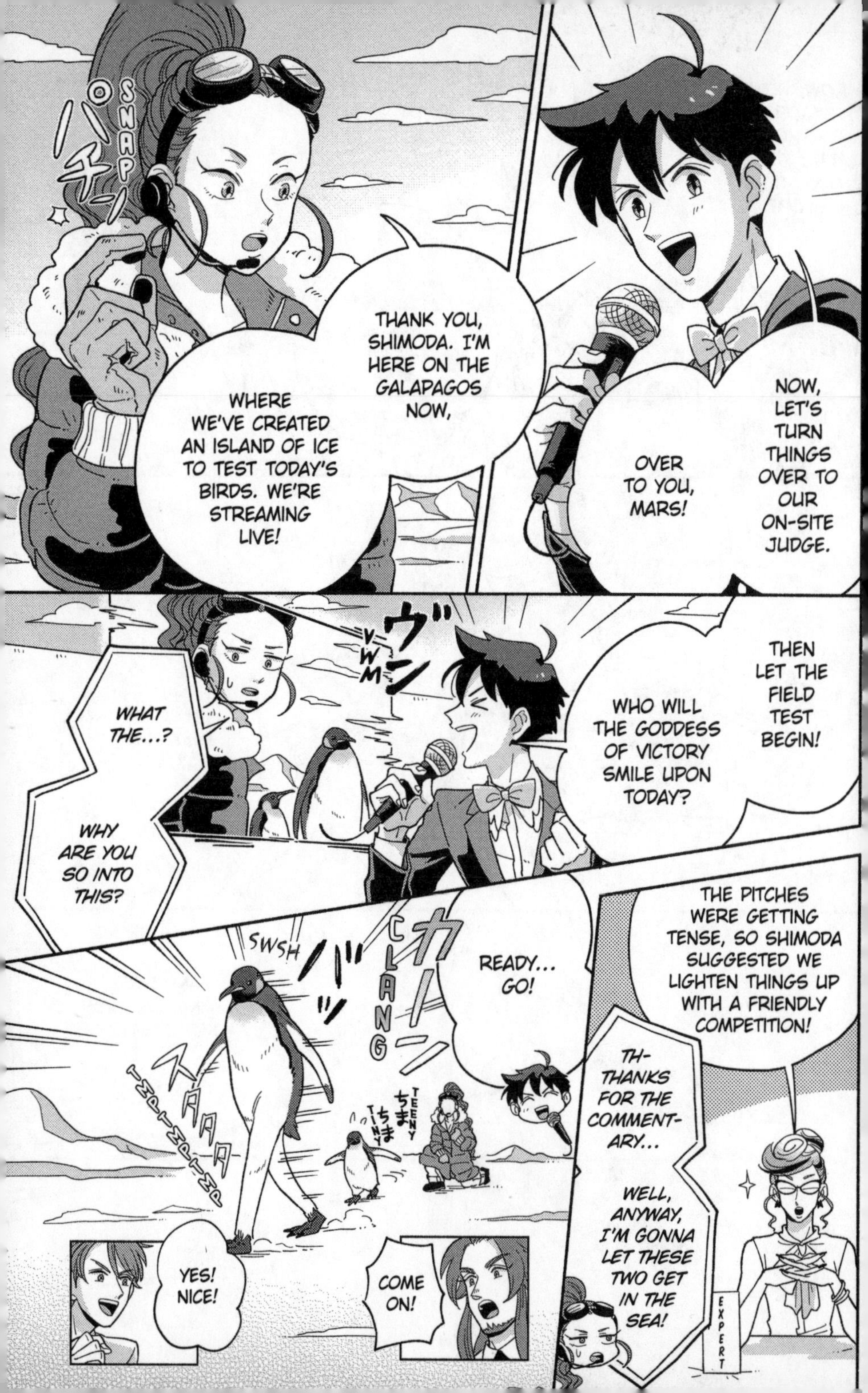
NOW, LET'S TURN THINGS OVER TO OUR ON-SITE JUDGE.
OVER TO YOU, MARS!
SNAP
THANK YOU, SHIMODA. I'M HERE ON THE GALAPAGOS NOW,
WHERE WE'VE CREATED AN ISLAND OF ICE TO TEST TODAY'S BIRDS. WE'RE STREAMING LIVE!
THEN LET THE FIELD TEST BEGIN!
WHO WILL THE GODDESS OF VICTORY SMILE UPON TODAY?
VWM
WHAT THE...?
WHY ARE YOU SO INTO THIS?
THE PITCHES WERE GETTING TENSE, SO SHIMODA SUGGESTED WE LIGHTEN THINGS UP WITH A FRIENDLY COMPETITION!
TH-THANKS FOR THE COMMENTARY...
WELL, ANYWAY, I'M GONNA LET THESE TWO GET IN THE SEA!
EXPERT
READY... GO!
CLANG
SWSH
TMP TMP TMP
ちま TEENY
ちま TINY
YES! NICE!
COME ON!

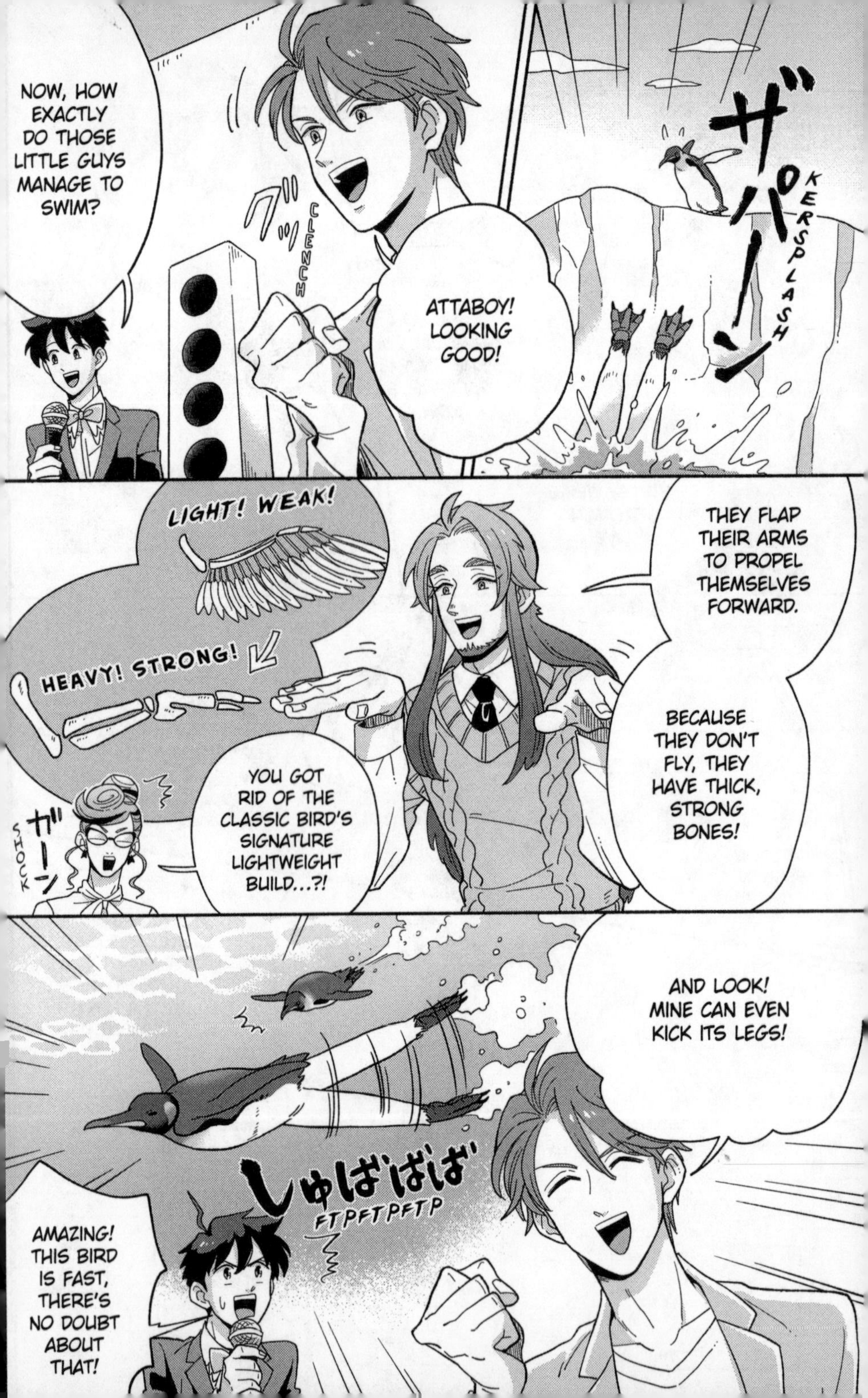
ザパーン
KERSPLASH
ATTABOY! LOOKING GOOD!
グッ
CLENCH
NOW, HOW EXACTLY DO THOSE LITTLE GUYS MANAGE TO SWIM?
THEY FLAP THEIR ARMS TO PROPEL THEMSELVES FORWARD.
BECAUSE THEY DON'T FLY, THEY HAVE THICK, STRONG BONES!
LIGHT! WEAK!
HEAVY! STRONG!
YOU GOT RID OF THE CLASSIC BIRD'S SIGNATURE LIGHTWEIGHT BUILD...?!
ガーン
SHOCK
AND LOOK! MINE CAN EVEN KICK ITS LEGS!
しゅばばば
FTPFTPFTP
AMAZING! THIS BIRD IS FAST, THERE'S NO DOUBT ABOUT THAT!

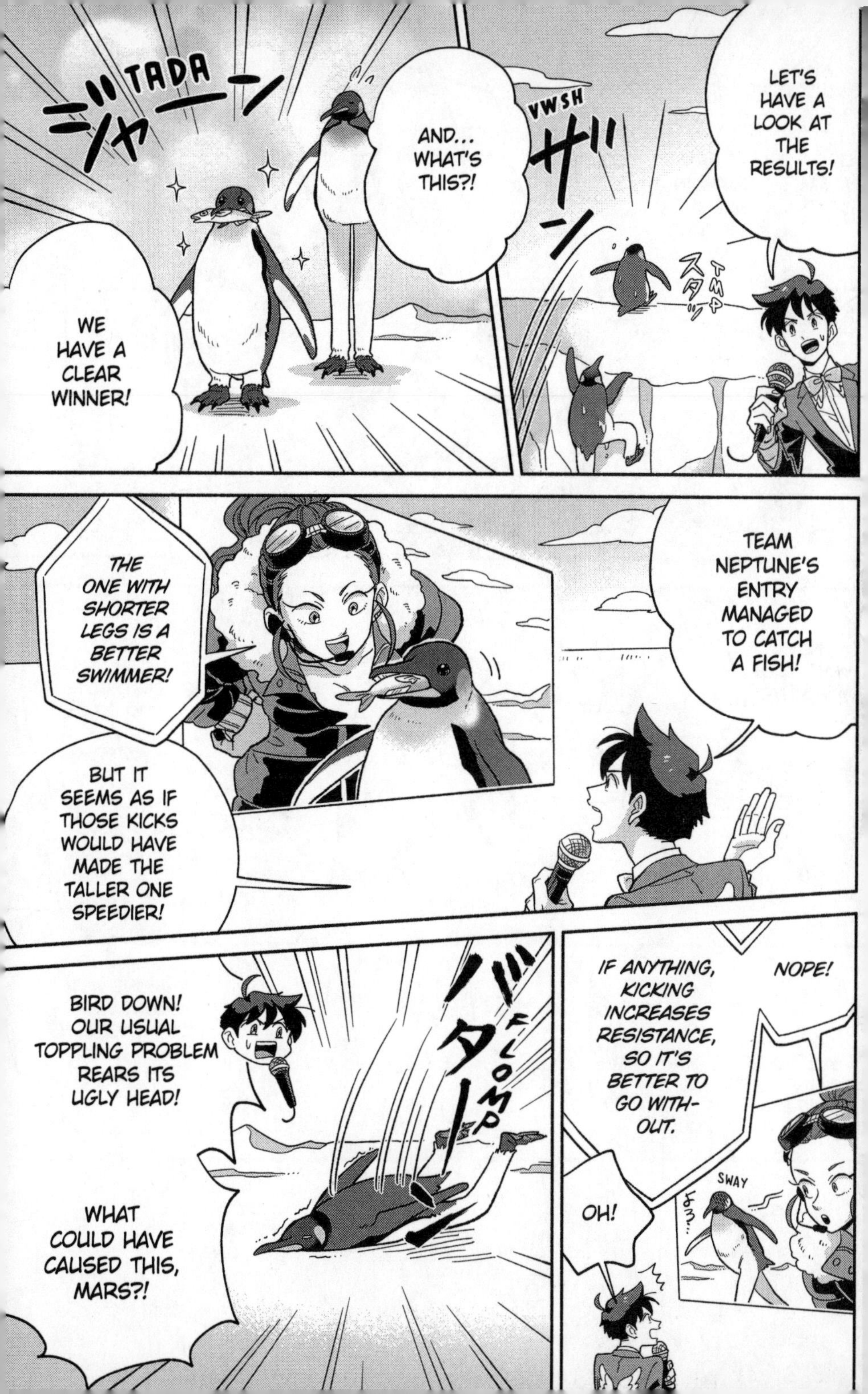
LET'S HAVE A LOOK AT THE RESULTS!
VWSH
TMP
AND... WHAT'S THIS?!
TADA
WE HAVE A CLEAR WINNER!
TEAM NEPTUNE'S ENTRY MANAGED TO CATCH A FISH!
THE ONE WITH SHORTER LEGS IS A BETTER SWIMMER!
BUT IT SEEMS AS IF THOSE KICKS WOULD HAVE MADE THE TALLER ONE SPEEDIER!
NOPE!
IF ANYTHING, KICKING INCREASES RESISTANCE, SO IT'S BETTER TO GO WITH-OUT.
SWAY
OH!
BIRD DOWN! OUR USUAL TOPPLING PROBLEM REARS ITS UGLY HEAD!
FLOMP
WHAT COULD HAVE CAUSED THIS, MARS?!

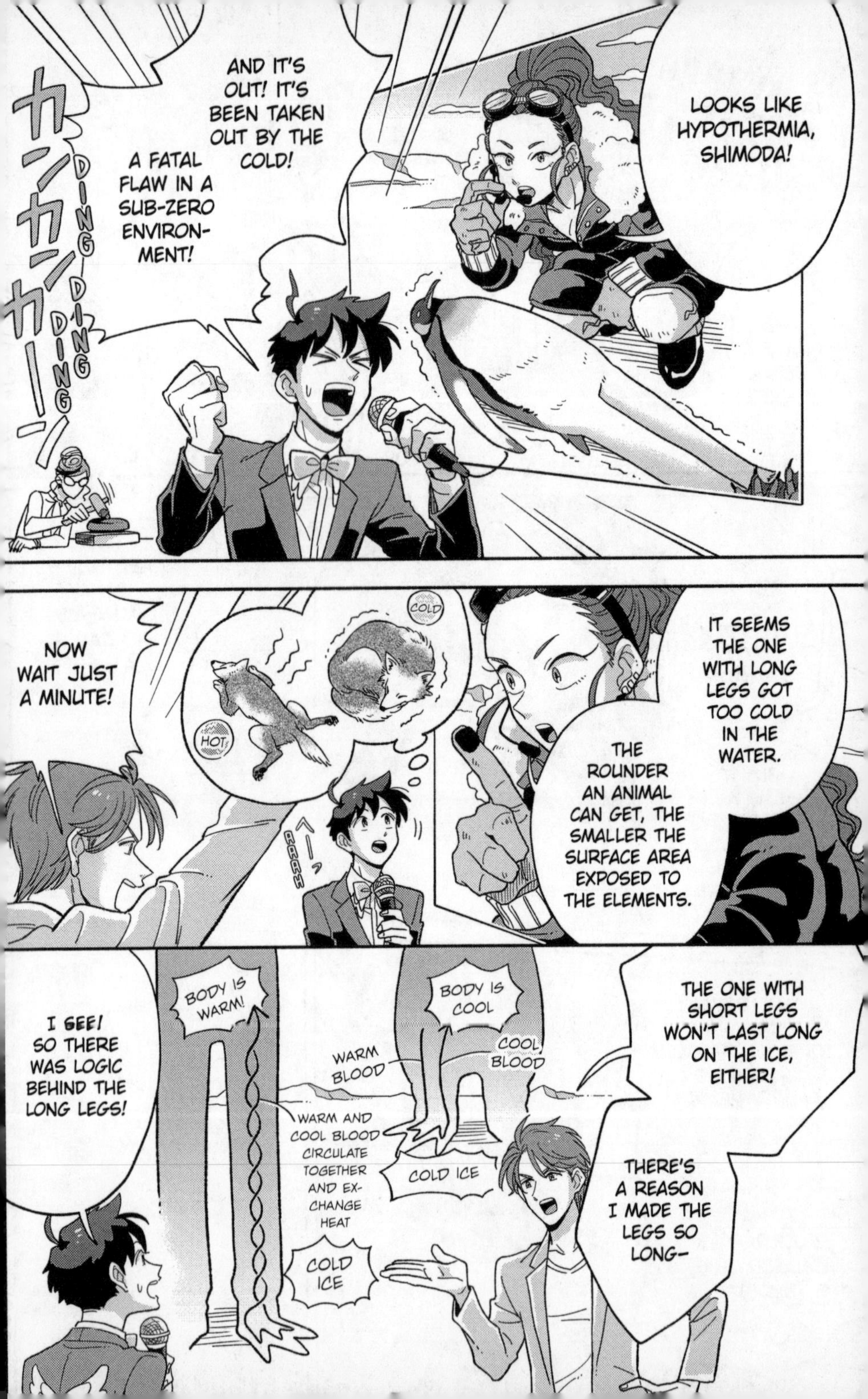

LOOKS LIKE HYPOTHERMIA, SHIMODA!
AND IT'S OUT! IT'S BEEN TAKEN OUT BY THE COLD!
A FATAL FLAW IN A SUB-ZERO ENVIRON-MENT!
カンカンカーン
DING DING DING DING
IT SEEMS THE ONE WITH LONG LEGS GOT TOO COLD IN THE WATER.
THE ROUNDER AN ANIMAL CAN GET, THE SMALLER THE SURFACE AREA EXPOSED TO THE ELEMENTS.
COLD
HOT
へー
RAAAH
NOW WAIT JUST A MINUTE!
THE ONE WITH SHORT LEGS WON'T LAST LONG ON THE ICE, EITHER!
THERE'S A REASON I MADE THE LEGS SO LONG—
BODY IS COOL
COOL BLOOD
COLD ICE
BODY IS WARM!
WARM BLOOD
WARM AND COOL BLOOD CIRCULATE TOGETHER AND EX-CHANGE HEAT
COLD ICE
I SEE! SO THERE WAS LOGIC BEHIND THE LONG LEGS!

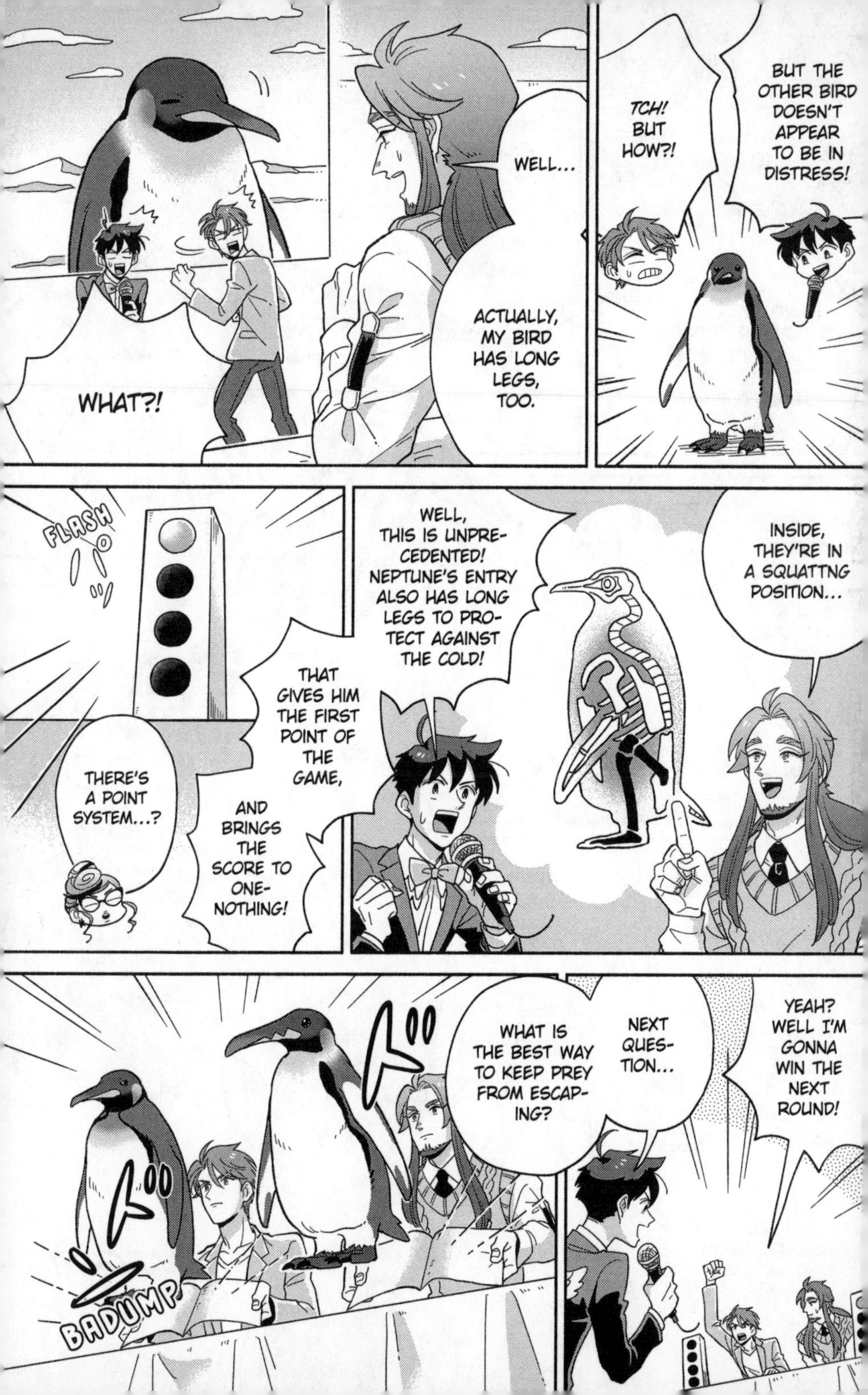
BUT THE OTHER BIRD DOESN'T APPEAR TO BE IN DISTRESS!
TCH! BUT HOW?!
WELL...
ACTUALLY, MY BIRD HAS LONG LEGS, TOO.
WHAT?!
INSIDE, THEY'RE IN A SQUATTNG POSITION...
WELL, THIS IS UNPRECEDENTED! NEPTUNE'S ENTRY ALSO HAS LONG LEGS TO PROTECT AGAINST THE COLD!
THAT GIVES HIM THE FIRST POINT OF THE GAME,
AND BRINGS THE SCORE TO ONE-NOTHING!
FLASH
THERE'S A POINT SYSTEM...?
YEAH? WELL I'M GONNA WIN THE NEXT ROUND!
NEXT QUESTION...
WHAT IS THE BEST WAY TO KEEP PREY FROM ESCAPING?
BADUMP

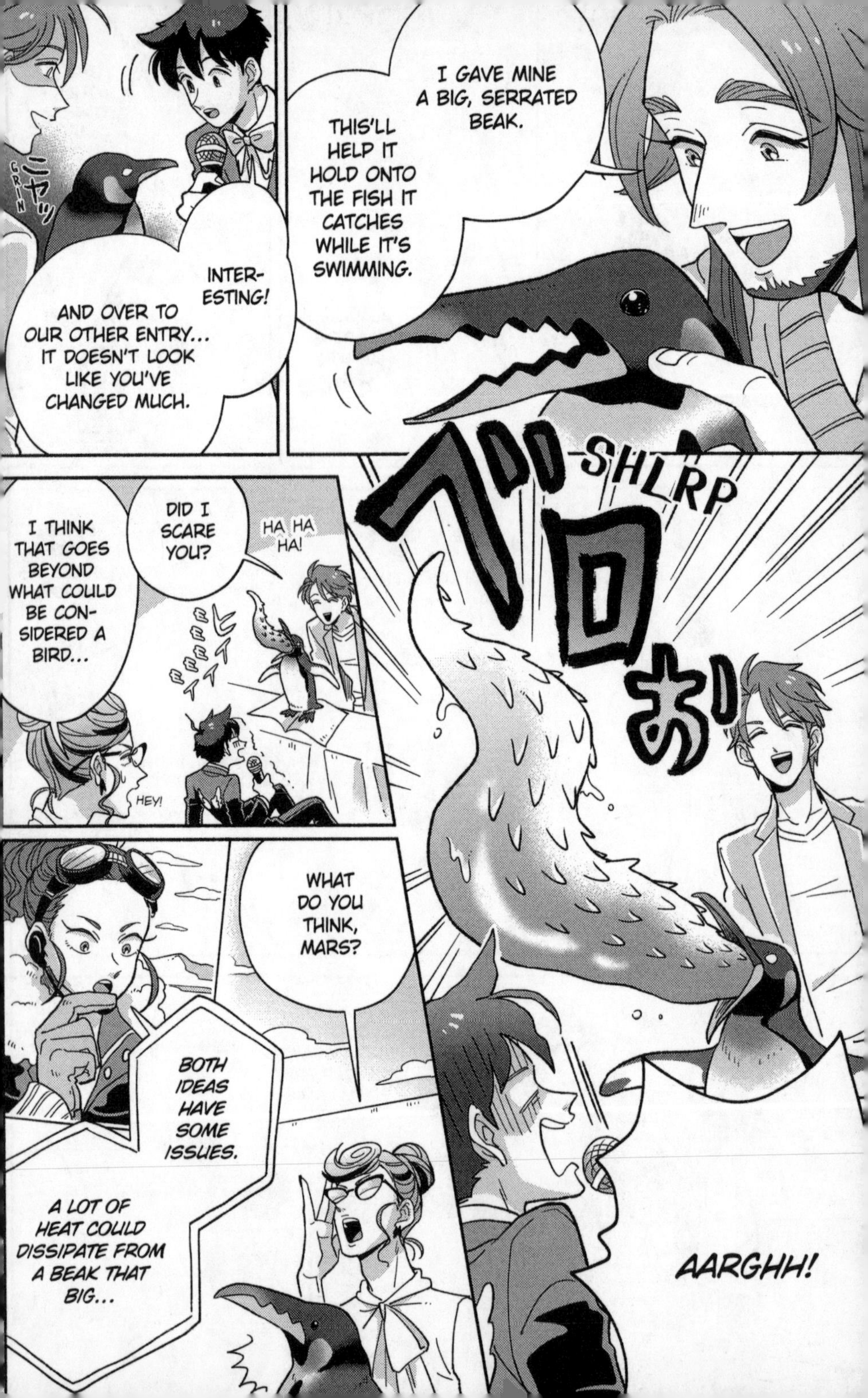
I GAVE MINE A BIG, SERRATED BEAK.
THIS'LL HELP IT HOLD ONTO THE FISH IT CATCHES WHILE IT'S SWIMMING.
ニヤッ GRIN
INTER-ESTING!
AND OVER TO OUR OTHER ENTRY… IT DOESN'T LOOK LIKE YOU'VE CHANGED MUCH.
SHLRP
お
AARGHH!
DID I SCARE YOU?
HA HA HA!
I THINK THAT GOES BEYOND WHAT COULD BE CON-SIDERED A BIRD…
HEY!
WHAT DO YOU THINK, MARS?
BOTH IDEAS HAVE SOME ISSUES.
A LOT OF HEAT COULD DISSIPATE FROM A BEAK THAT BIG…

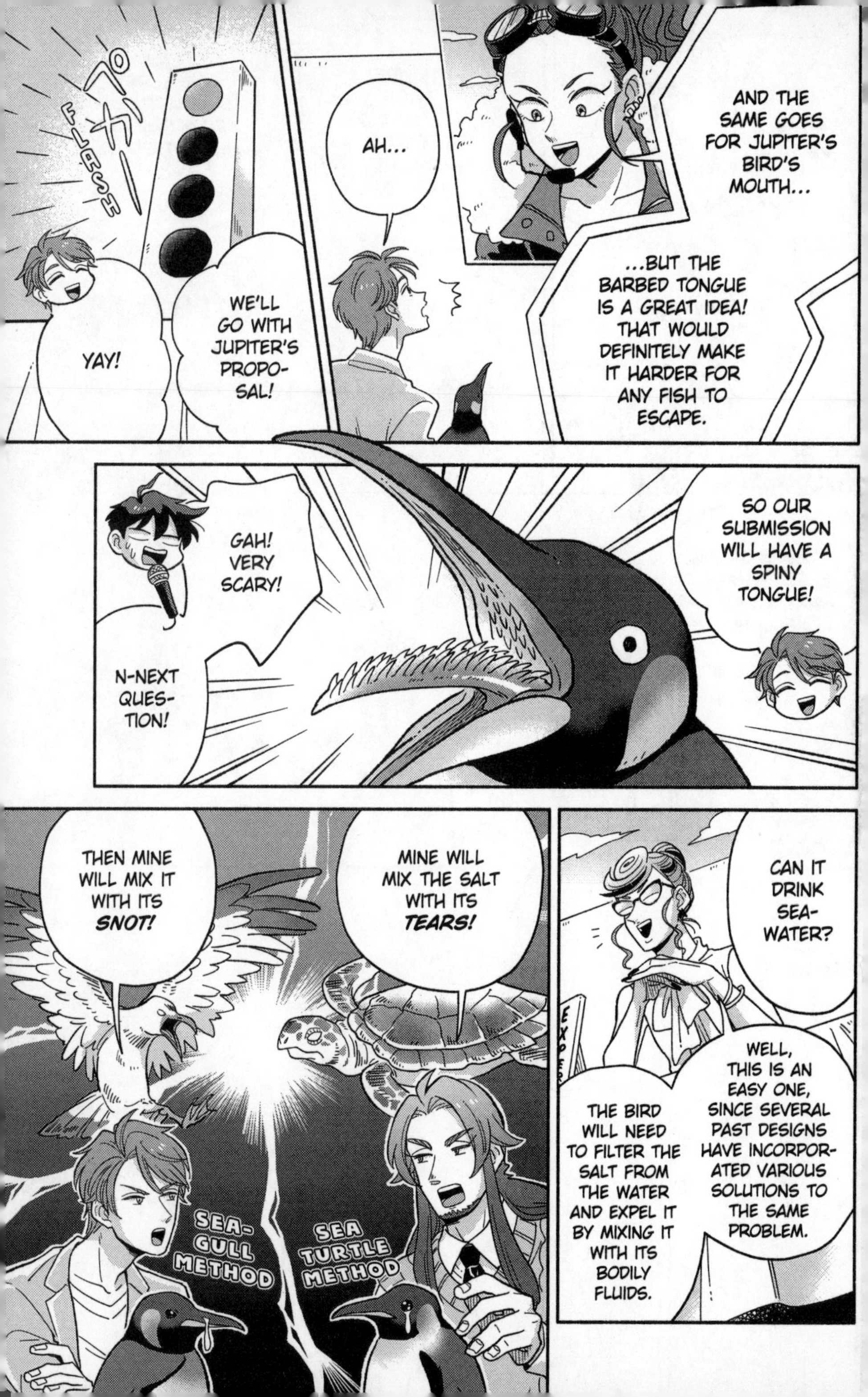
AND THE SAME GOES FOR JUPITER'S BIRD'S MOUTH...
...BUT THE BARBED TONGUE IS A GREAT IDEA! THAT WOULD DEFINITELY MAKE IT HARDER FOR ANY FISH TO ESCAPE.
AH...
ペカー
FLASH
WE'LL GO WITH JUPITER'S PROPO-SAL!
YAY!
SO OUR SUBMISSION WILL HAVE A SPINY TONGUE!
GAH! VERY SCARY!
N-NEXT QUES-TION!
CAN IT DRINK SEA-WATER?
WELL, THIS IS AN EASY ONE, SINCE SEVERAL PAST DESIGNS HAVE INCORPOR-ATED VARIOUS SOLUTIONS TO THE SAME PROBLEM.
THE BIRD WILL NEED TO FILTER THE SALT FROM THE WATER AND EXPEL IT BY MIXING IT WITH ITS BODILY FLUIDS.
MINE WILL MIX THE SALT WITH ITS *TEARS!*
THEN MINE WILL MIX IT WITH ITS *SNOT!*
SEA TURTLE METHOD
SEA-GULL METHOD

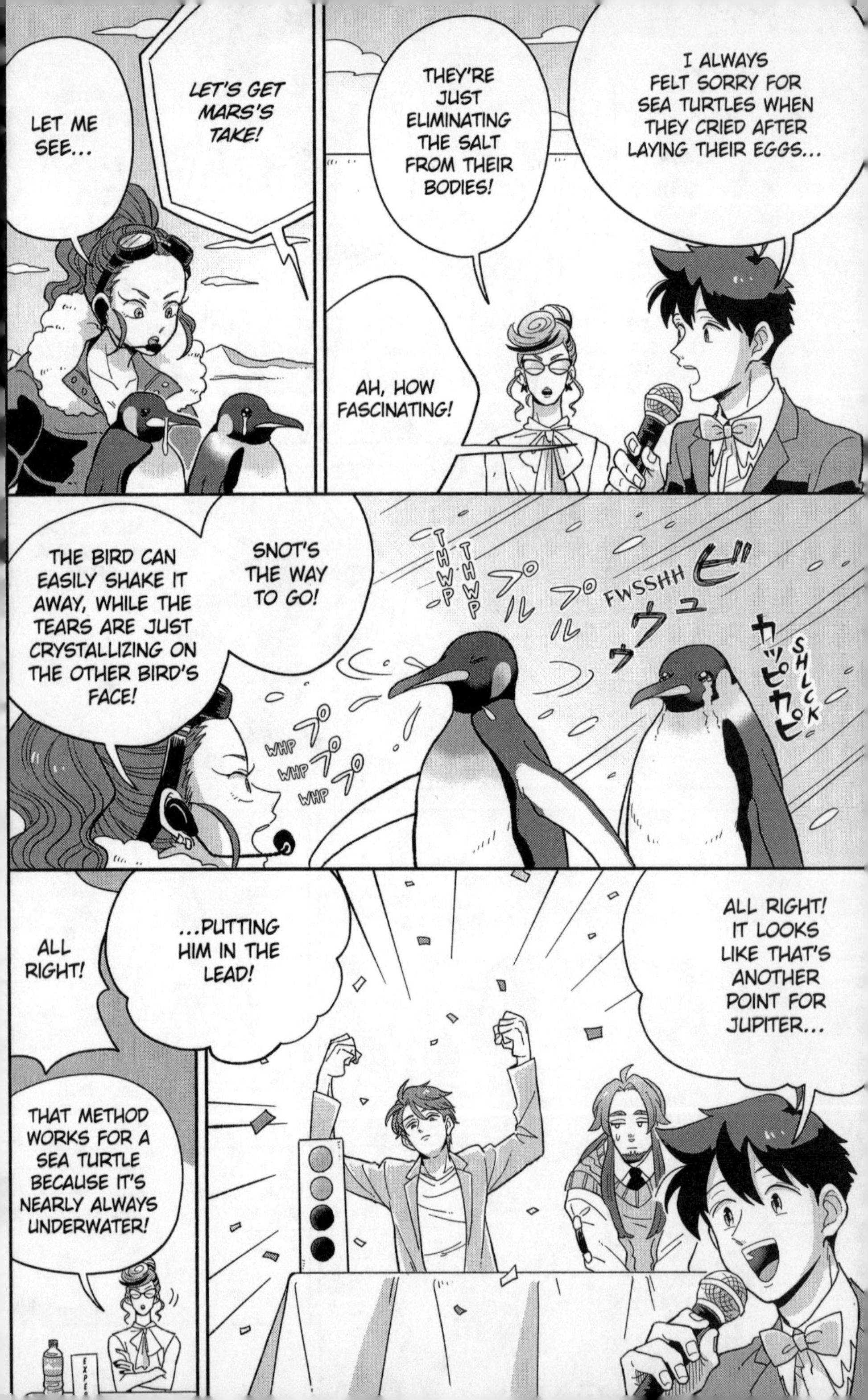
I ALWAYS FELT SORRY FOR SEA TURTLES WHEN THEY CRIED AFTER LAYING THEIR EGGS...
THEY'RE JUST ELIMINATING THE SALT FROM THEIR BODIES!
AH, HOW FASCINATING!
LET'S GET MARS'S TAKE!
LET ME SEE...
ビュウウ
FWSSHH
カッピカッピ
SHLCK
プルプル
THWP THWP
SNOT'S THE WAY TO GO!
THE BIRD CAN EASILY SHAKE IT AWAY, WHILE THE TEARS ARE JUST CRYSTALLIZING ON THE OTHER BIRD'S FACE!
プ WHP
プ WHP
プ WHP
ALL RIGHT! IT LOOKS LIKE THAT'S ANOTHER POINT FOR JUPITER...
...PUTTING HIM IN THE LEAD!
ALL RIGHT!
THAT METHOD WORKS FOR A SEA TURTLE BECAUSE IT'S NEARLY ALWAYS UNDERWATER!

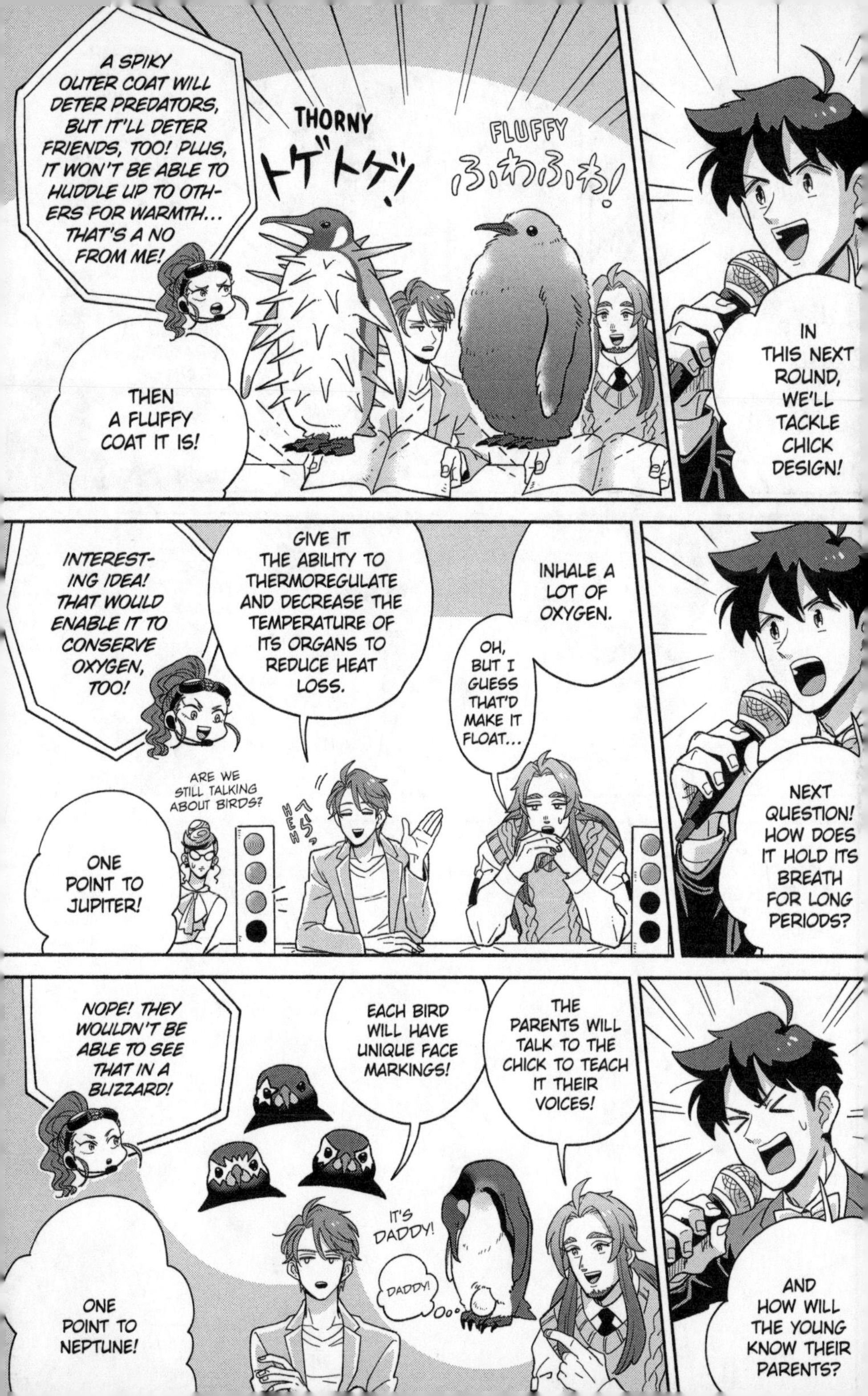

IN THIS NEXT ROUND, WE'LL TACKLE CHICK DESIGN!
FLUFFY
ふわふわ!
THORNY
トゲトゲ!
A SPIKY OUTER COAT WILL DETER PREDATORS, BUT IT'LL DETER FRIENDS, TOO! PLUS, IT WON'T BE ABLE TO HUDDLE UP TO OTHERS FOR WARMTH... THAT'S A NO FROM ME!
THEN A FLUFFY COAT IT IS!
NEXT QUESTION! HOW DOES IT HOLD ITS BREATH FOR LONG PERIODS?
INHALE A LOT OF OXYGEN.
OH, BUT I GUESS THAT'D MAKE IT FLOAT...
GIVE IT THE ABILITY TO THERMOREGULATE AND DECREASE THE TEMPERATURE OF ITS ORGANS TO REDUCE HEAT LOSS.
INTERESTING IDEA! THAT WOULD ENABLE IT TO CONSERVE OXYGEN, TOO!
HEH へら
ARE WE STILL TALKING ABOUT BIRDS?
ONE POINT TO JUPITER!
AND HOW WILL THE YOUNG KNOW THEIR PARENTS?
THE PARENTS WILL TALK TO THE CHICK TO TEACH IT THEIR VOICES!
EACH BIRD WILL HAVE UNIQUE FACE MARKINGS!
NOPE! THEY WOULDN'T BE ABLE TO SEE THAT IN A BLIZZARD!
IT'S DADDY!
DADDY!
ONE POINT TO NEPTUNE!

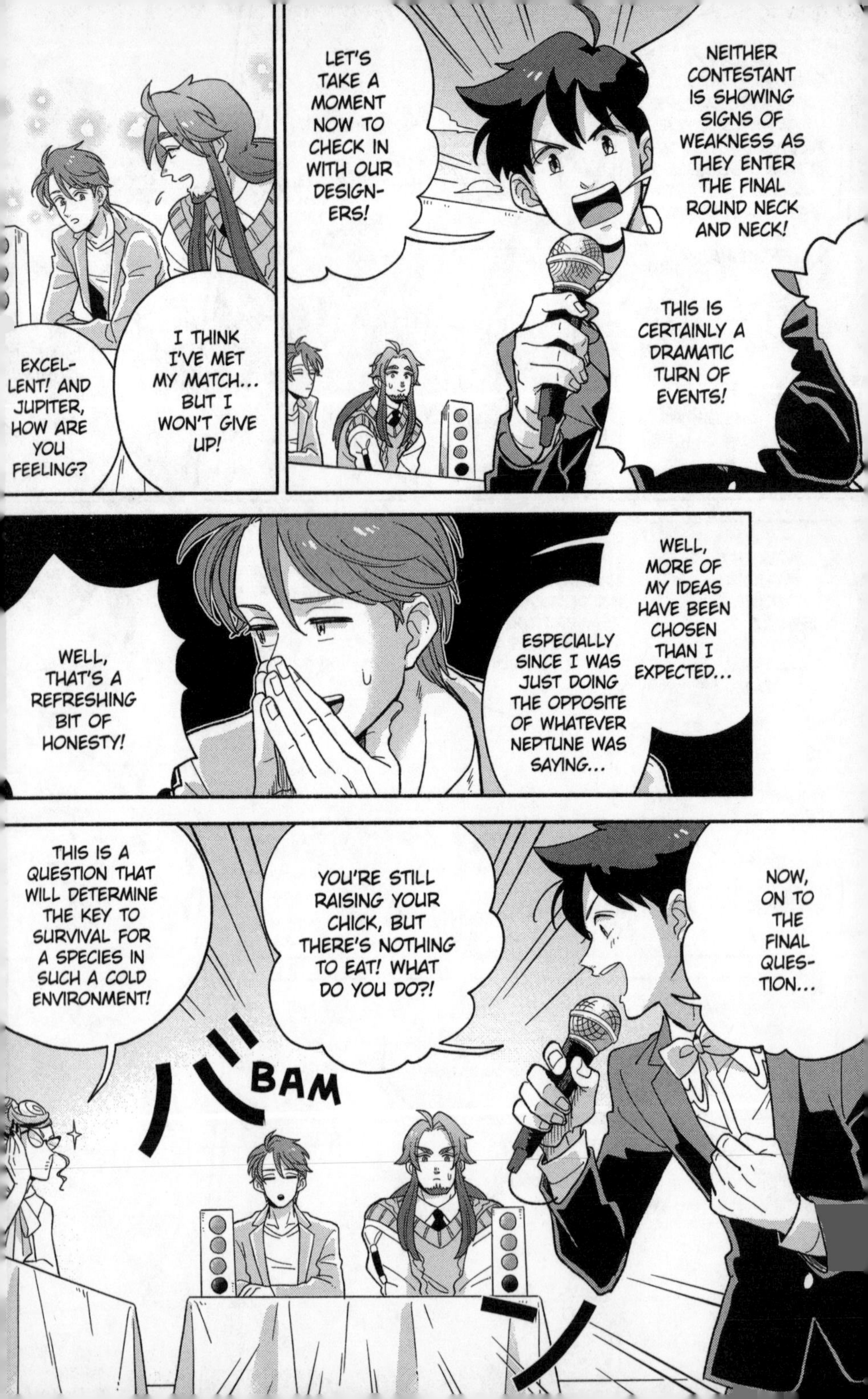
NEITHER CONTESTANT IS SHOWING SIGNS OF WEAKNESS AS THEY ENTER THE FINAL ROUND NECK AND NECK!
THIS IS CERTAINLY A DRAMATIC TURN OF EVENTS!
LET'S TAKE A MOMENT NOW TO CHECK IN WITH OUR DESIGNERS!
I THINK I'VE MET MY MATCH... BUT I WON'T GIVE UP!
EXCELLENT! AND JUPITER, HOW ARE YOU FEELING?
WELL, MORE OF MY IDEAS HAVE BEEN CHOSEN THAN I EXPECTED...
ESPECIALLY SINCE I WAS JUST DOING THE OPPOSITE OF WHATEVER NEPTUNE WAS SAYING...
WELL, THAT'S A REFRESHING BIT OF HONESTY!
NOW, ON TO THE FINAL QUESTION...
YOU'RE STILL RAISING YOUR CHICK, BUT THERE'S NOTHING TO EAT! WHAT DO YOU DO?!
THIS IS A QUESTION THAT WILL DETERMINE THE KEY TO SURVIVAL FOR A SPECIES IN SUCH A COLD ENVIRONMENT!
BAM

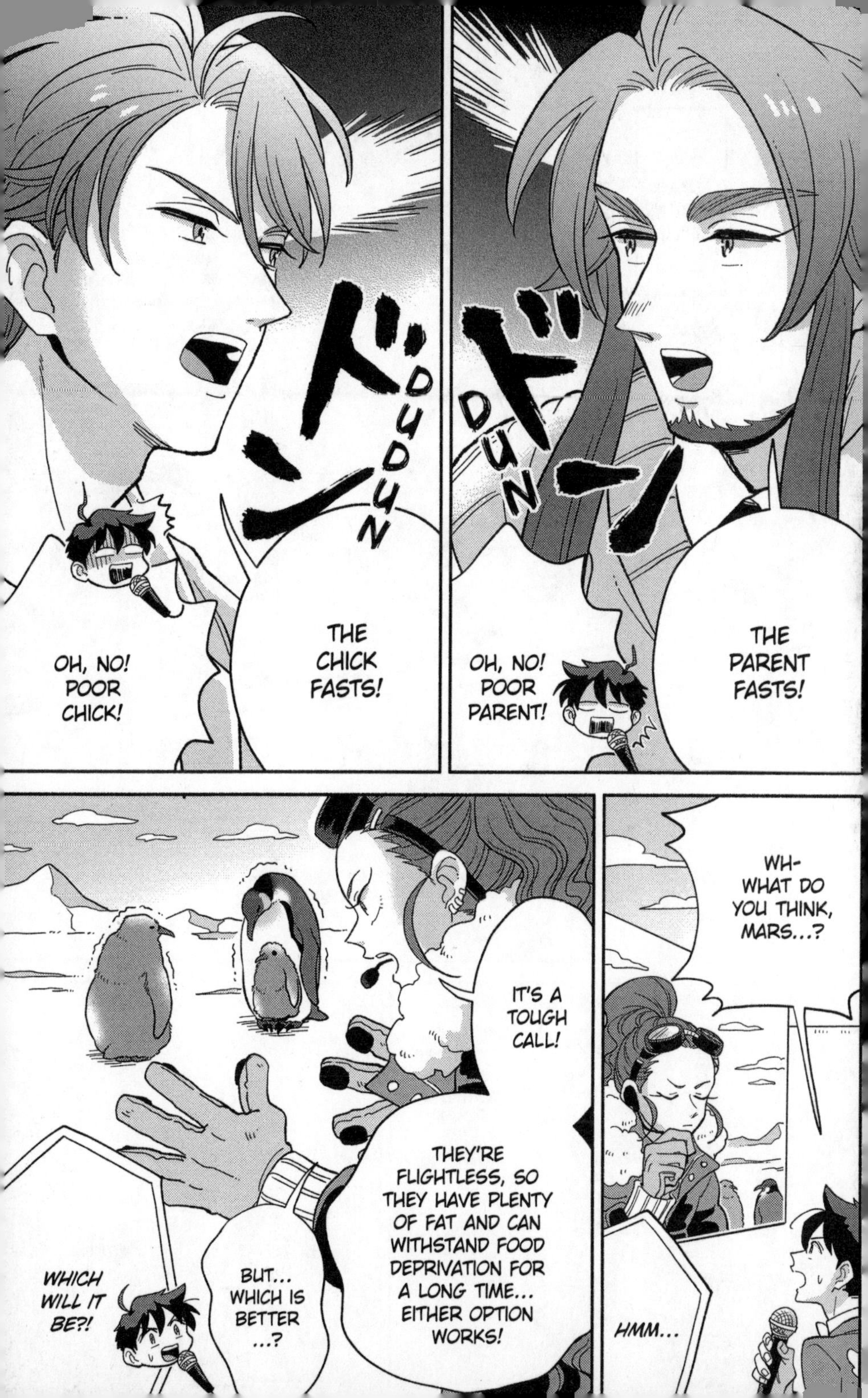
THE PARENT FASTS!
ドーン
DUN
OH, NO! POOR PARENT!
THE CHICK FASTS!
ドーン
DUDUN
OH, NO! POOR CHICK!
WH- WHAT DO YOU THINK, MARS...?
HMM...
IT'S A TOUGH CALL!
THEY'RE FLIGHTLESS, SO THEY HAVE PLENTY OF FAT AND CAN WITHSTAND FOOD DEPRIVATION FOR A LONG TIME... EITHER OPTION WORKS!
BUT... WHICH IS BETTER ...?
WHICH WILL IT BE?!

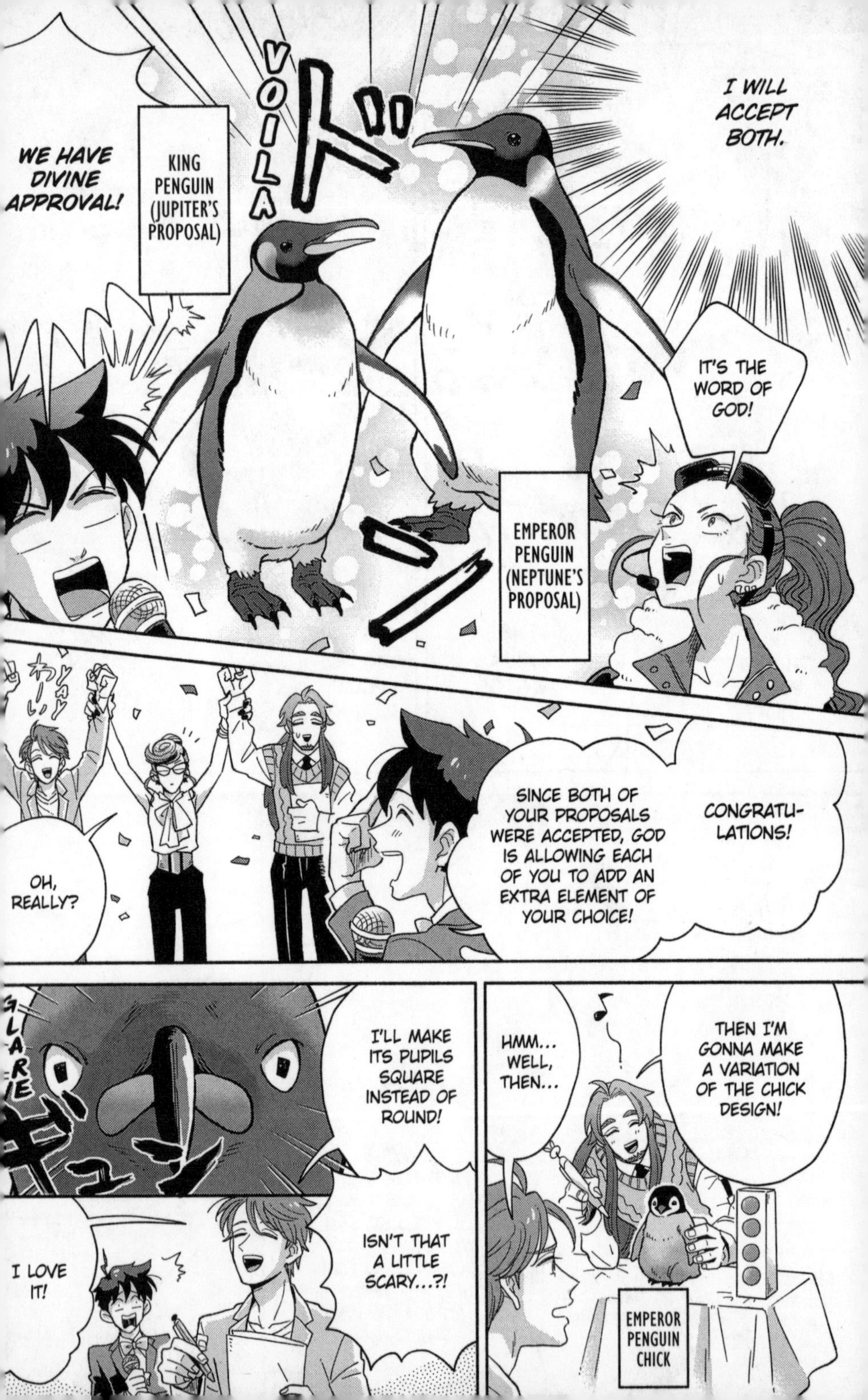
I WILL ACCEPT BOTH.
VOILA
KING PENGUIN (JUPITER'S PROPOSAL)
WE HAVE DIVINE APPROVAL!
IT'S THE WORD OF GOD!
EMPEROR PENGUIN (NEPTUNE'S PROPOSAL)
CONGRATULATIONS!
SINCE BOTH OF YOUR PROPOSALS WERE ACCEPTED, GOD IS ALLOWING EACH OF YOU TO ADD AN EXTRA ELEMENT OF YOUR CHOICE!
YAY
OH, REALLY?
THEN I'M GONNA MAKE A VARIATION OF THE CHICK DESIGN!
HMM... WELL, THEN...
EMPEROR PENGUIN CHICK
I'LL MAKE ITS PUPILS SQUARE INSTEAD OF ROUND!
GLARE
ISN'T THAT A LITTLE SCARY...?!
I LOVE IT!

THE ENCYCLOPEDIA OF REAL ANIMALS 26

ANIMAL 66 | KING PENGUIN

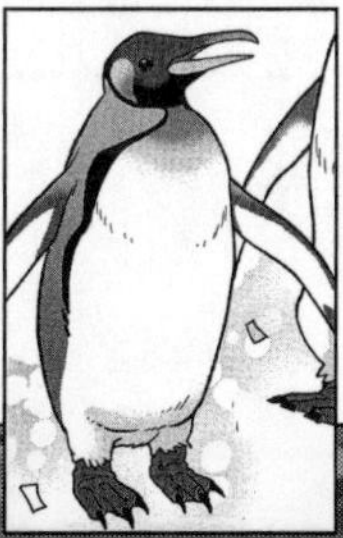

THE REAL THING

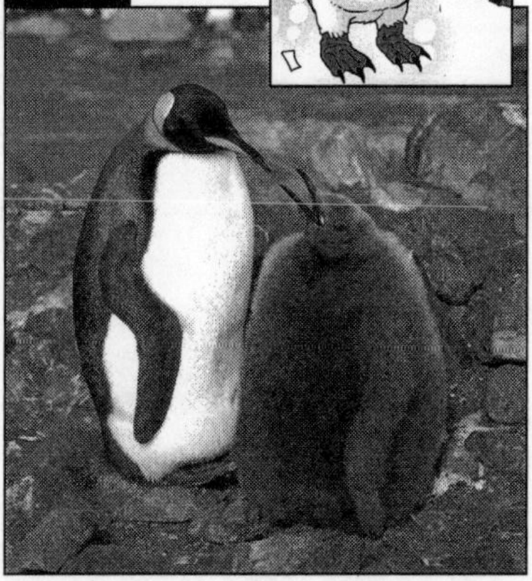

Parent and child. The chick is covered in brown feathers and is relatively large in size.

Photo: Minden Pictures/Aflo

[Name]	King penguin
[Classification]	Class: Aves Order: Sphenisciformes Family: Spheniscidae Genus: *Aptenodytes*
[Habitat]	The subantarctic islands
[Height]	95 cm (3 ft)

With the exception of the black band connecting the plumage on their faces and bodies, king penguins look very similar to their emperor counterparts. Penguins are often thought to have short legs, but this is an illusion caused by the fact that the legs are fixed in a permanently crouched position. This adaptation prevents the blood cooled by contact with ice from immediately cooling the rest of the body.

The penguin's tongue is quite frightening, with sharp barbs that allow it to hold onto its catch. In order to regulate its salt intake, the bird eliminates excess salt through its mucus. Unusually for a bird, it can thermoregulate, enabling it to stay submerged in water for long periods. Finally, it has square pupils for an unknown reason.

The king differs from the emperor penguin in the appearance of its young and in childrearing methods. King penguin young are covered in soft, fluffy brown feathers and are larger over-all than their counterparts. The young also fast while they wait for their parents to return from feeding in the sea.

ANIMAL 67 | EMPEROR PENGUIN

Chicks are covered in gray down with black heads and white masks. They are also relatively small.

THE REAL THING

Photo: Minden Pictures/Aflo

The largest extant penguin, the emperor penguin is known for its unusual childrearing habits. While the female is feeding at sea, it is the male's job to go without food for around 120 days while he incubates the egg. The mother returns when the chick has hatched, and she feeds it partially digested krill and other fish. If the mother is delayed, the male feeds the chick a crop milk from his mouth.

[Name]	*Aptenodytes forsteri*
[Classification]	Class: Aves Order: Sphenisciformes Family: Spheniscidae Genus: *Aptenodytes*
[Habitat]	Antarctica
[Height]	120 cm (3.9 ft)

SPECIAL FEATURE | SEA TURTLE TEARS

The sea turtle is able to drink seawater thanks to a well-developed filtration system that eliminates the excess salt by mixing the ions with tears and excreting them through the tear glands positioned behind the eyes. What appears to be an emotional reaction to laying eggs is simply a biological function designed to regulate the body's salt levels, and the turtle actually "cries" constantly (though it is not visible underwater).

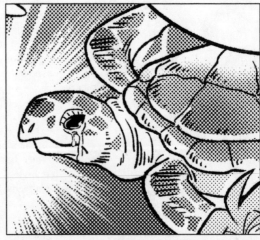

As a reptile, the turtle breathes using its lungs, but as long as it isn't overly active, it can remain underwater for up to five hours.

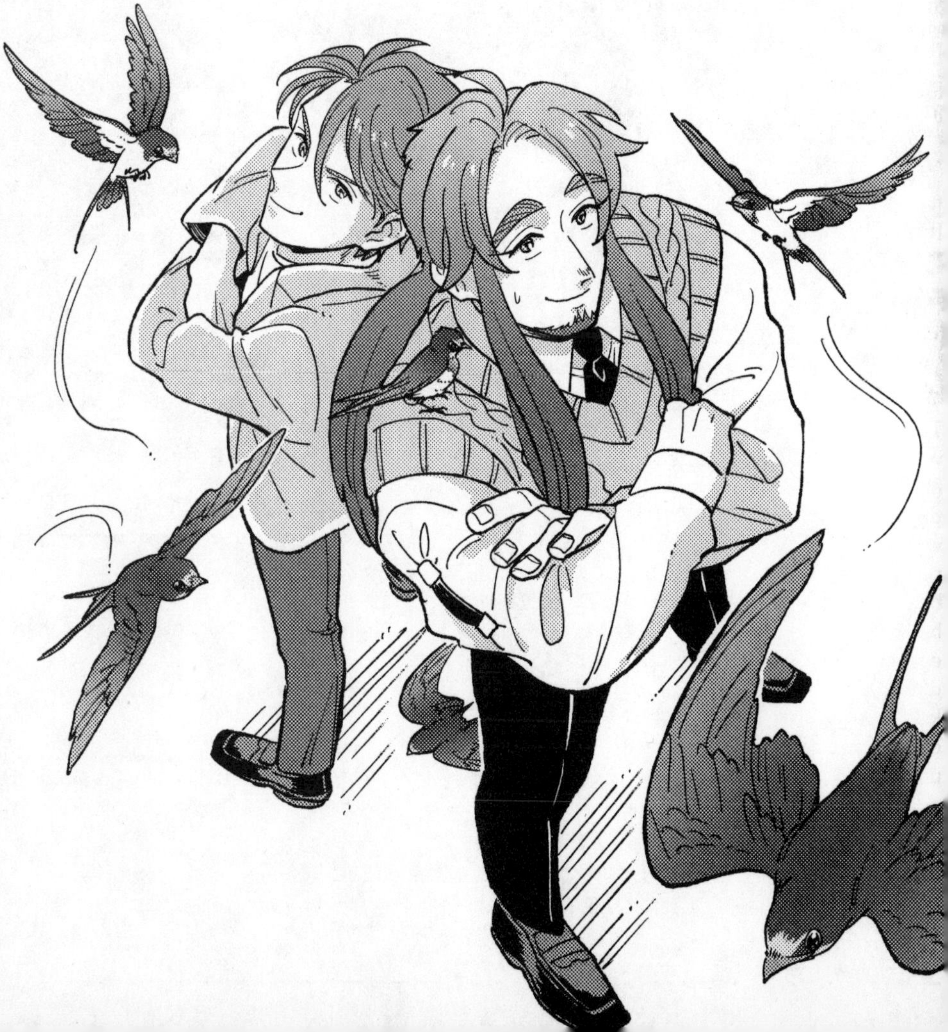

HEAVEN'S DESIGN TEAM

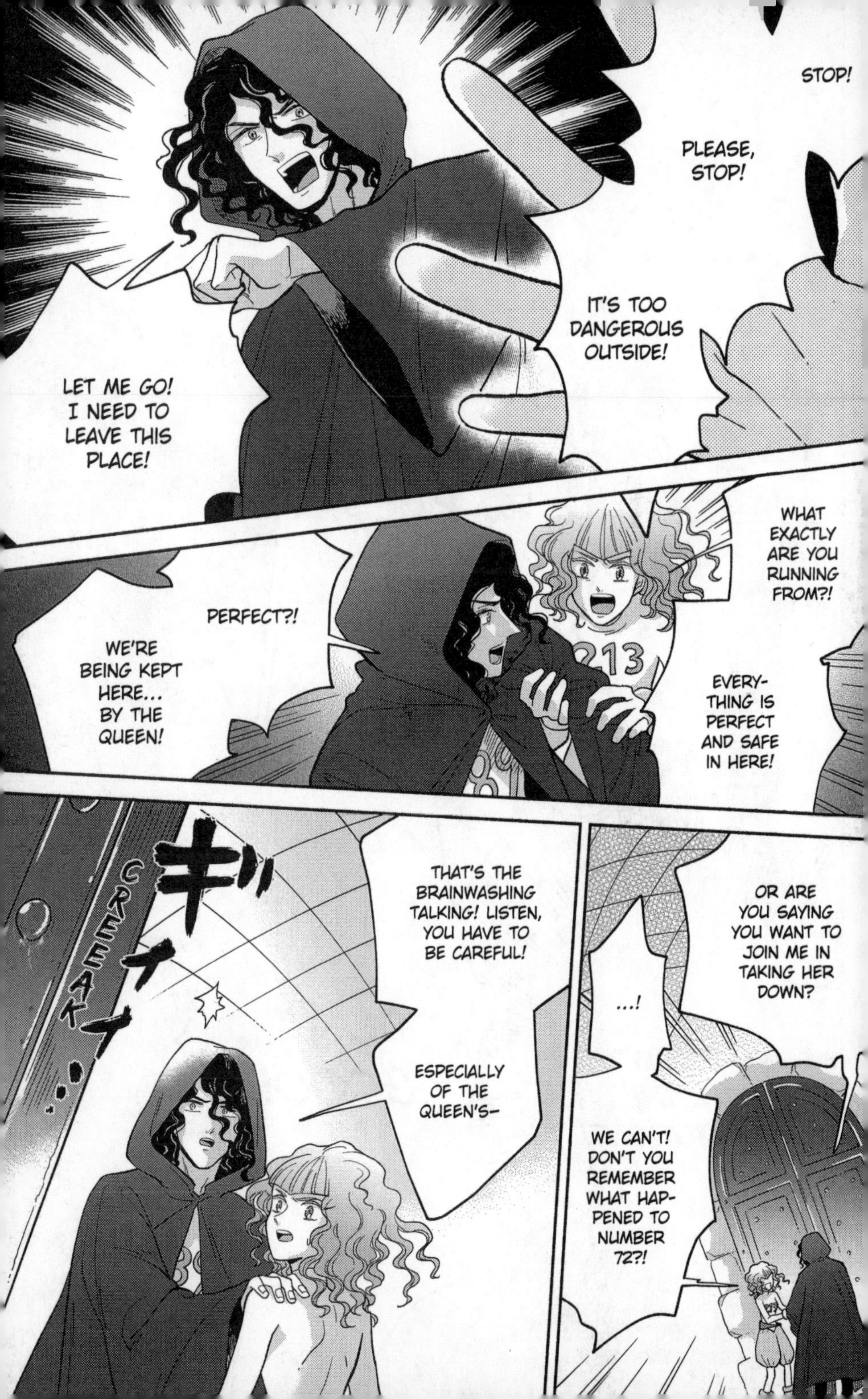
STOP!
PLEASE, STOP!
IT'S TOO DANGEROUS OUTSIDE!
LET ME GO! I NEED TO LEAVE THIS PLACE!
WHAT EXACTLY ARE YOU RUNNING FROM?!
EVERYTHING IS PERFECT AND SAFE IN HERE!
PERFECT?!
WE'RE BEING KEPT HERE... BY THE QUEEN!
OR ARE YOU SAYING YOU WANT TO JOIN ME IN TAKING HER DOWN?
...!
WE CAN'T! DON'T YOU REMEMBER WHAT HAPPENED TO NUMBER 72?!
THAT'S THE BRAINWASHING TALKING! LISTEN, YOU HAVE TO BE CAREFUL!
ESPECIALLY OF THE QUEEN'S–
CREEAK...

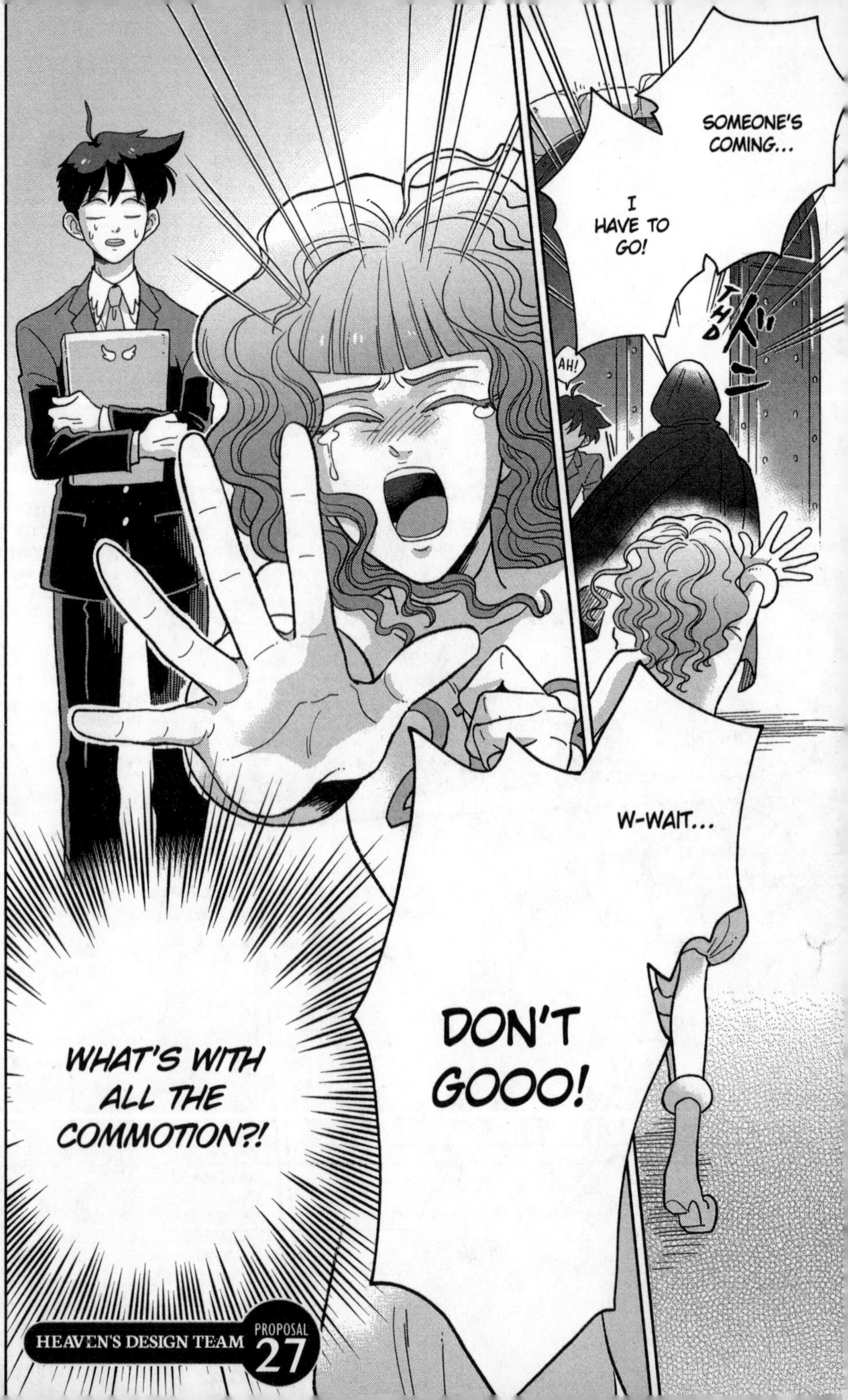
SOMEONE'S COMING...
I HAVE TO GO!
THD
AH!
W-WAIT...
DON'T GOOO!
WHAT'S WITH ALL THE COMMOTION?!
HEAVEN'S DESIGN TEAM PROPOSAL 27

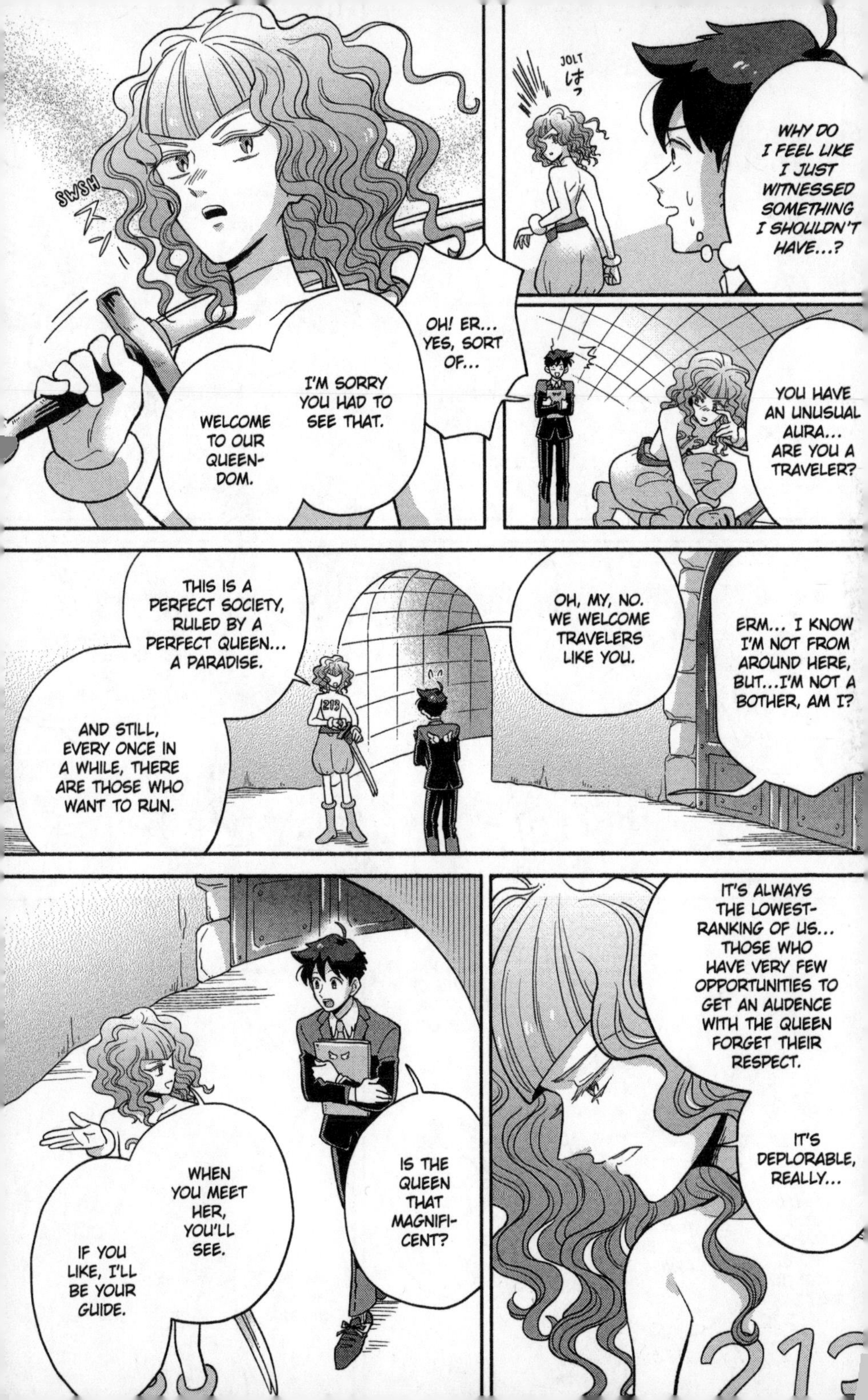
JOLT
はっ
WHY DO I FEEL LIKE I JUST WITNESSED SOMETHING I SHOULDN'T HAVE...?
YOU HAVE AN UNUSUAL AURA... ARE YOU A TRAVELER?
OH! ER... YES, SORT OF...
SWSH
I'M SORRY YOU HAD TO SEE THAT.
WELCOME TO OUR QUEEN-DOM.
ERM... I KNOW I'M NOT FROM AROUND HERE, BUT...I'M NOT A BOTHER, AM I?
OH, MY, NO. WE WELCOME TRAVELERS LIKE YOU.
THIS IS A PERFECT SOCIETY, RULED BY A PERFECT QUEEN... A PARADISE.
AND STILL, EVERY ONCE IN A WHILE, THERE ARE THOSE WHO WANT TO RUN.
IT'S ALWAYS THE LOWEST-RANKING OF US... THOSE WHO HAVE VERY FEW OPPORTUNITIES TO GET AN AUDENCE WITH THE QUEEN FORGET THEIR RESPECT.
IT'S DEPLORABLE, REALLY...
IS THE QUEEN THAT MAGNIFI-CENT?
WHEN YOU MEET HER, YOU'LL SEE.
IF YOU LIKE, I'LL BE YOUR GUIDE.

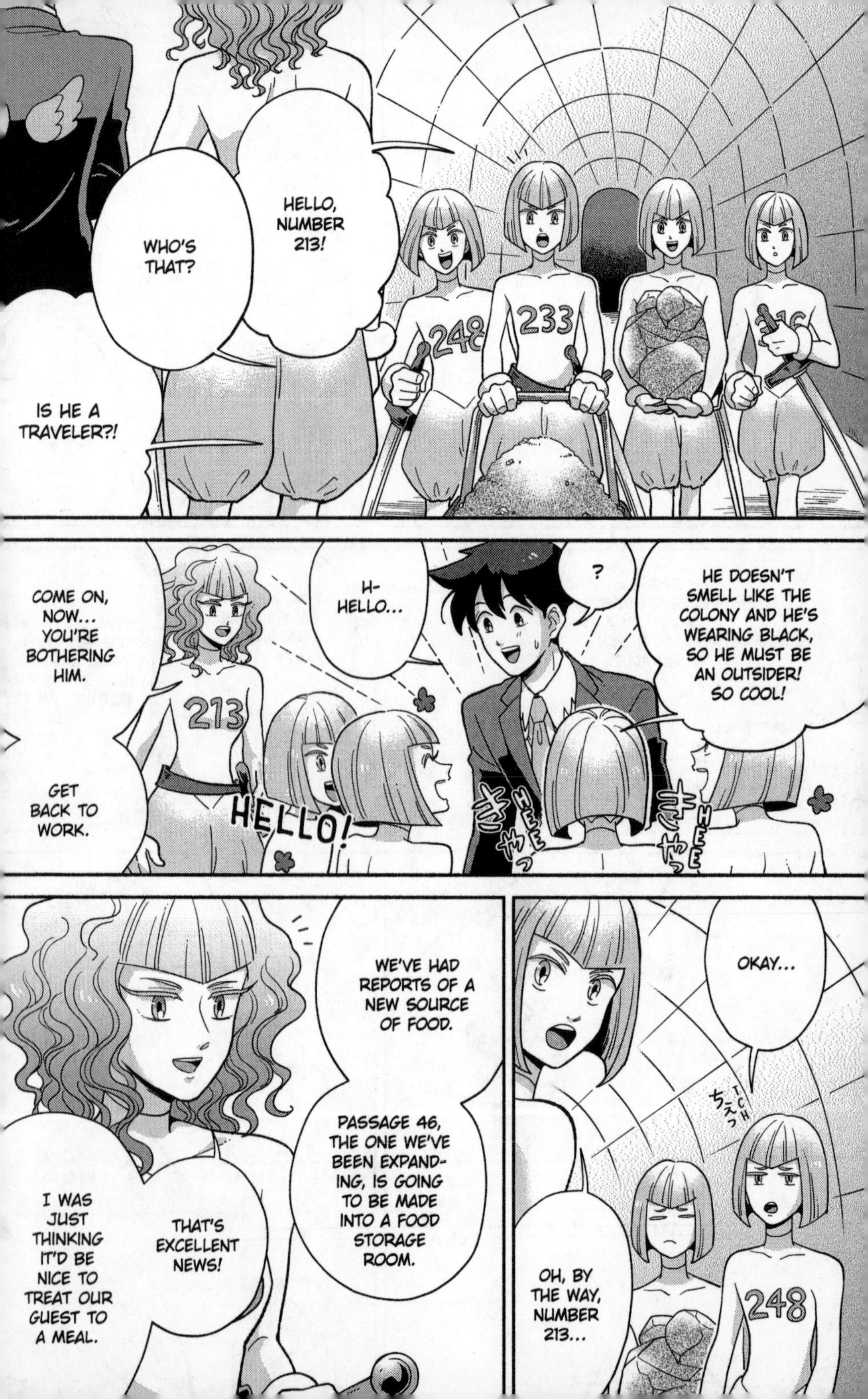
HELLO, NUMBER 213!
WHO'S THAT?
IS HE A TRAVELER?!
248
233
213
HE DOESN'T SMELL LIKE THE COLONY AND HE'S WEARING BLACK, SO HE MUST BE AN OUTSIDER! SO COOL!
?
H- HELLO...
COME ON, NOW... YOU'RE BOTHERING HIM.
GET BACK TO WORK.
きゃっ HEEE
きゃっ HEEE
HELLO!
OKAY...
ちぇっ TCH
OH, BY THE WAY, NUMBER 213...
248
WE'VE HAD REPORTS OF A NEW SOURCE OF FOOD.
PASSAGE 46, THE ONE WE'VE BEEN EXPAND-ING, IS GOING TO BE MADE INTO A FOOD STORAGE ROOM.
THAT'S EXCELLENT NEWS!
I WAS JUST THINKING IT'D BE NICE TO TREAT OUR GUEST TO A MEAL.

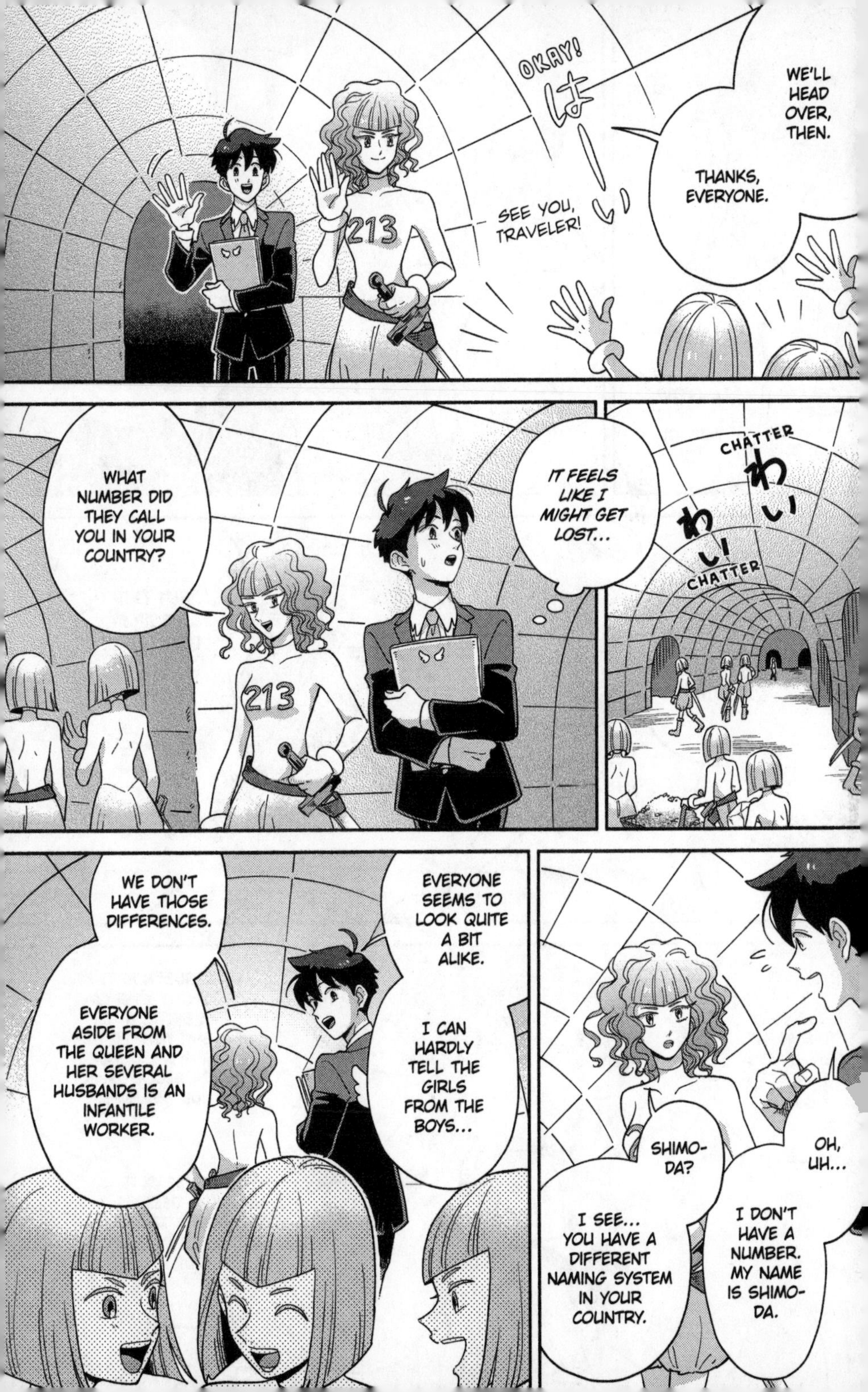
WE'LL HEAD OVER, THEN.
THANKS, EVERYONE.
OKAY!
はーい
SEE YOU, TRAVELER!
213
CHATTER
わい
わい
CHATTER
IT FEELS LIKE I MIGHT GET LOST...
WHAT NUMBER DID THEY CALL YOU IN YOUR COUNTRY?
213
OH, UH...
I DON'T HAVE A NUMBER. MY NAME IS SHIMO-DA.
SHIMO-DA?
I SEE... YOU HAVE A DIFFERENT NAMING SYSTEM IN YOUR COUNTRY.
EVERYONE SEEMS TO LOOK QUITE A BIT ALIKE.
I CAN HARDLY TELL THE GIRLS FROM THE BOYS...
WE DON'T HAVE THOSE DIFFERENCES.
EVERYONE ASIDE FROM THE QUEEN AND HER SEVERAL HUSBANDS IS AN INFANTILE WORKER.

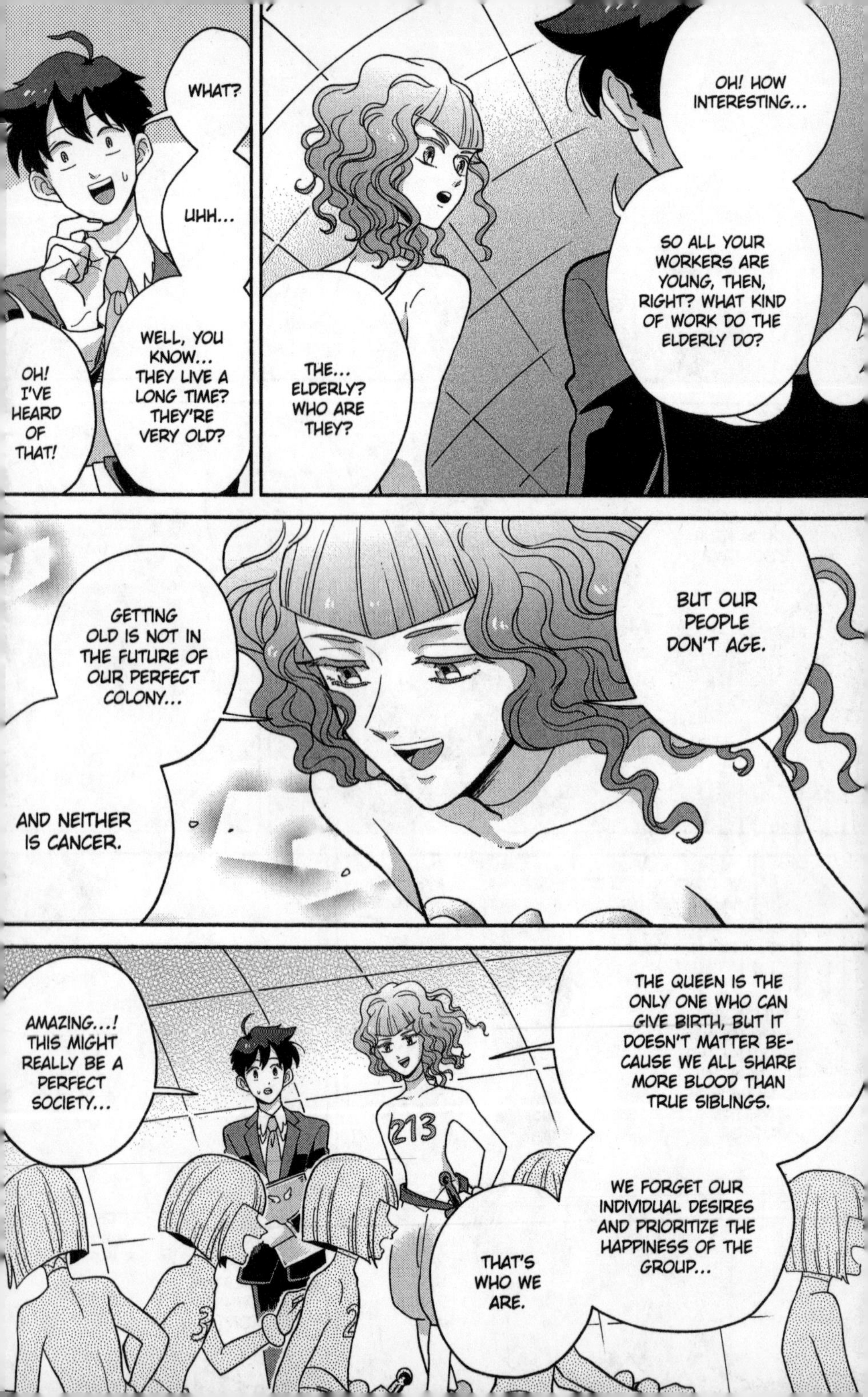
OH! HOW INTERESTING...
SO ALL YOUR WORKERS ARE YOUNG, THEN, RIGHT? WHAT KIND OF WORK DO THE ELDERLY DO?
THE... ELDERLY? WHO ARE THEY?
WHAT?
UHH...
WELL, YOU KNOW... THEY LIVE A LONG TIME? THEY'RE VERY OLD?
OH! I'VE HEARD OF THAT!
BUT OUR PEOPLE DON'T AGE.
GETTING OLD IS NOT IN THE FUTURE OF OUR PERFECT COLONY...
AND NEITHER IS CANCER.
THE QUEEN IS THE ONLY ONE WHO CAN GIVE BIRTH, BUT IT DOESN'T MATTER BE-CAUSE WE ALL SHARE MORE BLOOD THAN TRUE SIBLINGS.
WE FORGET OUR INDIVIDUAL DESIRES AND PRIORITIZE THE HAPPINESS OF THE GROUP...
THAT'S WHO WE ARE.
213
AMAZING...! THIS MIGHT REALLY BE A PERFECT SOCIETY...

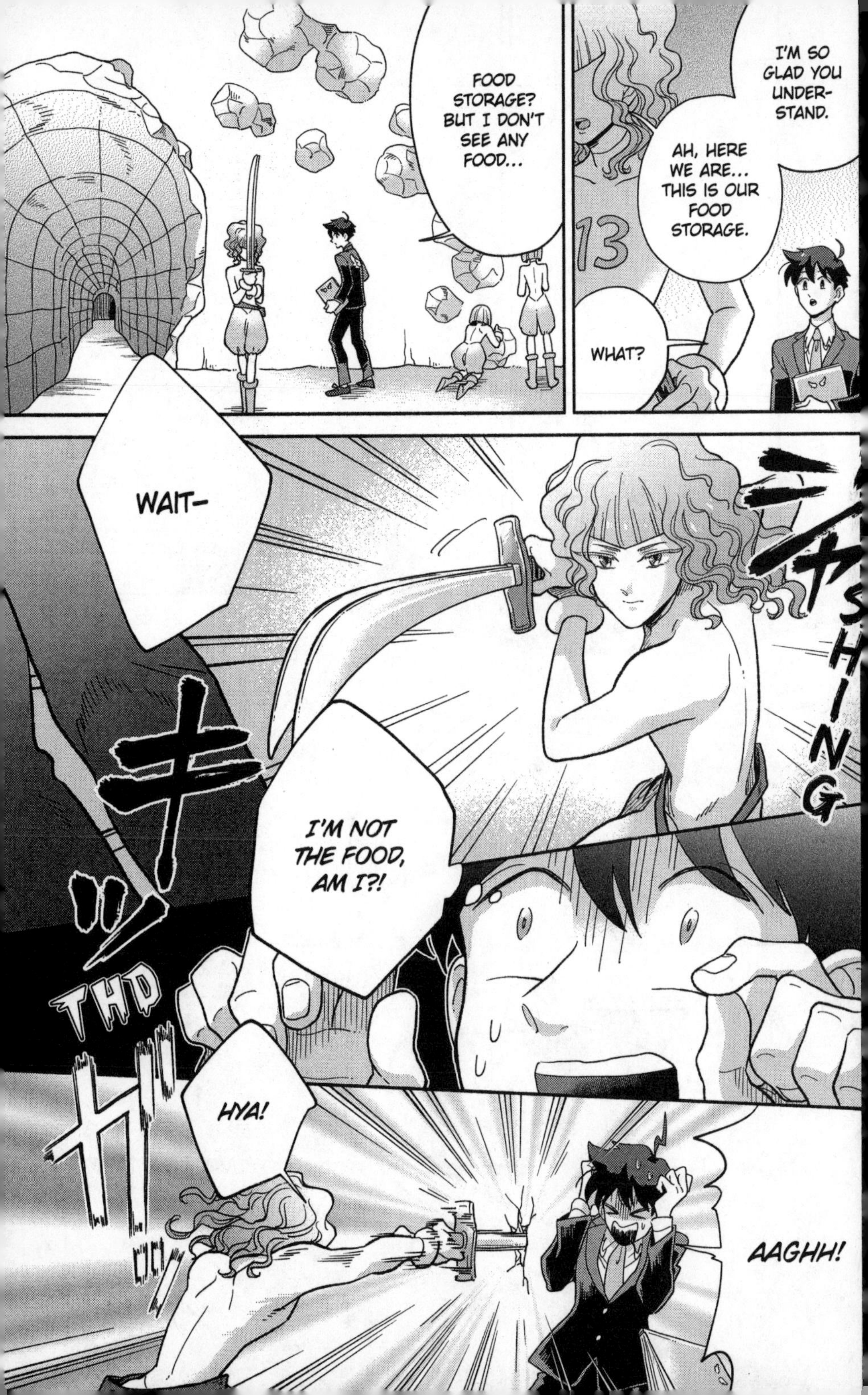
I'M SO GLAD YOU UNDER-STAND.
AH, HERE WE ARE... THIS IS OUR FOOD STORAGE.
WHAT?
FOOD STORAGE? BUT I DON'T SEE ANY FOOD...
SHING
WAIT-
I'M NOT THE FOOD, AM I?!
THD
HYA!
AAGHH!

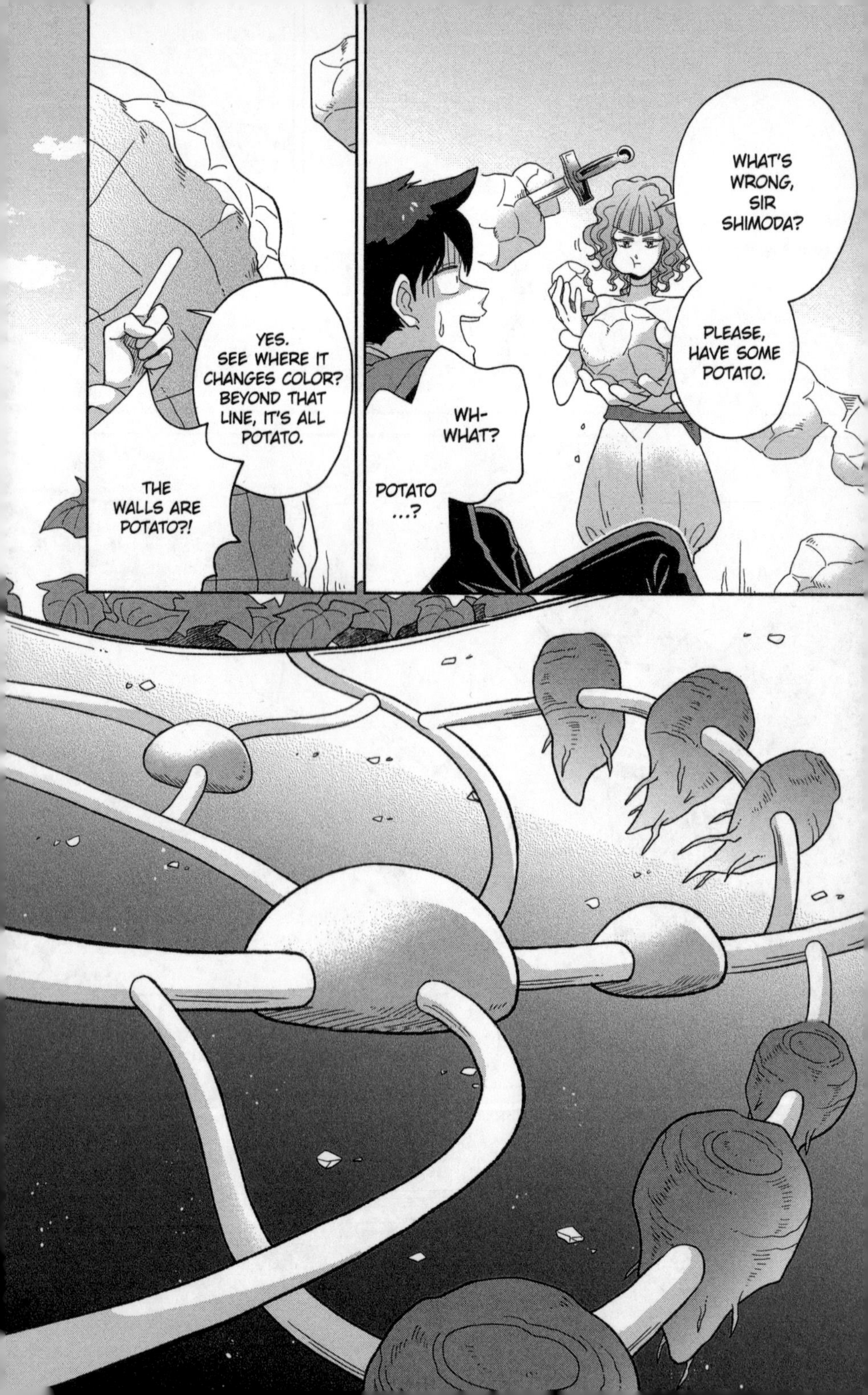
WHAT'S WRONG, SIR SHIMODA?
PLEASE, HAVE SOME POTATO.
WH-WHAT?
POTATO ...?
YES. SEE WHERE IT CHANGES COLOR? BEYOND THAT LINE, IT'S ALL POTATO.
THE WALLS ARE POTATO?!

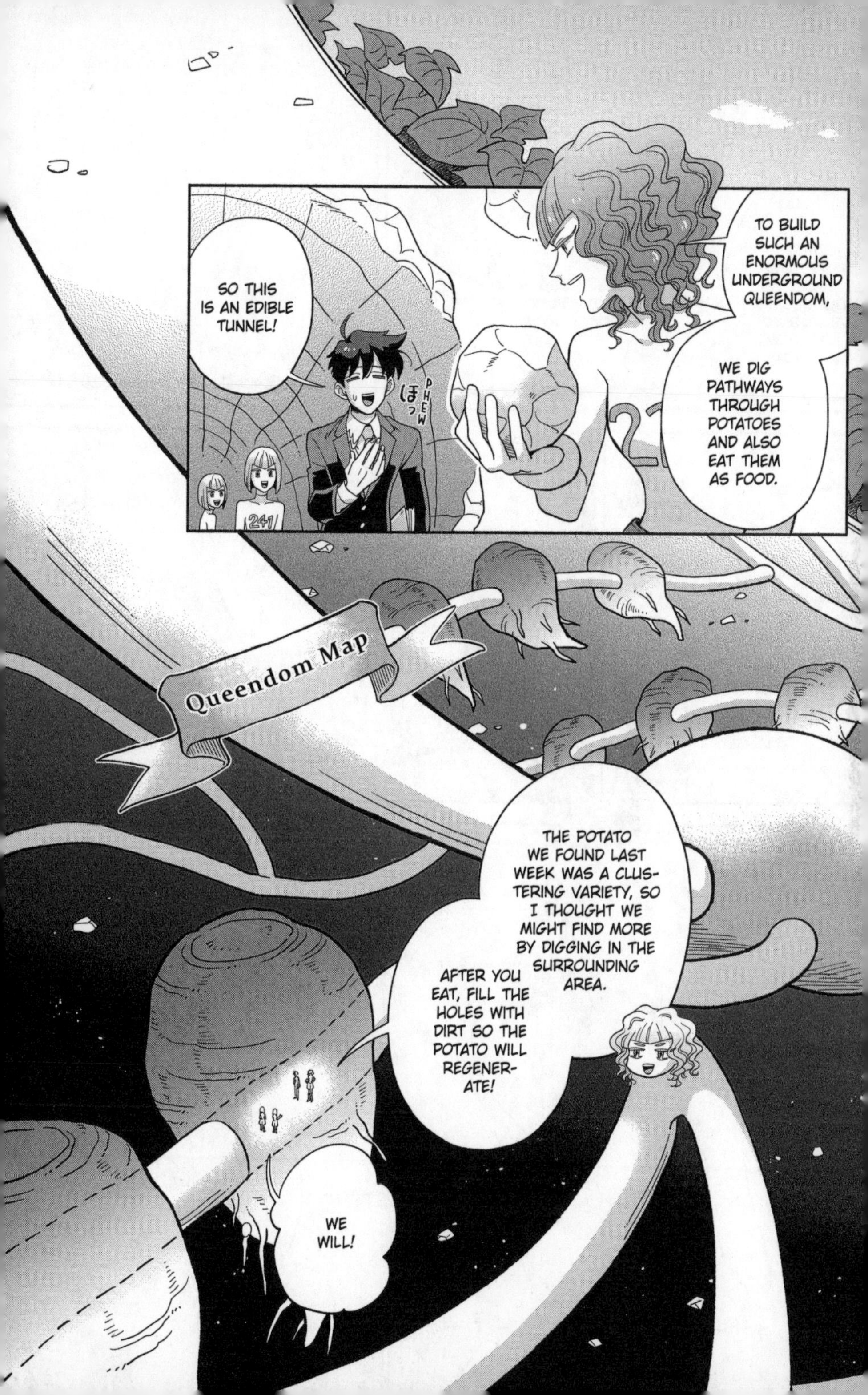
TO BUILD SUCH AN ENORMOUS UNDERGROUND QUEENDOM,
WE DIG PATHWAYS THROUGH POTATOES AND ALSO EAT THEM AS FOOD.
ほっ PHEW
SO THIS IS AN EDIBLE TUNNEL!
Queendom Map
THE POTATO WE FOUND LAST WEEK WAS A CLUS-TERING VARIETY, SO I THOUGHT WE MIGHT FIND MORE BY DIGGING IN THE SURROUNDING AREA.
AFTER YOU EAT, FILL THE HOLES WITH DIRT SO THE POTATO WILL REGENER-ATE!
WE WILL!

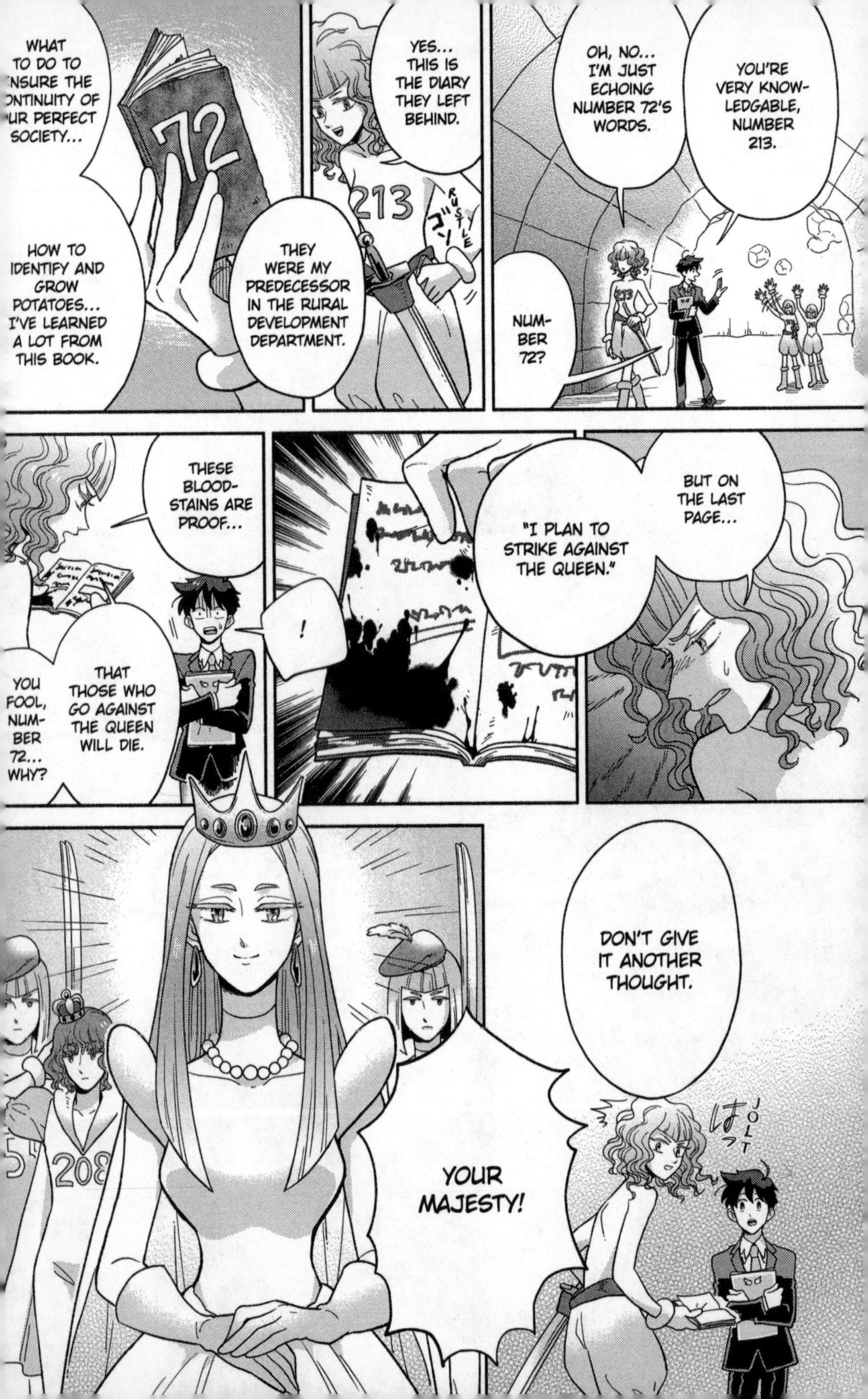

YOU'RE VERY KNOWLEDGABLE, NUMBER 213.
OH, NO... I'M JUST ECHOING NUMBER 72'S WORDS.
NUMBER 72?
YES... THIS IS THE DIARY THEY LEFT BEHIND.
RUSTLE
THEY WERE MY PREDECESSOR IN THE RURAL DEVELOPMENT DEPARTMENT.
WHAT TO DO TO NSURE THE ONTINUITY OF UR PERFECT SOCIETY...
HOW TO IDENTIFY AND GROW POTATOES... I'VE LEARNED A LOT FROM THIS BOOK.
BUT ON THE LAST PAGE...
"I PLAN TO STRIKE AGAINST THE QUEEN."
!
THESE BLOODSTAINS ARE PROOF...
THAT THOSE WHO GO AGAINST THE QUEEN WILL DIE.
YOU FOOL, NUMBER 72... WHY?
DON'T GIVE IT ANOTHER THOUGHT.
JOLT
YOUR MAJESTY!

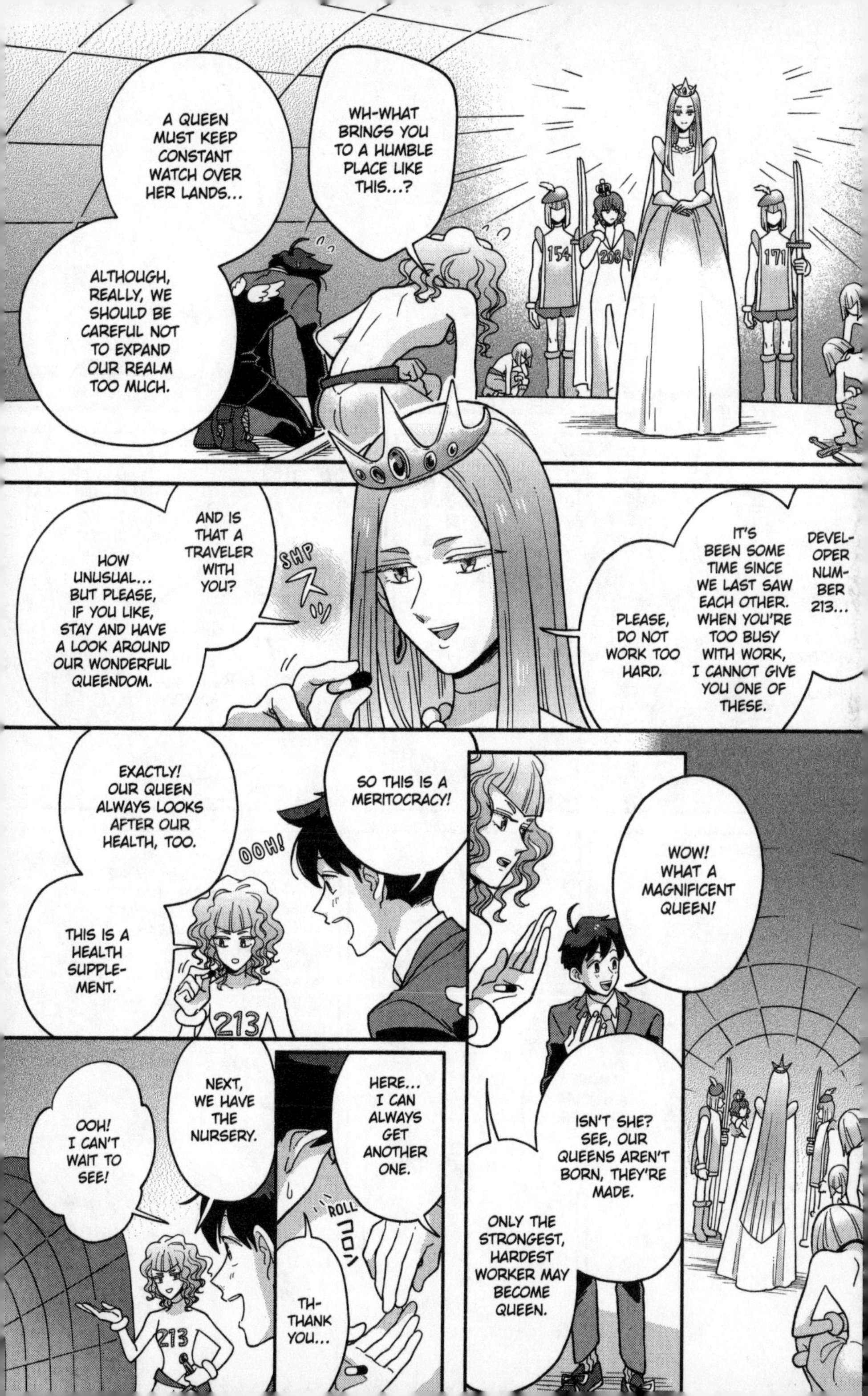
WH-WHAT BRINGS YOU TO A HUMBLE PLACE LIKE THIS...?
A QUEEN MUST KEEP CONSTANT WATCH OVER HER LANDS...
ALTHOUGH, REALLY, WE SHOULD BE CAREFUL NOT TO EXPAND OUR REALM TOO MUCH.
154
208
171
DEVELOPER NUMBER 213...
IT'S BEEN SOME TIME SINCE WE LAST SAW EACH OTHER. WHEN YOU'RE TOO BUSY WITH WORK, I CANNOT GIVE YOU ONE OF THESE.
PLEASE, DO NOT WORK TOO HARD.
SHP ス ッ
AND IS THAT A TRAVELER WITH YOU?
HOW UNUSUAL... BUT PLEASE, IF YOU LIKE, STAY AND HAVE A LOOK AROUND OUR WONDERFUL QUEENDOM.
WOW! WHAT A MAGNIFICENT QUEEN!
SO THIS IS A MERITOCRACY!
OOH!
EXACTLY! OUR QUEEN ALWAYS LOOKS AFTER OUR HEALTH, TOO.
THIS IS A HEALTH SUPPLEMENT.
213
ISN'T SHE? SEE, OUR QUEENS AREN'T BORN, THEY'RE MADE.
ONLY THE STRONGEST, HARDEST WORKER MAY BECOME QUEEN.
HERE... I CAN ALWAYS GET ANOTHER ONE.
ROLL コロン
TH-THANK YOU...
NEXT, WE HAVE THE NURSERY.
OOH! I CAN'T WAIT TO SEE!
213

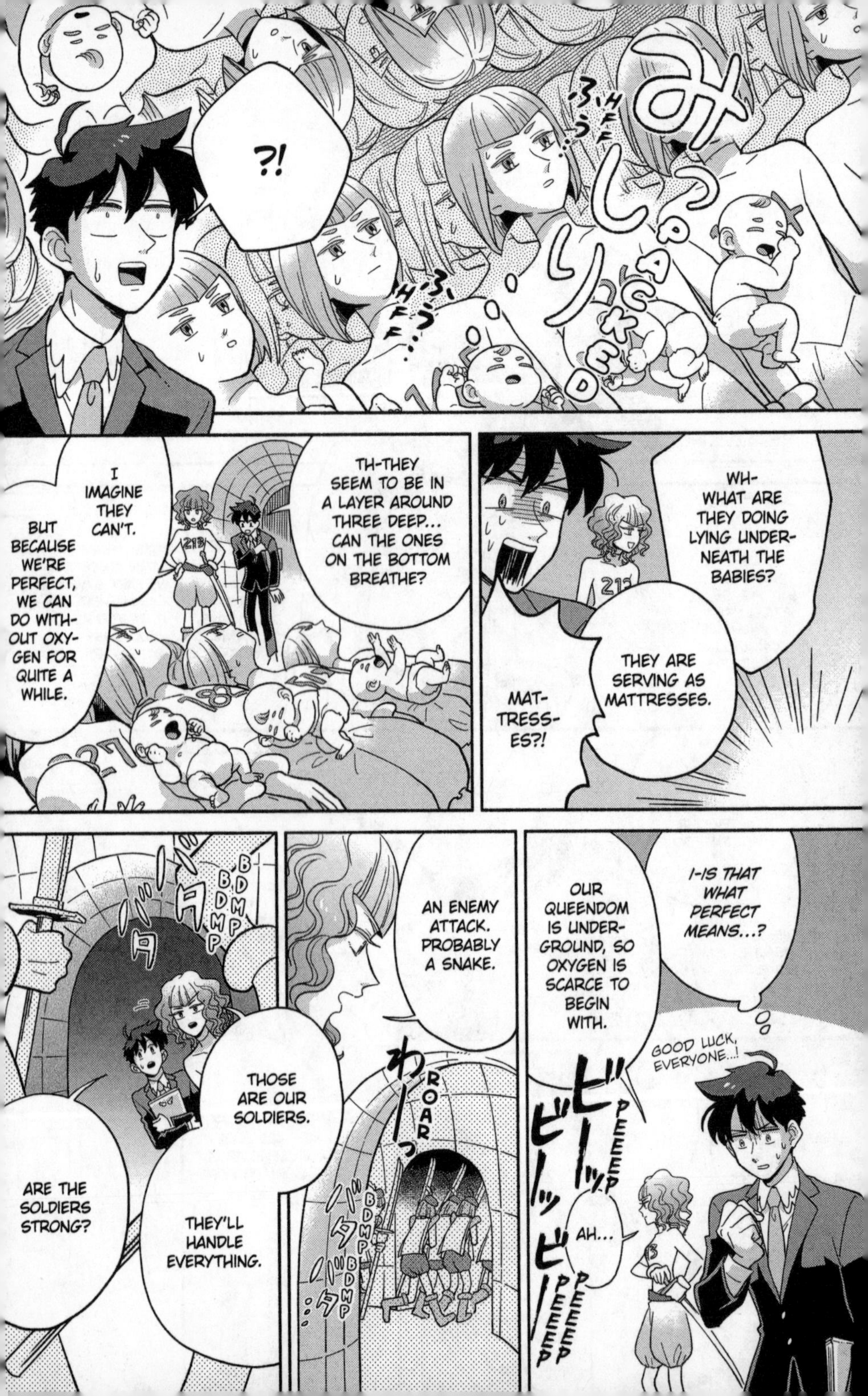
?!
ふう HFF
ふう HFF
みっしり PACKED
WH-WHAT ARE THEY DOING LYING UNDER-NEATH THE BABIES?
THEY ARE SERVING AS MATTRESSES.
MAT-TRESS-ES?!
TH-THEY SEEM TO BE IN A LAYER AROUND THREE DEEP... CAN THE ONES ON THE BOTTOM BREATHE?
I IMAGINE THEY CAN'T.
BUT BECAUSE WE'RE PERFECT, WE CAN DO WITH-OUT OXY-GEN FOR QUITE A WHILE.
I-IS THAT WHAT PERFECT MEANS...?
OUR QUEENDOM IS UNDER-GROUND, SO OXYGEN IS SCARCE TO BEGIN WITH.
GOOD LUCK, EVERYONE...!
ビーッ PEEEP
ビーッ PEEEP
ビー PEEEP
AH...
AN ENEMY ATTACK. PROBABLY A SNAKE.
わーっ ROAR
バタ BDMP
バタ BDMP
バタ BDMP
BDMP
BDMP
THOSE ARE OUR SOLDIERS.
ARE THE SOLDIERS STRONG?
THEY'LL HANDLE EVERYTHING.

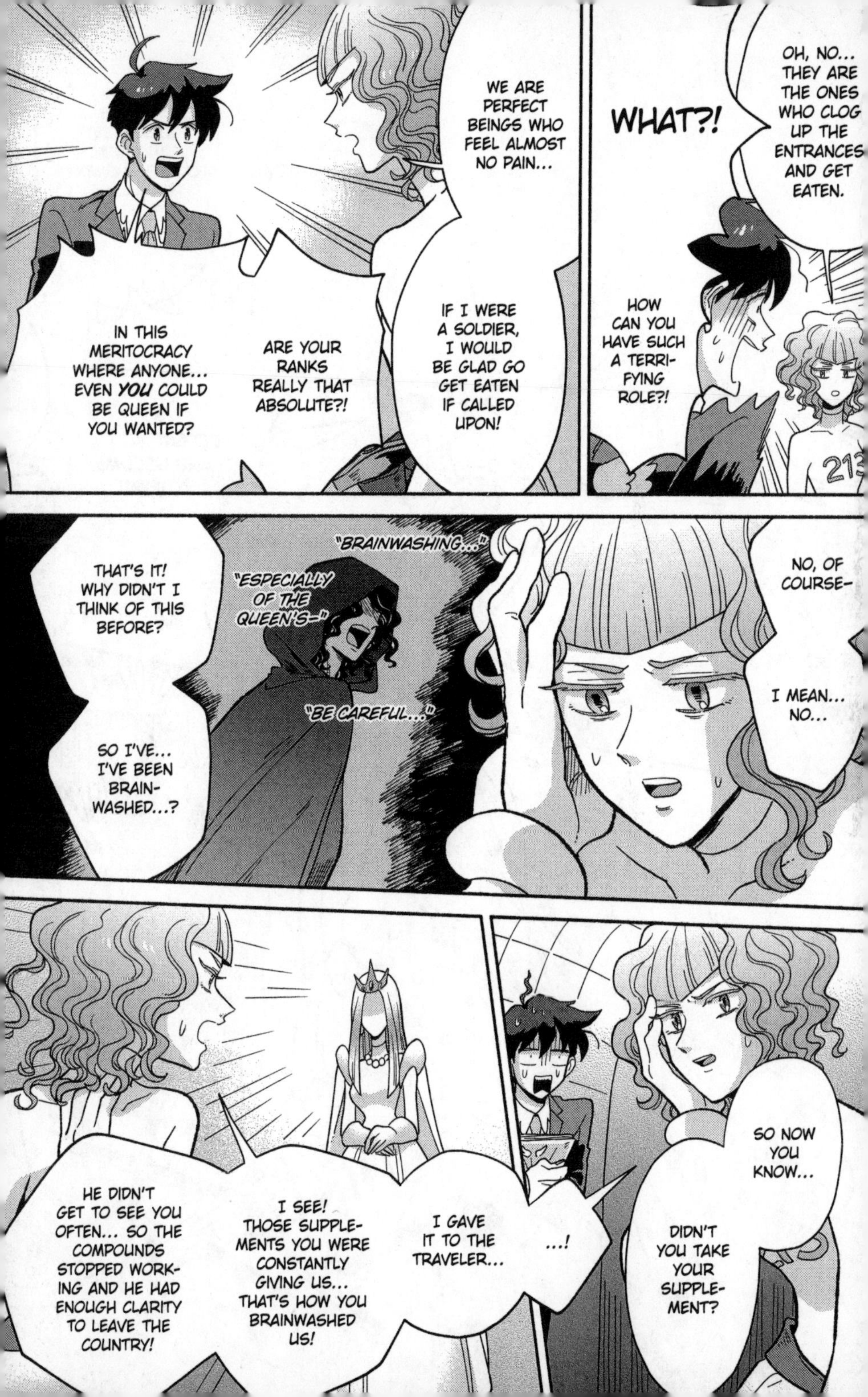
OH, NO... THEY ARE THE ONES WHO CLOG UP THE ENTRANCES AND GET EATEN.
WHAT?!
HOW CAN YOU HAVE SUCH A TERRI-FYING ROLE?!
WE ARE PERFECT BEINGS WHO FEEL ALMOST NO PAIN...
IF I WERE A SOLDIER, I WOULD BE GLAD GO GET EATEN IF CALLED UPON!
ARE YOUR RANKS REALLY THAT ABSOLUTE?!
IN THIS MERITOCRACY WHERE ANYONE... EVEN *YOU* COULD BE QUEEN IF YOU WANTED?
NO, OF COURSE-
I MEAN... NO...
"BRAINWASHING..."
"ESPECIALLY OF THE QUEEN'S-"
"BE CAREFUL..."
THAT'S IT! WHY DIDN'T I THINK OF THIS BEFORE?
SO I'VE... I'VE BEEN BRAIN-WASHED...?
SO NOW YOU KNOW...
DIDN'T YOU TAKE YOUR SUPPLE-MENT?
...!
I GAVE IT TO THE TRAVELER...
I SEE! THOSE SUPPLE-MENTS YOU WERE CONSTANTLY GIVING US... THAT'S HOW YOU BRAINWASHED US!
HE DIDN'T GET TO SEE YOU OFTEN... SO THE COMPOUNDS STOPPED WORK-ING AND HE HAD ENOUGH CLARITY TO LEAVE THE COUNTRY!

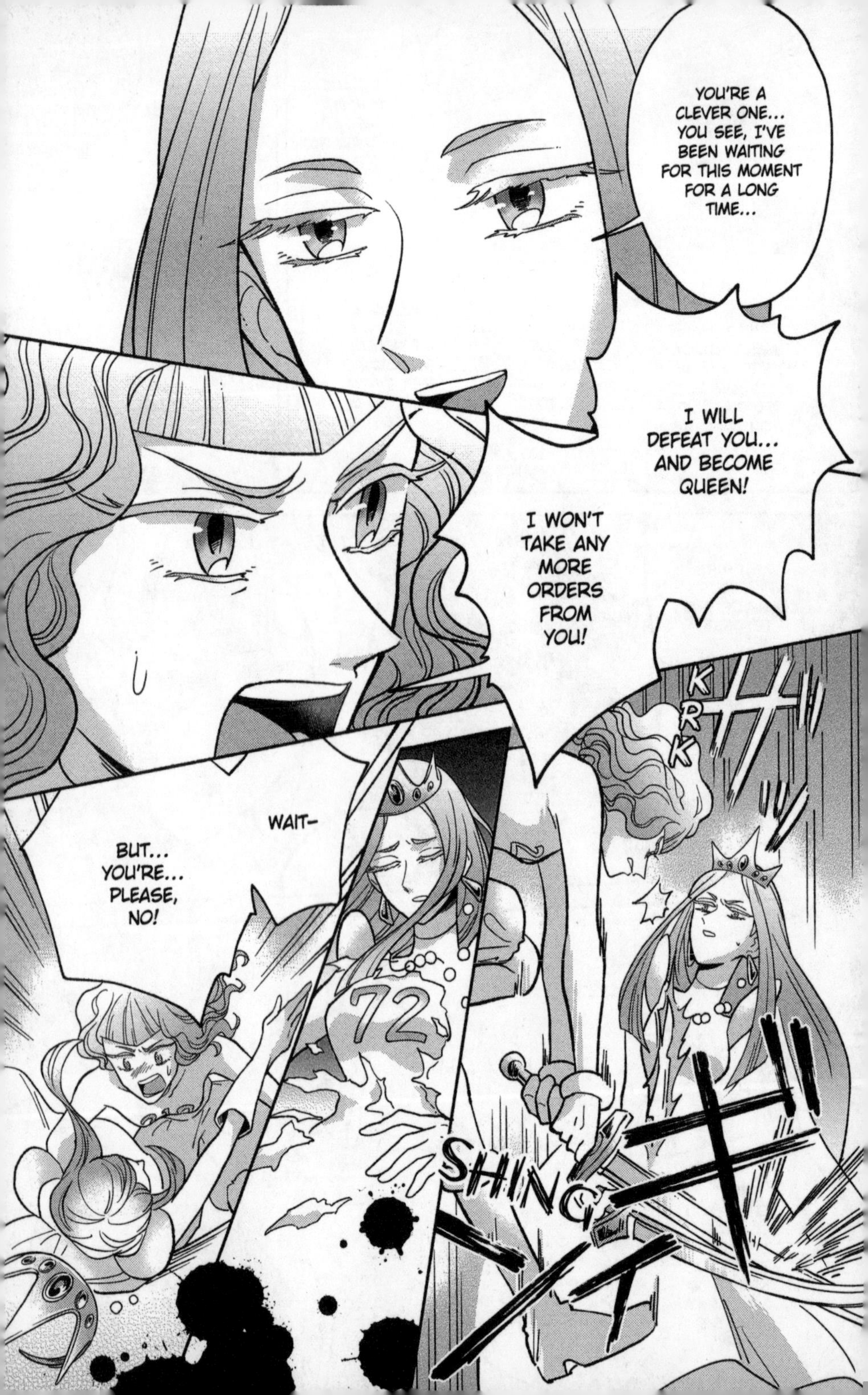
YOU'RE A CLEVER ONE... YOU SEE, I'VE BEEN WAITING FOR THIS MOMENT FOR A LONG TIME...
I WILL DEFEAT YOU... AND BECOME QUEEN!
I WON'T TAKE ANY MORE ORDERS FROM YOU!
KRK
SHING
72
WAIT-
BUT... YOU'RE... PLEASE, NO!

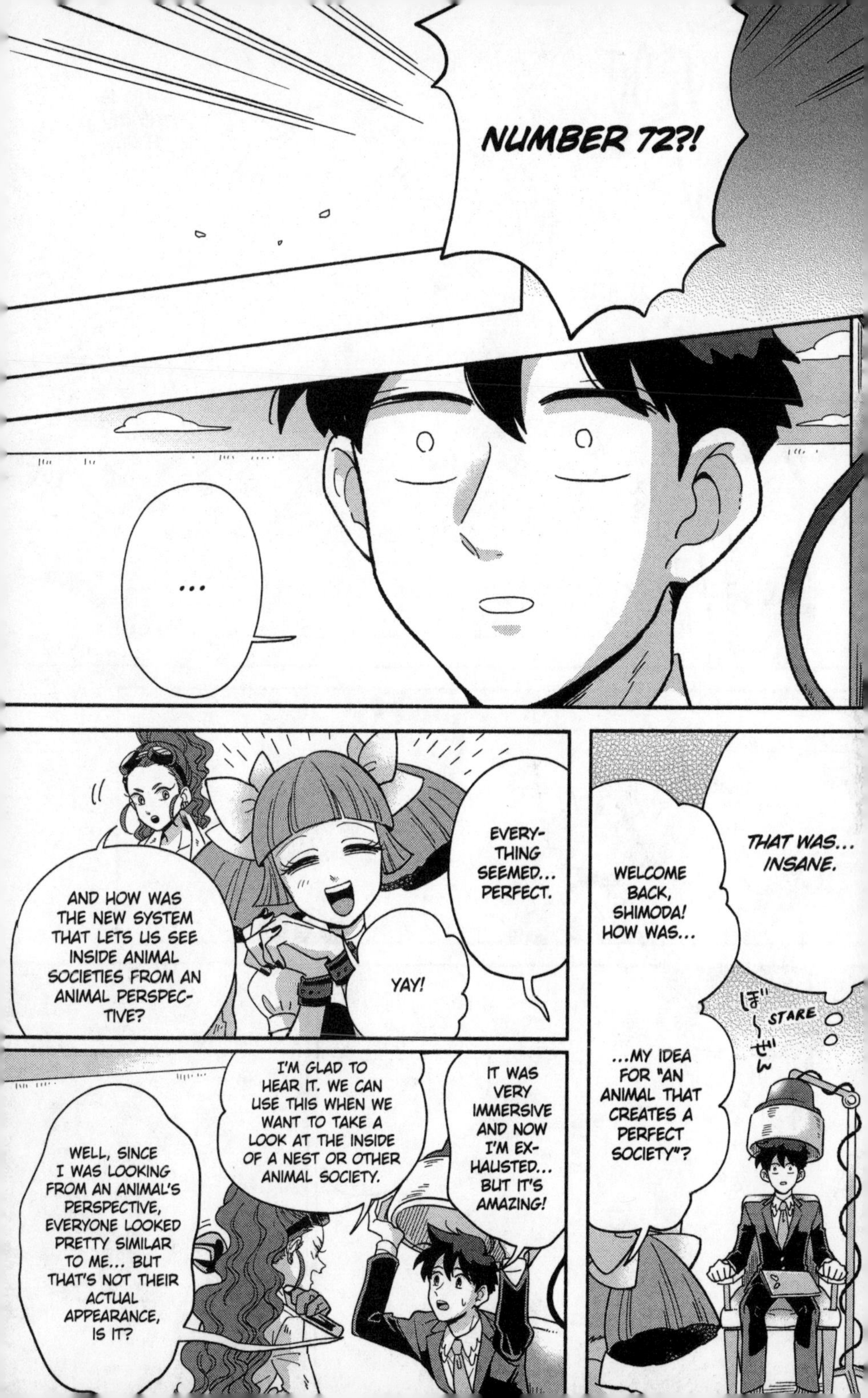
NUMBER 72?!
...
THAT WAS... INSANE.
WELCOME BACK, SHIMODA! HOW WAS...
...MY IDEA FOR "AN ANIMAL THAT CREATES A PERFECT SOCIETY"?
ぼ～ぜん
STARE
EVERYTHING SEEMED... PERFECT.
YAY!
AND HOW WAS THE NEW SYSTEM THAT LETS US SEE INSIDE ANIMAL SOCIETIES FROM AN ANIMAL PERSPECTIVE?
IT WAS VERY IMMERSIVE AND NOW I'M EXHAUSTED... BUT IT'S AMAZING!
I'M GLAD TO HEAR IT. WE CAN USE THIS WHEN WE WANT TO TAKE A LOOK AT THE INSIDE OF A NEST OR OTHER ANIMAL SOCIETY.
WELL, SINCE I WAS LOOKING FROM AN ANIMAL'S PERSPECTIVE, EVERYONE LOOKED PRETTY SIMILAR TO ME... BUT THAT'S NOT THEIR ACTUAL APPEARANCE, IS IT?

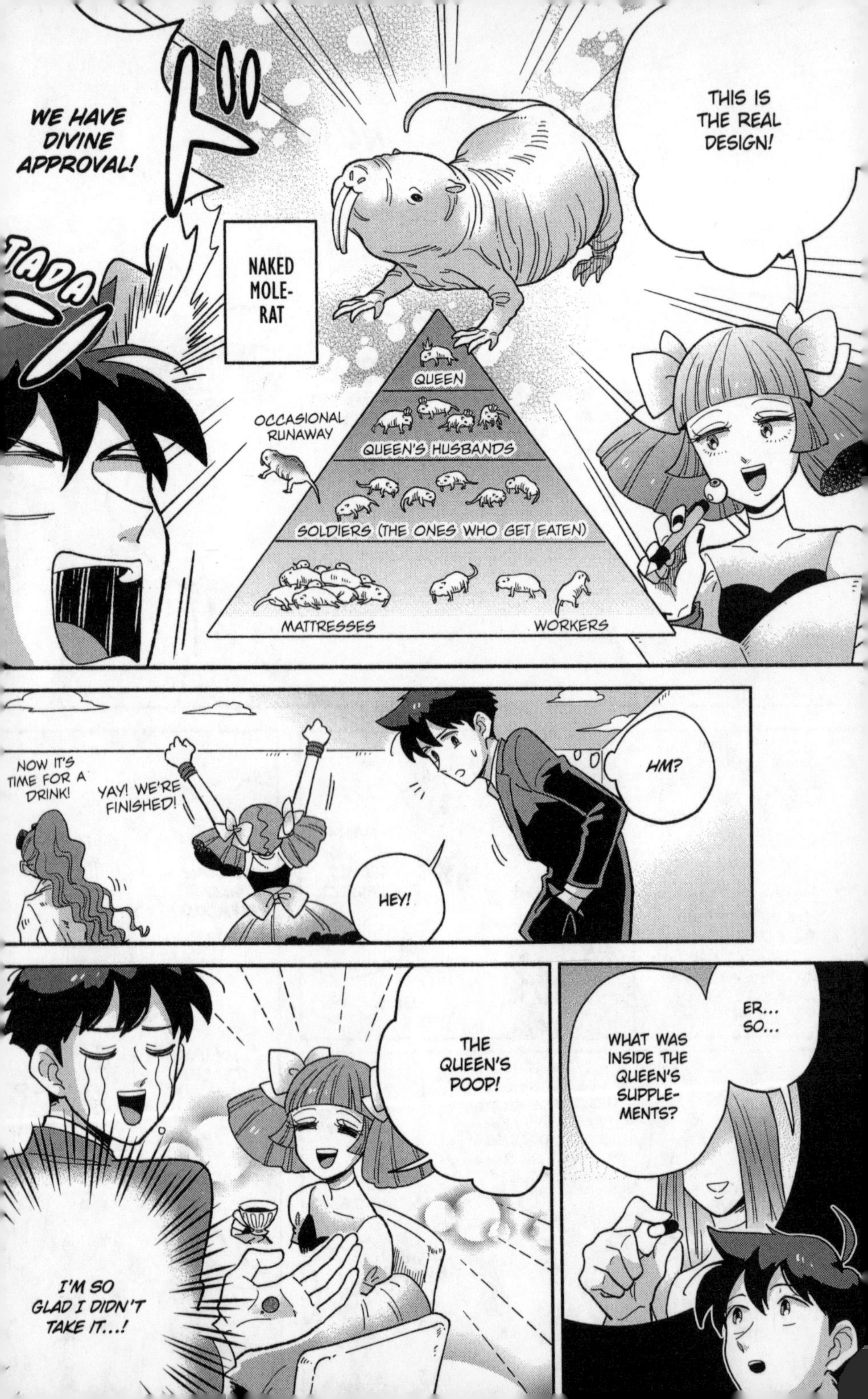
THIS IS THE REAL DESIGN!
NAKED MOLE-RAT
QUEEN
QUEEN'S HUSBANDS
OCCASIONAL RUNAWAY
SOLDIERS (THE ONES WHO GET EATEN)
WORKERS
MATTRESSES
TADA
WE HAVE DIVINE APPROVAL!
HM?
HEY!
YAY! WE'RE FINISHED!
NOW IT'S TIME FOR A DRINK!
ER... SO...
WHAT WAS INSIDE THE QUEEN'S SUPPLEMENTS?
THE QUEEN'S POOP!
I'M SO GLAD I DIDN'T TAKE IT...!

THE ENCYCLOPEDIA OF REAL ANIMALS 27

ANIMAL 68 | NAKED MOLE-RAT

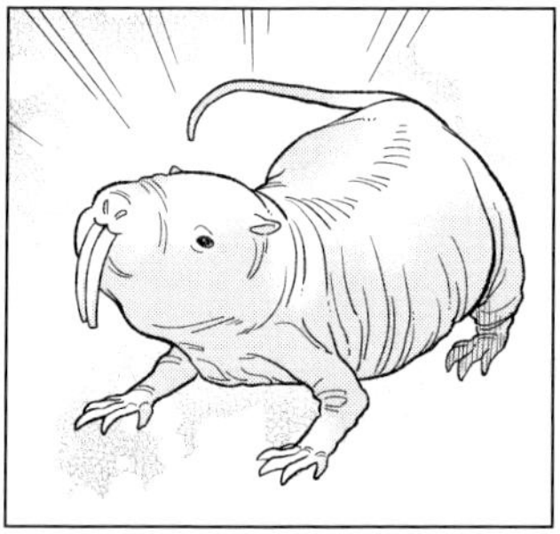

THE REAL THING

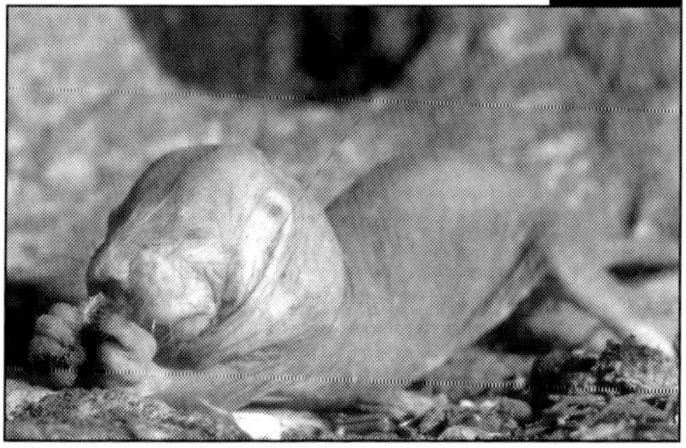

A naked mole-rat eating its queen's feces.

Photo: Science Photo Library/Aflo

[Name] *Heterocephalus glaber*
[Classification] Class: Mammalia
Order: Rodentia
Family: Heterocephalidae
Genus: *Heterocephalus*
[Habitat] East Africa
[Length] About 8-9 cm (3.1-3.5 in)

The naked mole-rat is competely hairless, as its name suggests, and has distinctive front teeth. It is one of only a few mammals that lives in eusocial groups, in which only one female (the queen) and a few males reproduce and the remaining members are organized by role in a highly structured society. These worker roles include husband to the queen, nest builder, soldiers to be sacrificed and eaten by the enemy, and mattresses for the young. It's said that the year-round warm temperatures of the mole-rat's equatorial habitat is the reason for its lack of fur and thermoregulatory system. Young pups, on the other hand, lose heat quickly and need to lie on top of mattress workers to stay warm.

When mole-rats find their staple food of giant tubers or yams, they connect it to their network of tunnels and create a combination passageway and pantry. They're careful not to eat the entire thing and pack dirt into the holes they create in order to encourage regeneration.

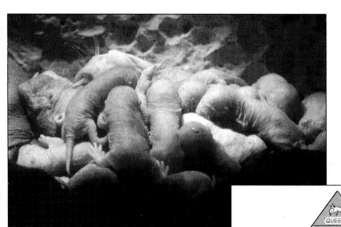

Naked mole-rats often play the role of a mattress in the colony. The queen's place is at the top of the pile.

Photo: Science Photo Library/Aflo

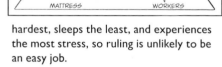

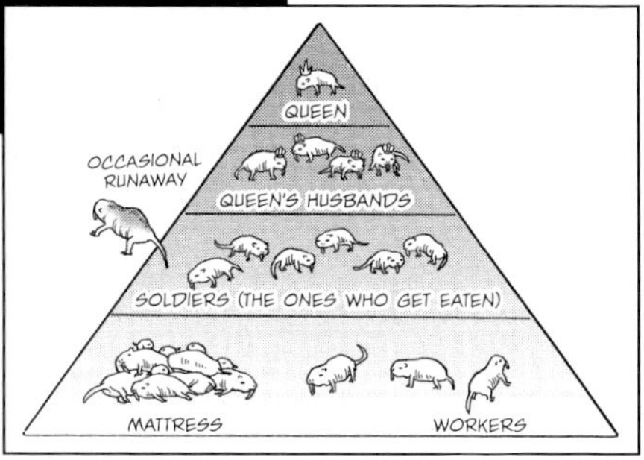

QUEEN

OCCASIONAL RUNAWAY

QUEEN'S HUSBANDS

SOLDIERS (THE ONES WHO GET EATEN)

MATTRESS

WORKERS

The naked mole rat lives an exceptionally long life, with specimens in captivity reaching up to 30 years of age. That combined with other factors such as their apparent lack of a normal aging process, their resistance to cancer, and their ability to survive in oxygen-deprived environments have earned them the nickname "the miraculous mammal."

Causes of death include periodontitis and being eaten by predators. As described in this chapter, some members of the colony may attempt to escape. Before its journey to the surface, the mole-rat's back fur will darken to mimic the coloration of the ground.

Males who display their fortitude by joining the colony independently from the outside are highly popular among the females. Queens are not decided by birth but rather by shows of strength and organizational skill. It's said that the queen works the hardest, sleeps the least, and experiences the most stress, so ruling is unlikely to be an easy job.

The queen's feces contain large amounts of estrogen, and by feeding it to the workers, both male and female, she can command them to take care of her young. When the colony has grown too large or a superior queen is born, the mole-rats stage a coup and the victor is declared the new queen.

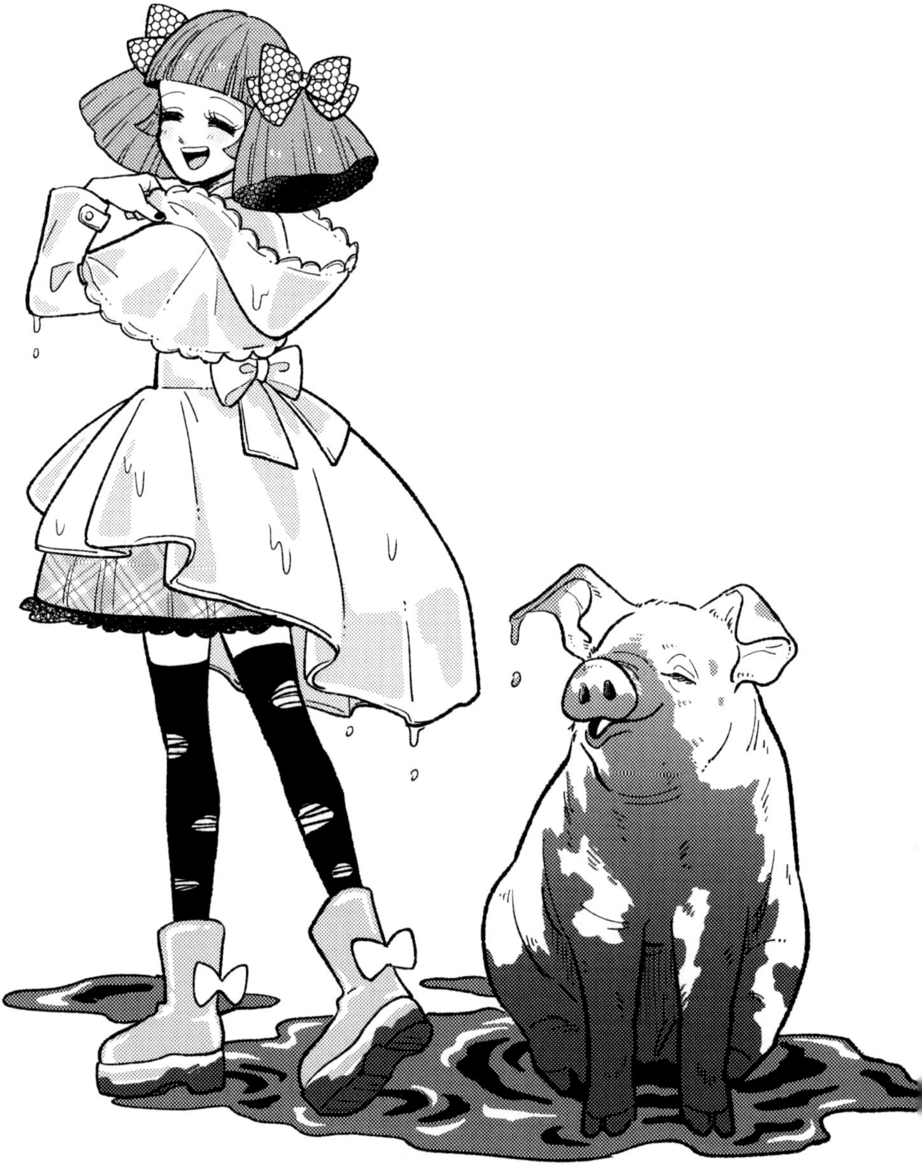

HEAVEN'S
DESIGN TEAM

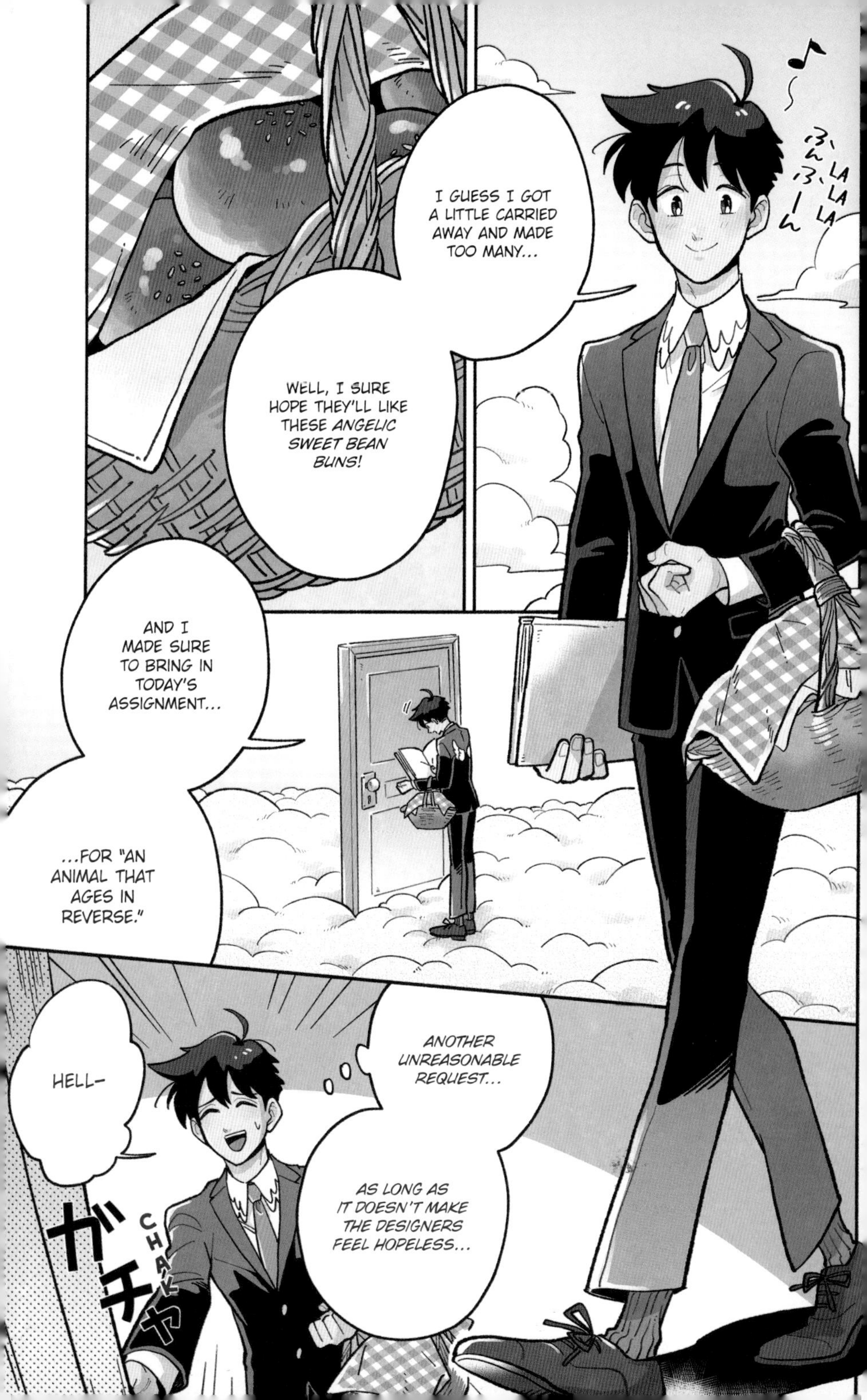

ふんふーん
LA LA LA
I GUESS I GOT A LITTLE CARRIED AWAY AND MADE TOO MANY...
WELL, I SURE HOPE THEY'LL LIKE THESE *ANGELIC SWEET BEAN BUNS!*
AND I MADE SURE TO BRING IN TODAY'S ASSIGNMENT...
...FOR "AN ANIMAL THAT AGES IN REVERSE."
ANOTHER UNREASONABLE REQUEST...
HELL-
AS LONG AS IT DOESN'T MAKE THE DESIGNERS FEEL HOPELESS...
ガチャ
CHAK

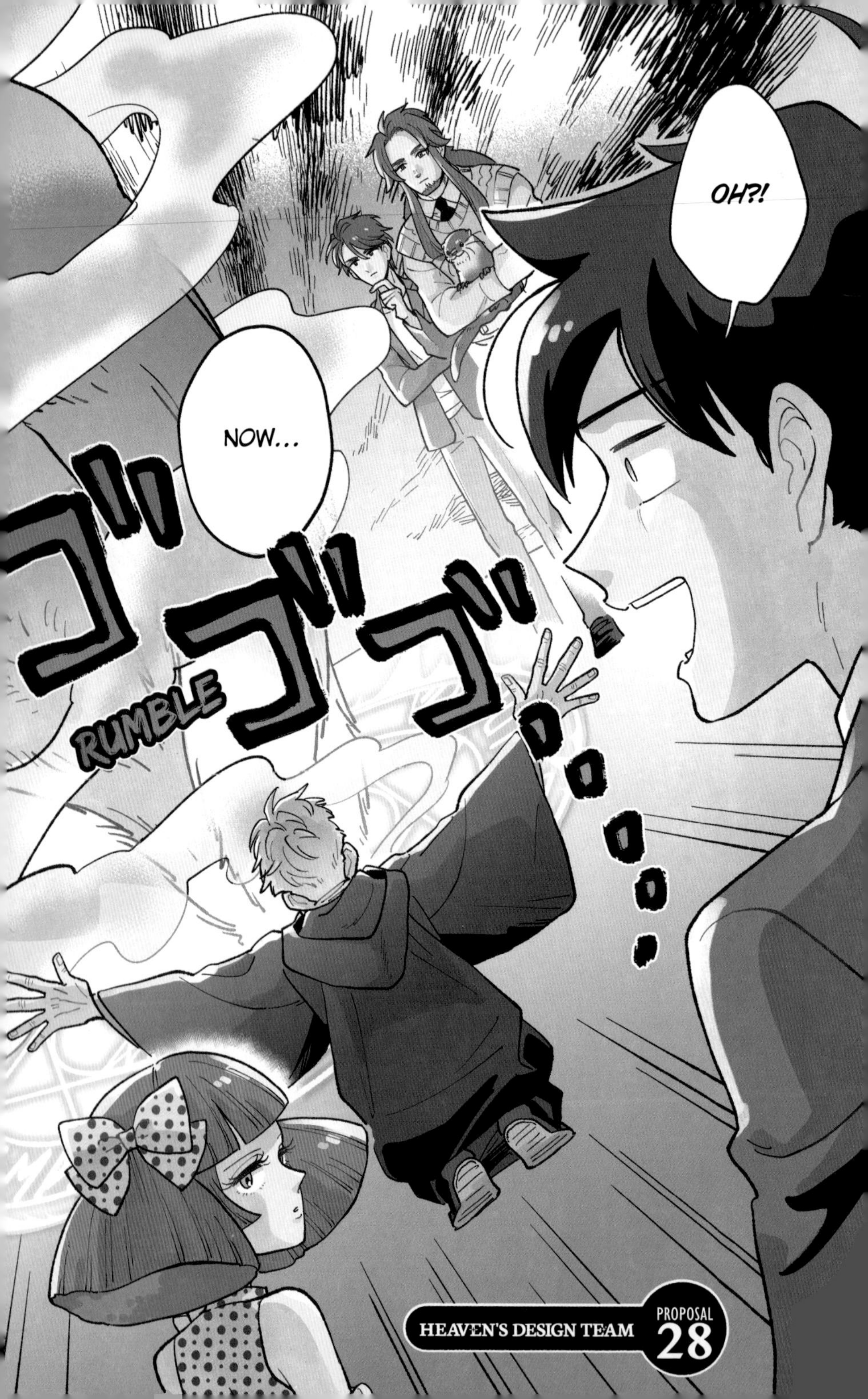
OH?!
NOW...
ゴゴゴゴ
RUMBLE
HEAVEN'S DESIGN TEAM
PROPOSAL
28

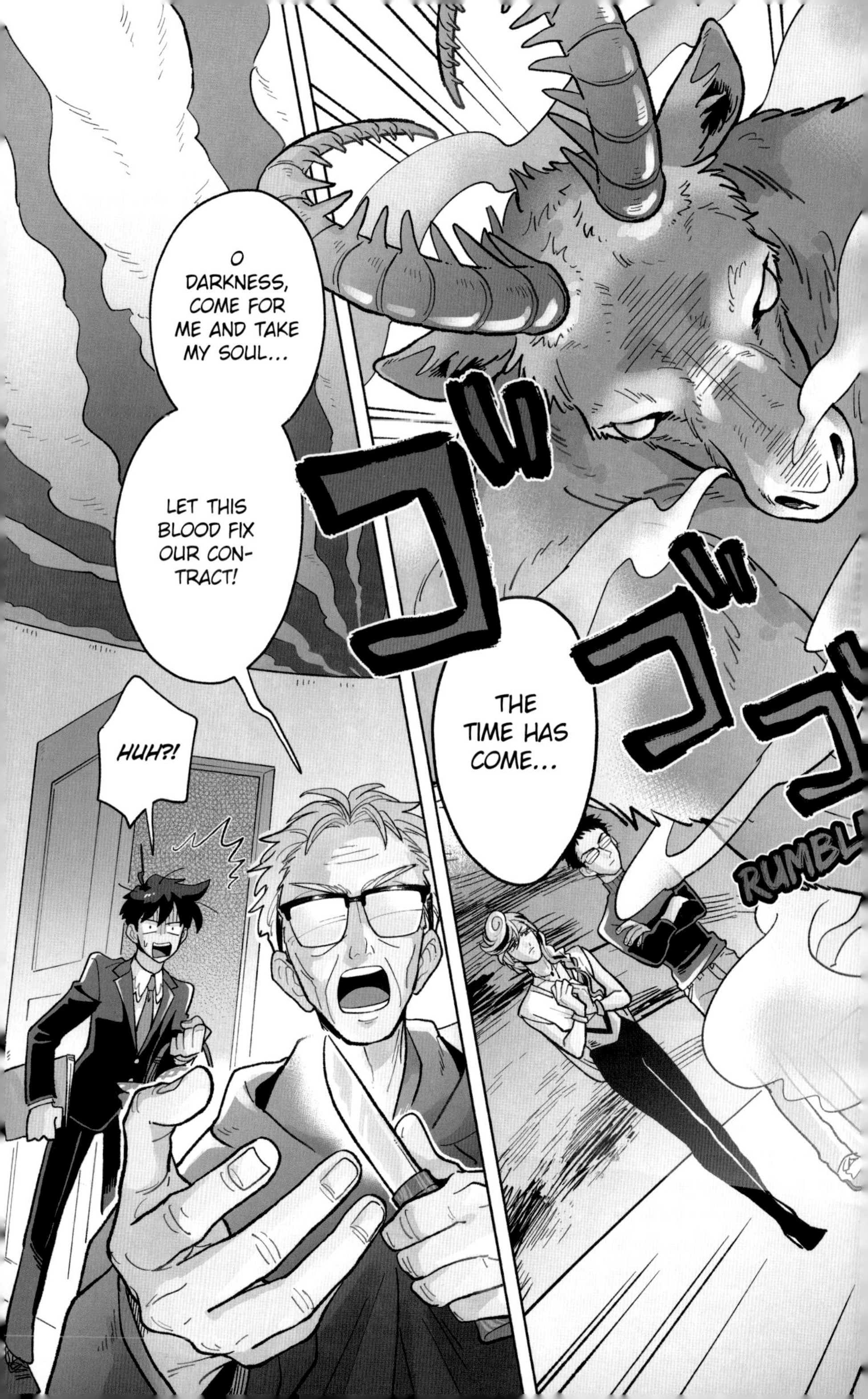
THE TIME HAS COME...
ゴゴゴ
RUMBL
O DARKNESS, COME FOR ME AND TAKE MY SOUL...
LET THIS BLOOD FIX OUR CON-TRACT!
HUH?!

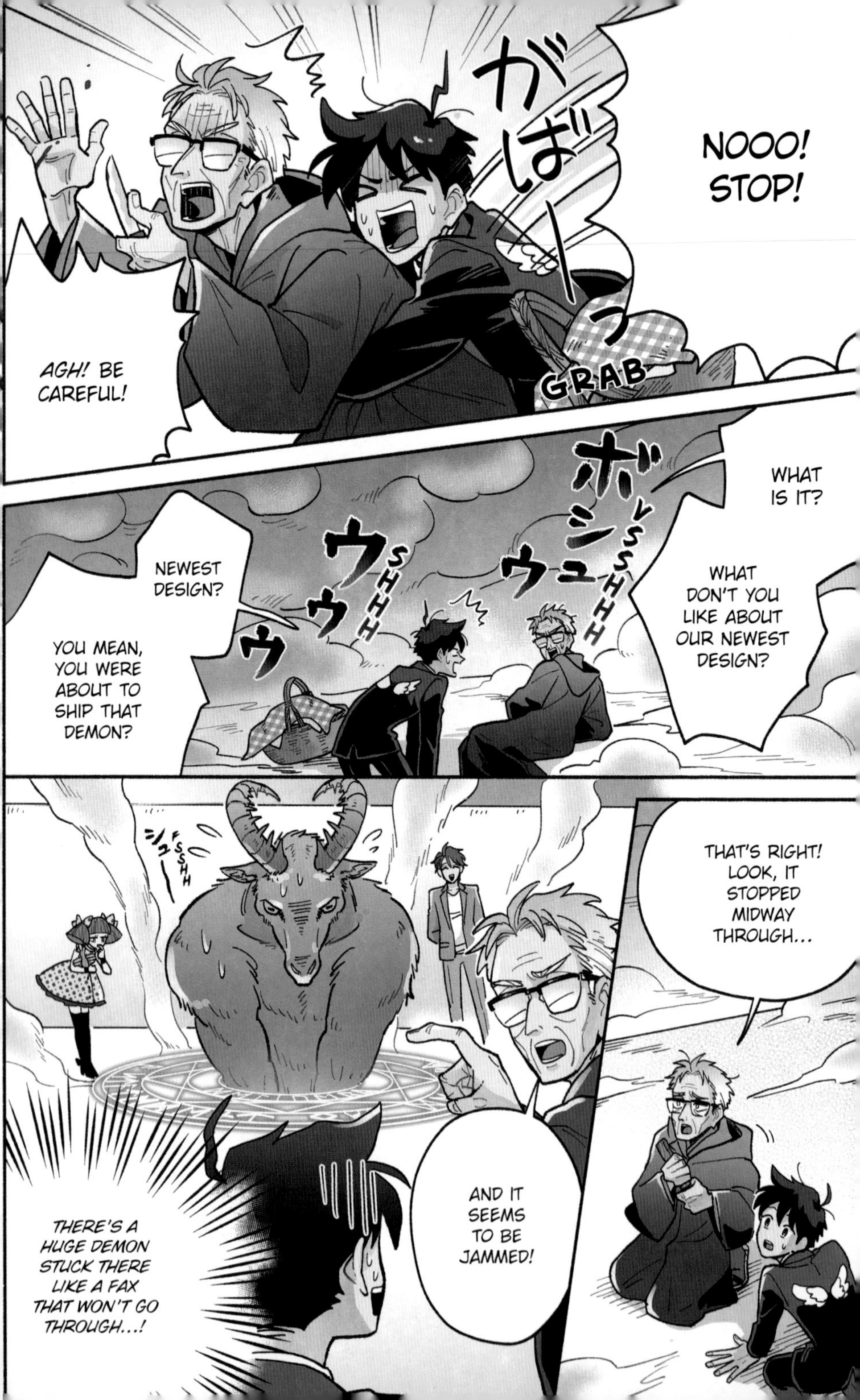
NOOO! STOP!
がばっ
GRAB
AGH! BE CAREFUL!
WHAT IS IT?
WHAT DON'T YOU LIKE ABOUT OUR NEWEST DESIGN?
ボシュウウウ
VSSHHHH
SHHHH
NEWEST DESIGN?
YOU MEAN, YOU WERE ABOUT TO SHIP THAT DEMON?
THAT'S RIGHT! LOOK, IT STOPPED MIDWAY THROUGH...
シュー
FSSHH
AND IT SEEMS TO BE JAMMED!
THERE'S A HUGE DEMON STUCK THERE LIKE A FAX THAT WON'T GO THROUGH...!

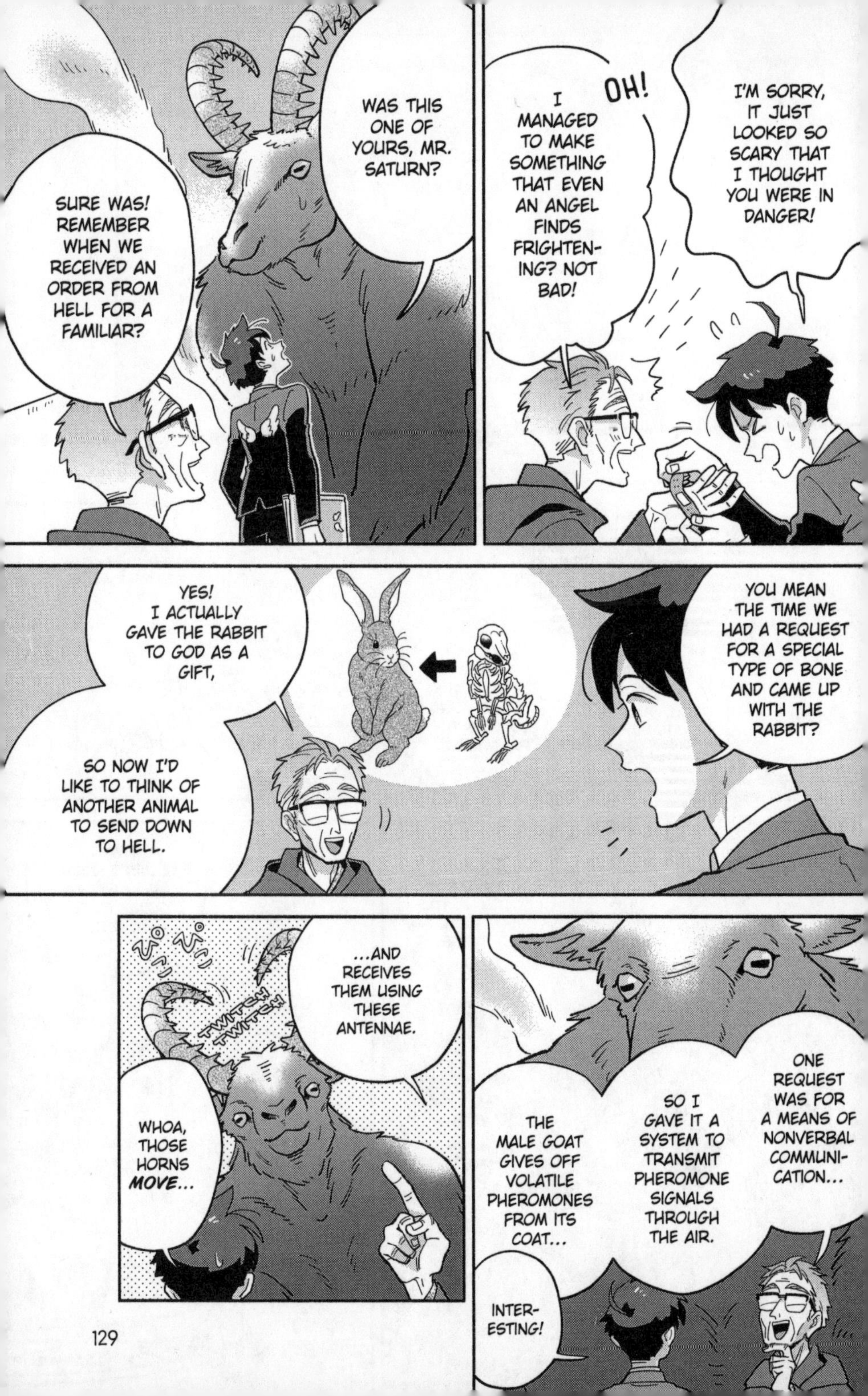
I'M SORRY, IT JUST LOOKED SO SCARY THAT I THOUGHT YOU WERE IN DANGER!
OH!
I MANAGED TO MAKE SOMETHING THAT EVEN AN ANGEL FINDS FRIGHTEN-ING? NOT BAD!
WAS THIS ONE OF YOURS, MR. SATURN?
SURE WAS! REMEMBER WHEN WE RECEIVED AN ORDER FROM HELL FOR A FAMILIAR?
YOU MEAN THE TIME WE HAD A REQUEST FOR A SPECIAL TYPE OF BONE AND CAME UP WITH THE RABBIT?
YES! I ACTUALLY GAVE THE RABBIT TO GOD AS A GIFT,
SO NOW I'D LIKE TO THINK OF ANOTHER ANIMAL TO SEND DOWN TO HELL.
ONE REQUEST WAS FOR A MEANS OF NONVERBAL COMMUNI-CATION...
SO I GAVE IT A SYSTEM TO TRANSMIT PHEROMONE SIGNALS THROUGH THE AIR.
THE MALE GOAT GIVES OFF VOLATILE PHEROMONES FROM ITS COAT...
INTER-ESTING!
...AND RECEIVES THEM USING THESE ANTENNAE.
TWITCH TWITCH
WHOA, THOSE HORNS ***MOVE***...

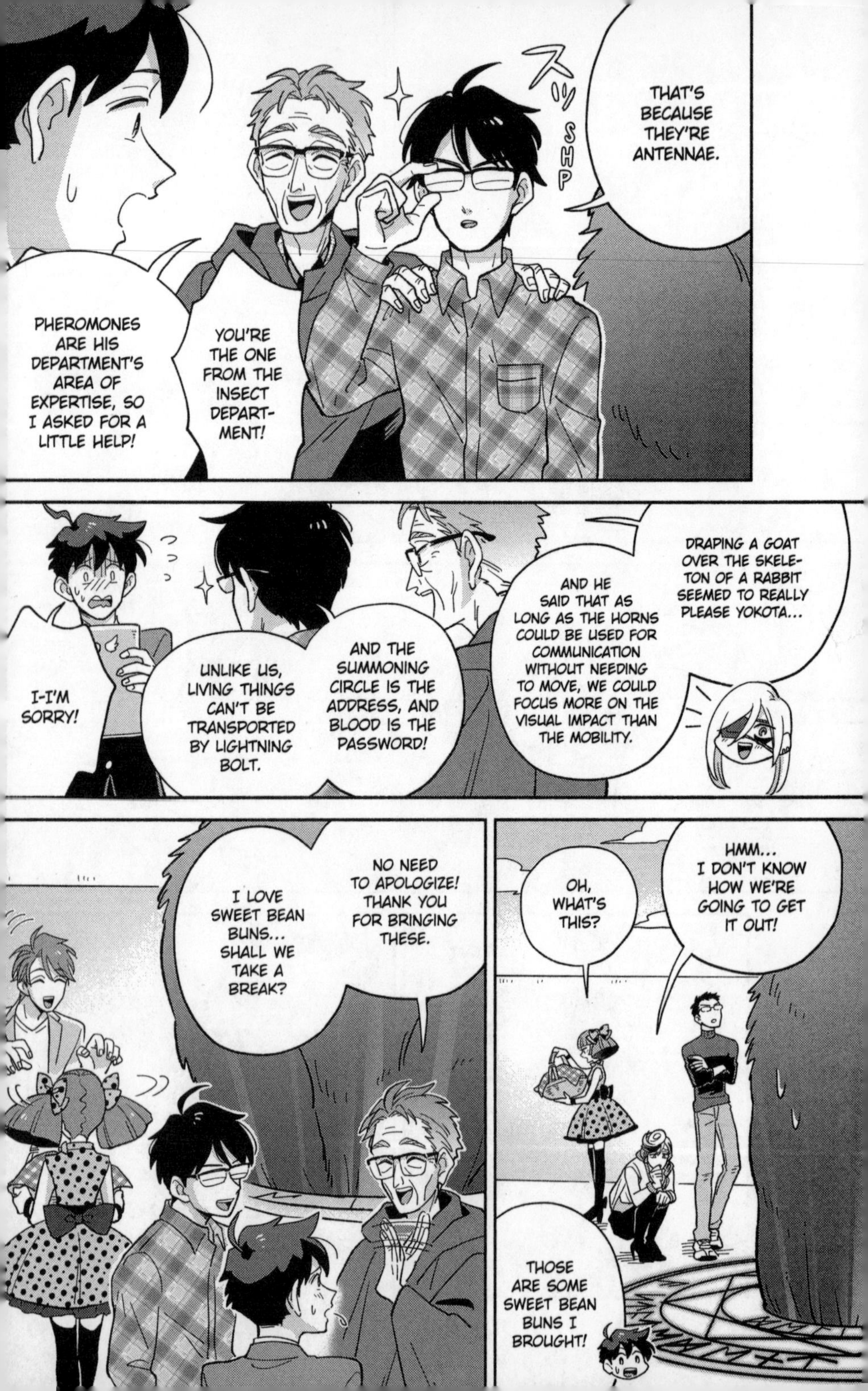
THAT'S BECAUSE THEY'RE ANTENNAE.
SHP
YOU'RE THE ONE FROM THE INSECT DEPART-MENT!
PHEROMONES ARE HIS DEPARTMENT'S AREA OF EXPERTISE, SO I ASKED FOR A LITTLE HELP!
DRAPING A GOAT OVER THE SKELE-TON OF A RABBIT SEEMED TO REALLY PLEASE YOKOTA...
AND HE SAID THAT AS LONG AS THE HORNS COULD BE USED FOR COMMUNICATION WITHOUT NEEDING TO MOVE, WE COULD FOCUS MORE ON THE VISUAL IMPACT THAN THE MOBILITY.
AND THE SUMMONING CIRCLE IS THE ADDRESS, AND BLOOD IS THE PASSWORD!
UNLIKE US, LIVING THINGS CAN'T BE TRANSPORTED BY LIGHTNING BOLT.
I-I'M SORRY!
HMM... I DON'T KNOW HOW WE'RE GOING TO GET IT OUT!
OH, WHAT'S THIS?
THOSE ARE SOME SWEET BEAN BUNS I BROUGHT!
NO NEED TO APOLOGIZE! THANK YOU FOR BRINGING THESE.
I LOVE SWEET BEAN BUNS... SHALL WE TAKE A BREAK?

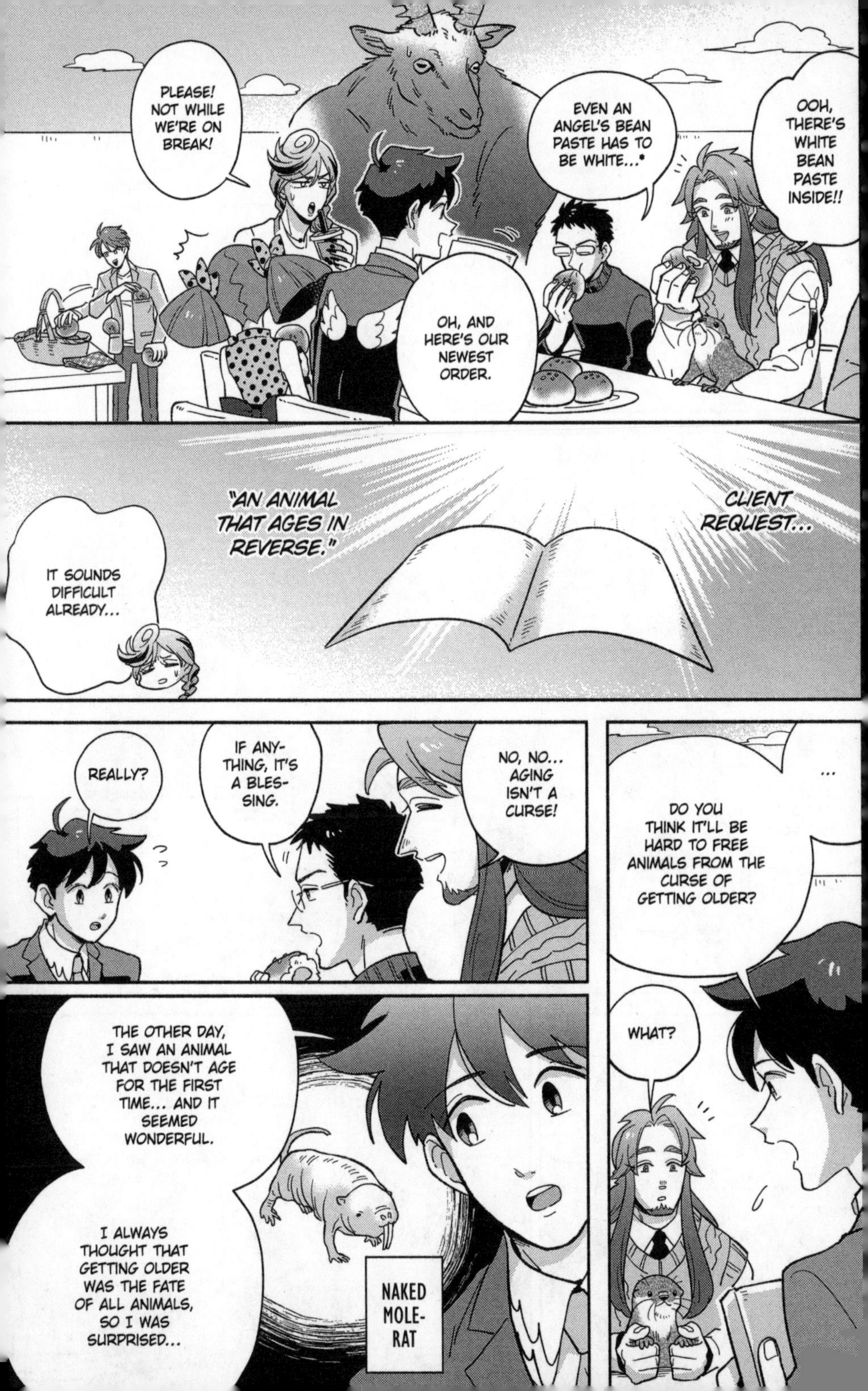
OOH, THERE'S WHITE BEAN PASTE INSIDE!!
EVEN AN ANGEL'S BEAN PASTE HAS TO BE WHITE...*
PLEASE! NOT WHILE WE'RE ON BREAK!
OH, AND HERE'S OUR NEWEST ORDER.
CLIENT REQUEST...
"AN ANIMAL THAT AGES IN REVERSE."
IT SOUNDS DIFFICULT ALREADY...
...
DO YOU THINK IT'LL BE HARD TO FREE ANIMALS FROM THE CURSE OF GETTING OLDER?
NO, NO... AGING ISN'T A CURSE!
IF ANYTHING, IT'S A BLESSING.
REALLY?
WHAT?
THE OTHER DAY, I SAW AN ANIMAL THAT DOESN'T AGE FOR THE FIRST TIME... AND IT SEEMED WONDERFUL.
NAKED MOLE-RAT
I ALWAYS THOUGHT THAT GETTING OLDER WAS THE FATE OF ALL ANIMALS, SO I WAS SURPRISED...

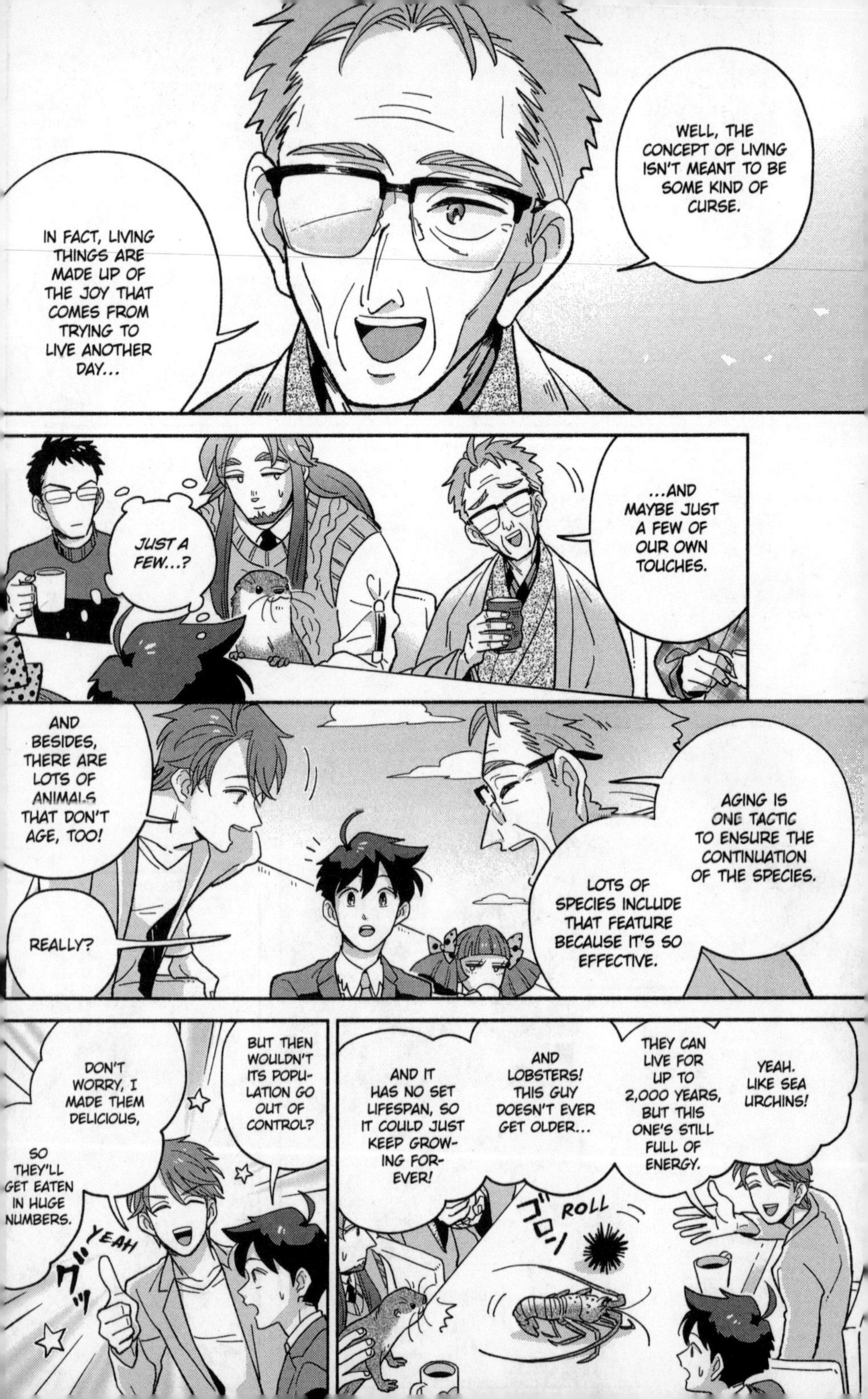
WELL, THE CONCEPT OF LIVING ISN'T MEANT TO BE SOME KIND OF CURSE.
IN FACT, LIVING THINGS ARE MADE UP OF THE JOY THAT COMES FROM TRYING TO LIVE ANOTHER DAY...
...AND MAYBE JUST A FEW OF OUR OWN TOUCHES.
JUST A FEW...?
AGING IS ONE TACTIC TO ENSURE THE CONTINUATION OF THE SPECIES.
LOTS OF SPECIES INCLUDE THAT FEATURE BECAUSE IT'S SO EFFECTIVE.
AND BESIDES, THERE ARE LOTS OF ANIMALS THAT DON'T AGE, TOO!
REALLY?
YEAH. LIKE SEA URCHINS!
THEY CAN LIVE FOR UP TO 2,000 YEARS, BUT THIS ONE'S STILL FULL OF ENERGY.
AND LOBSTERS! THIS GUY DOESN'T EVER GET OLDER...
AND IT HAS NO SET LIFESPAN, SO IT COULD JUST KEEP GROWING FOREVER!
ゴロッ ROLL
BUT THEN WOULDN'T ITS POPULATION GO OUT OF CONTROL?
DON'T WORRY, I MADE THEM DELICIOUS,
SO THEY'LL GET EATEN IN HUGE NUMBERS.
グッ YEAH

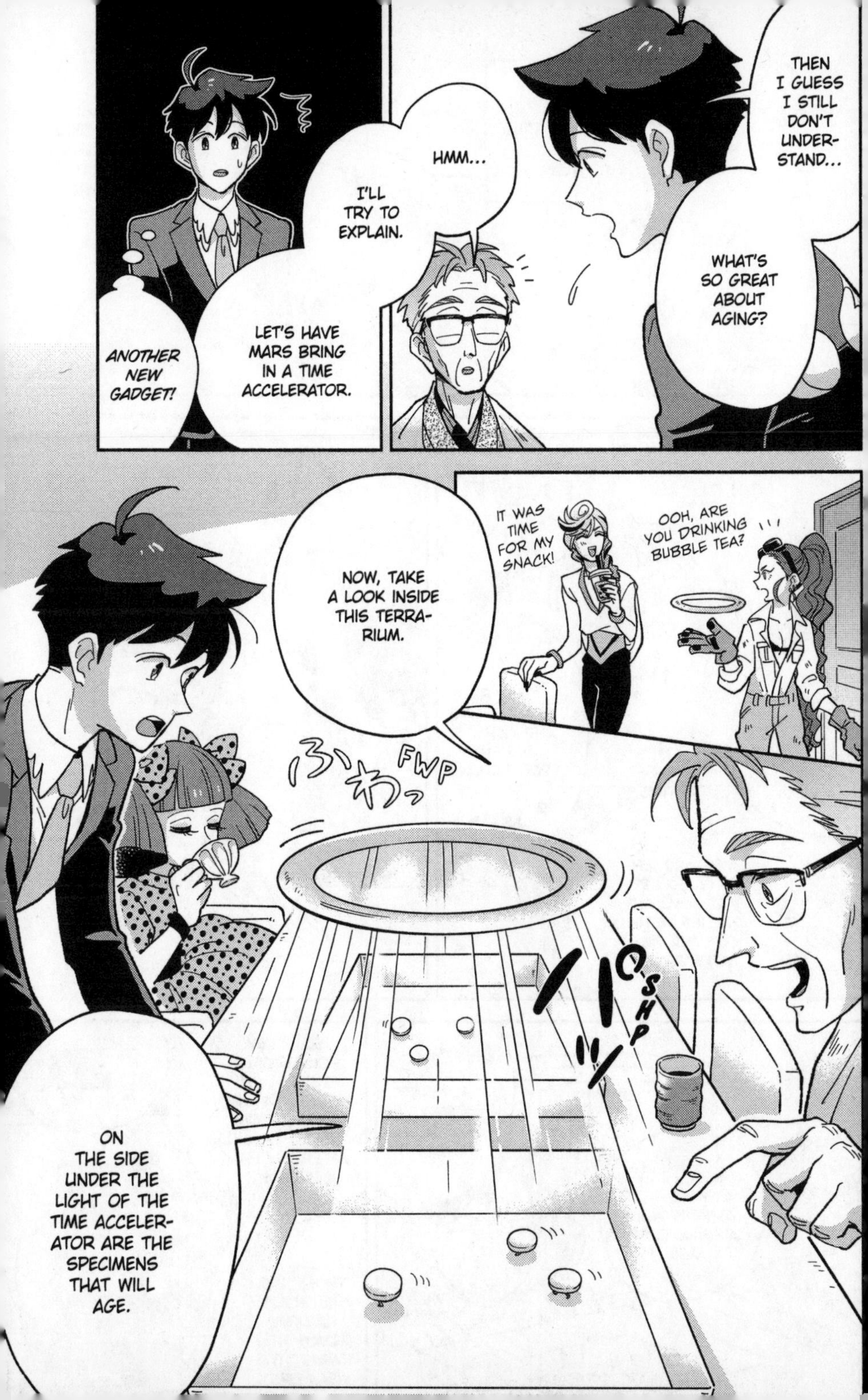
THEN I GUESS I STILL DON'T UNDER-STAND...
WHAT'S SO GREAT ABOUT AGING?
HMM...
I'LL TRY TO EXPLAIN.
LET'S HAVE MARS BRING IN A TIME ACCELERATOR.
ANOTHER NEW GADGET!
OOH, ARE YOU DRINKING BUBBLE TEA?
IT WAS TIME FOR MY SNACK!
NOW, TAKE A LOOK INSIDE THIS TERRA-RIUM.
ふわっ
FWP
C-SHP
ON THE SIDE UNDER THE LIGHT OF THE TIME ACCELER-ATOR ARE THE SPECIMENS THAT WILL AGE.

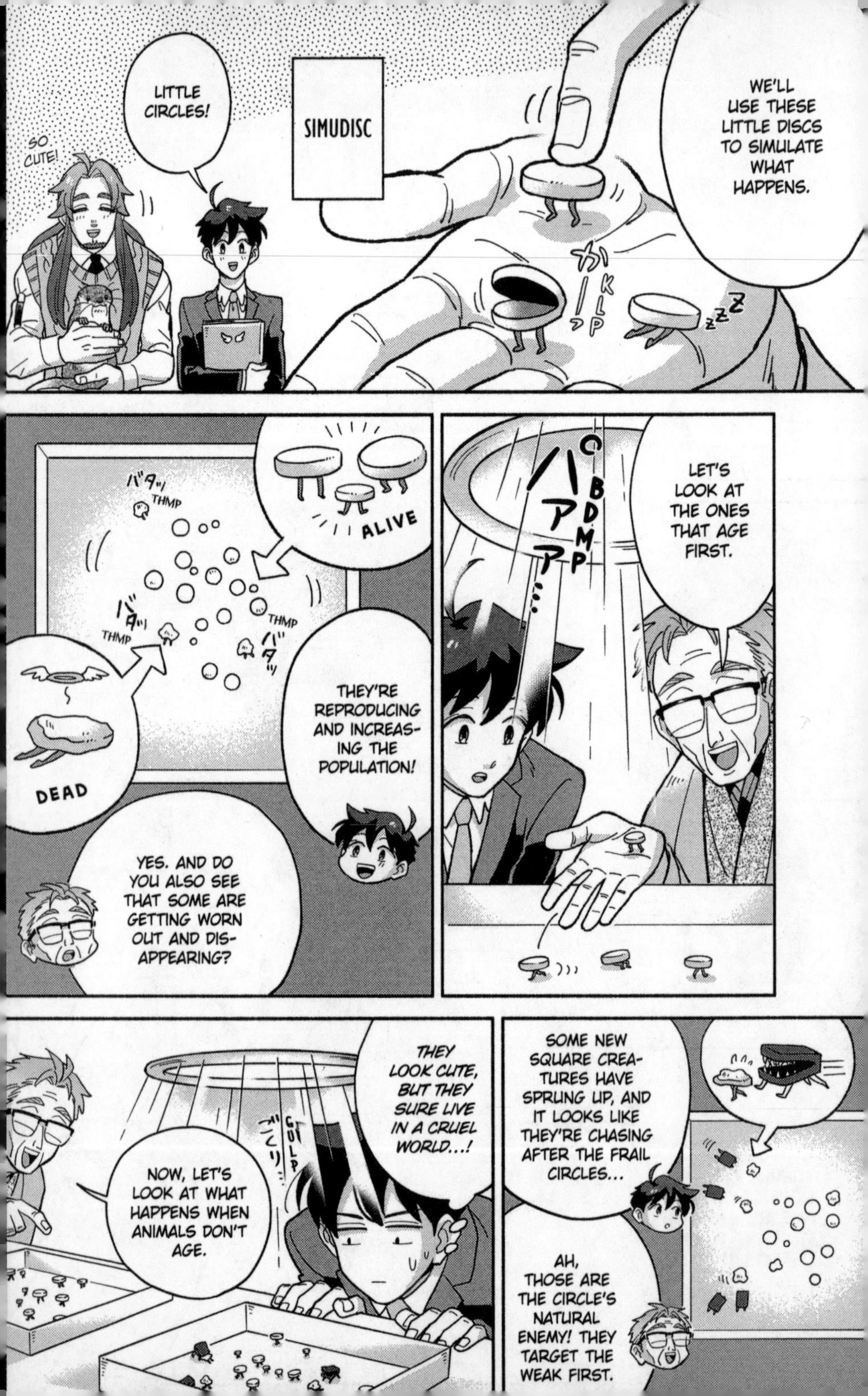
WE'LL USE THESE LITTLE DISCS TO SIMULATE WHAT HAPPENS.
SIMUDISC
KLLP
ZZZ
LITTLE CIRCLES!
SO CUTE!
LET'S LOOK AT THE ONES THAT AGE FIRST.
BDMP
ALIVE
THMP
THMP
THMP
THEY'RE REPRODUCING AND INCREASING THE POPULATION!
DEAD
YES. AND DO YOU ALSO SEE THAT SOME ARE GETTING WORN OUT AND DISAPPEARING?
SOME NEW SQUARE CREATURES HAVE SPRUNG UP, AND IT LOOKS LIKE THEY'RE CHASING AFTER THE FRAIL CIRCLES...
AH, THOSE ARE THE CIRCLE'S NATURAL ENEMY! THEY TARGET THE WEAK FIRST.
THEY LOOK CUTE, BUT THEY SURE LIVE IN A CRUEL WORLD...!
GULP
NOW, LET'S LOOK AT WHAT HAPPENS WHEN ANIMALS DON'T AGE.

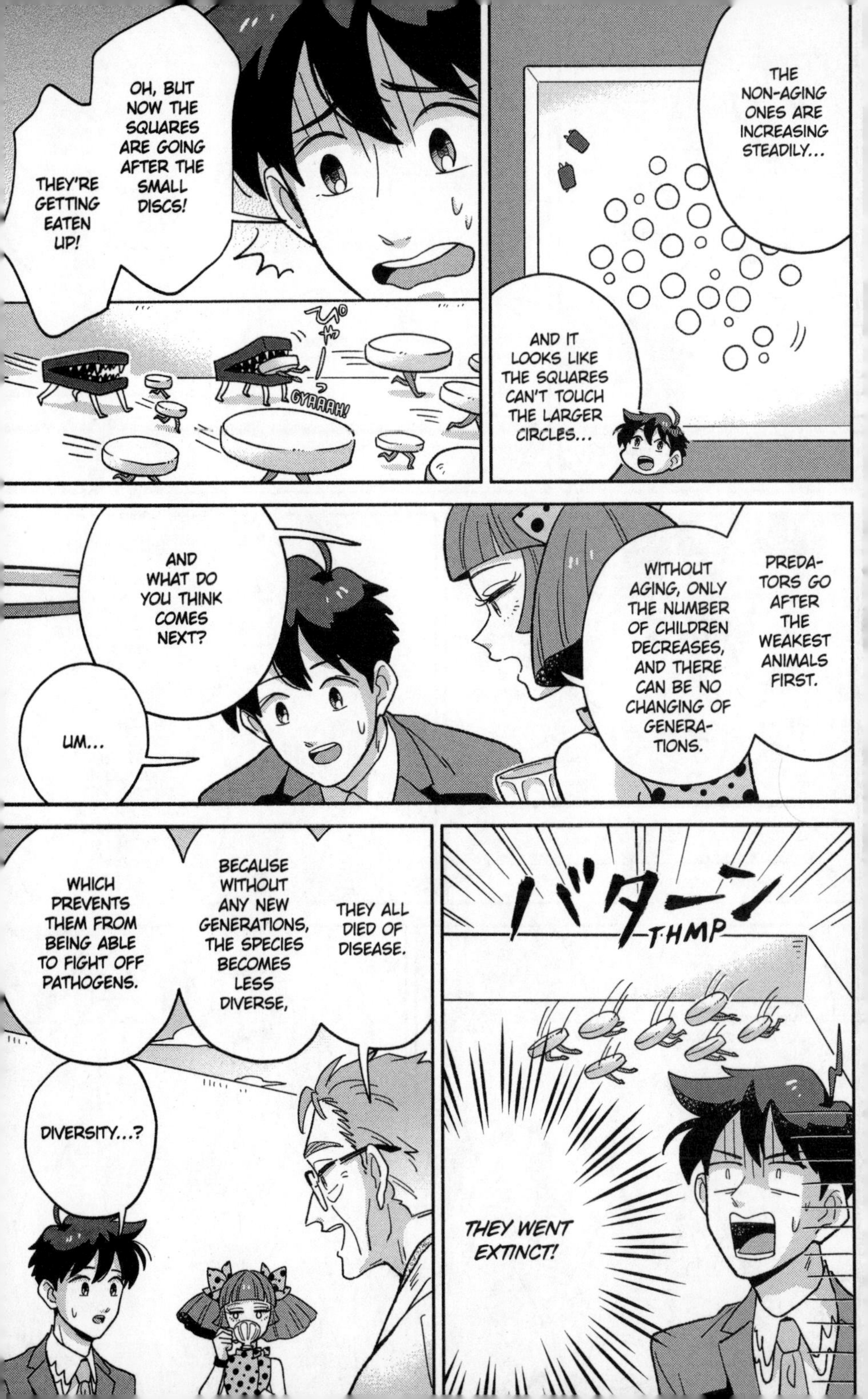
THE NON-AGING ONES ARE INCREASING STEADILY...
AND IT LOOKS LIKE THE SQUARES CAN'T TOUCH THE LARGER CIRCLES...
OH, BUT NOW THE SQUARES ARE GOING AFTER THE SMALL DISCS!
THEY'RE GETTING EATEN UP!
GYAAAAH!
PREDATORS GO AFTER THE WEAKEST ANIMALS FIRST.
WITHOUT AGING, ONLY THE NUMBER OF CHILDREN DECREASES, AND THERE CAN BE NO CHANGING OF GENERATIONS.
AND WHAT DO YOU THINK COMES NEXT?
UM...
バターン
T·HMP
THEY WENT EXTINCT!
THEY ALL DIED OF DISEASE.
BECAUSE WITHOUT ANY NEW GENERATIONS, THE SPECIES BECOMES LESS DIVERSE,
WHICH PREVENTS THEM FROM BEING ABLE TO FIGHT OFF PATHOGENS.
DIVERSITY...?

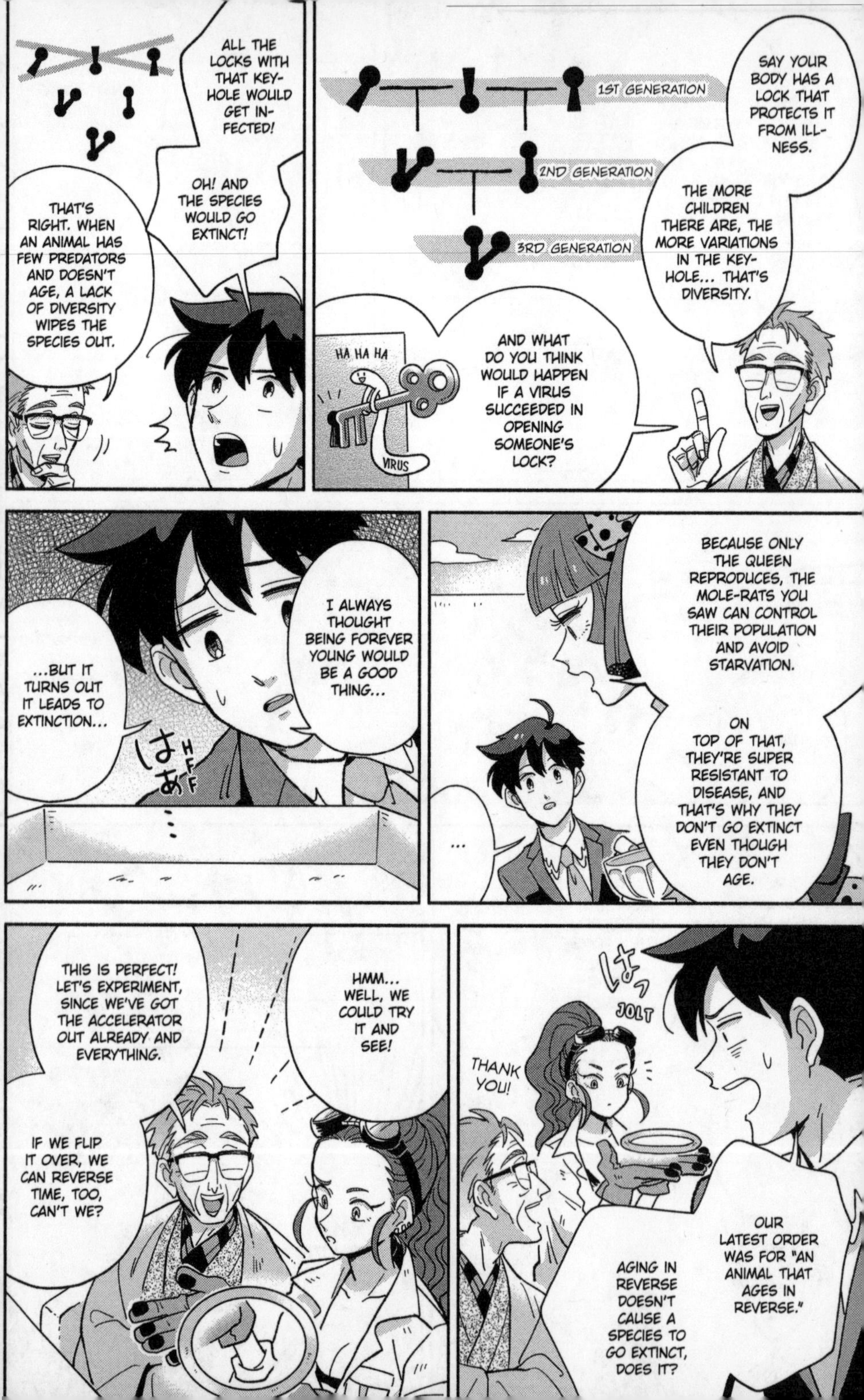
SAY YOUR BODY HAS A LOCK THAT PROTECTS IT FROM ILL-NESS.
1ST GENERATION
2ND GENERATION
3RD GENERATION
THE MORE CHILDREN THERE ARE, THE MORE VARIATIONS IN THE KEY-HOLE... THAT'S DIVERSITY.
AND WHAT DO YOU THINK WOULD HAPPEN IF A VIRUS SUCCEEDED IN OPENING SOMEONE'S LOCK?
HA HA HA
VIRUS
ALL THE LOCKS WITH THAT KEY-HOLE WOULD GET IN-FECTED!
OH! AND THE SPECIES WOULD GO EXTINCT!
THAT'S RIGHT. WHEN AN ANIMAL HAS FEW PREDATORS AND DOESN'T AGE, A LACK OF DIVERSITY WIPES THE SPECIES OUT.
BECAUSE ONLY THE QUEEN REPRODUCES, THE MOLE-RATS YOU SAW CAN CONTROL THEIR POPULATION AND AVOID STARVATION.
ON TOP OF THAT, THEY'RE SUPER RESISTANT TO DISEASE, AND THAT'S WHY THEY DON'T GO EXTINCT EVEN THOUGH THEY DON'T AGE.
...
I ALWAYS THOUGHT BEING FOREVER YOUNG WOULD BE A GOOD THING...
...BUT IT TURNS OUT IT LEADS TO EXTINCTION...
はあ HFF
...
はっ JOLT
OUR LATEST ORDER WAS FOR "AN ANIMAL THAT AGES IN REVERSE."
AGING IN REVERSE DOESN'T CAUSE A SPECIES TO GO EXTINCT, DOES IT?
THANK YOU!
HMM... WELL, WE COULD TRY IT AND SEE!
THIS IS PERFECT! LET'S EXPERIMENT, SINCE WE'VE GOT THE ACCELERATOR OUT ALREADY AND EVERYTHING.
IF WE FLIP IT OVER, WE CAN REVERSE TIME, TOO, CAN'T WE?

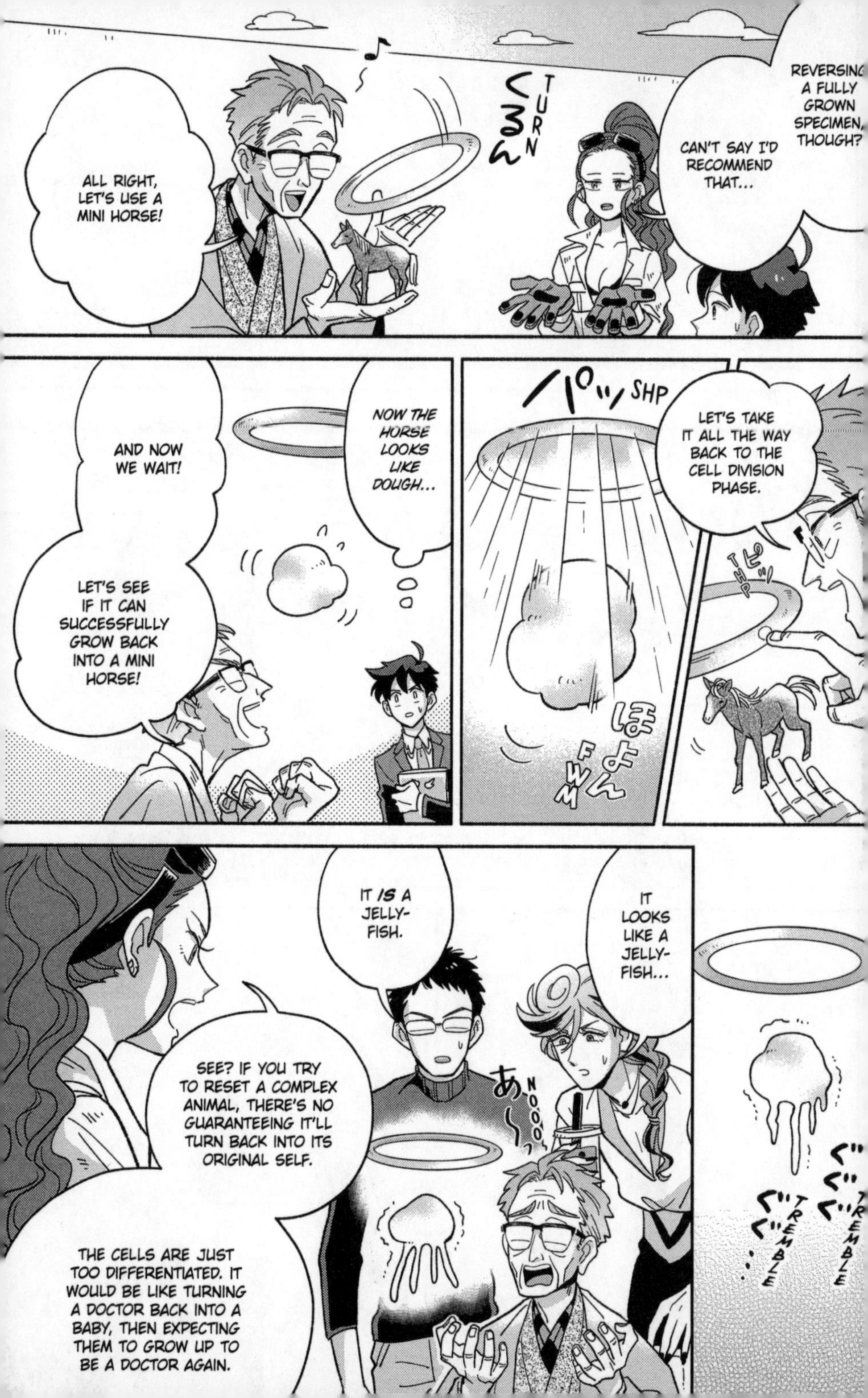
REVERSING A FULLY GROWN SPECIMEN, THOUGH?
CAN'T SAY I'D RECOMMEND THAT...
くるん TURN
ALL RIGHT, LET'S USE A MINI HORSE!
LET'S TAKE IT ALL THE WAY BACK TO THE CELL DIVISION PHASE.
ピッ THP
パッ SHP
ほよん FWM
NOW THE HORSE LOOKS LIKE DOUGH...
AND NOW WE WAIT!
LET'S SEE IF IT CAN SUCCESSFULLY GROW BACK INTO A MINI HORSE!
ぐぐぐ TREMBLE
ぐぐぐ TREMBLE
IT LOOKS LIKE A JELLY-FISH...
IT *IS* A JELLY-FISH.
あ〜っ NOOOO
SEE? IF YOU TRY TO RESET A COMPLEX ANIMAL, THERE'S NO GUARANTEEING IT'LL TURN BACK INTO ITS ORIGINAL SELF.
THE CELLS ARE JUST TOO DIFFERENTIATED. IT WOULD BE LIKE TURNING A DOCTOR BACK INTO A BABY, THEN EXPECTING THEM TO GROW UP TO BE A DOCTOR AGAIN.

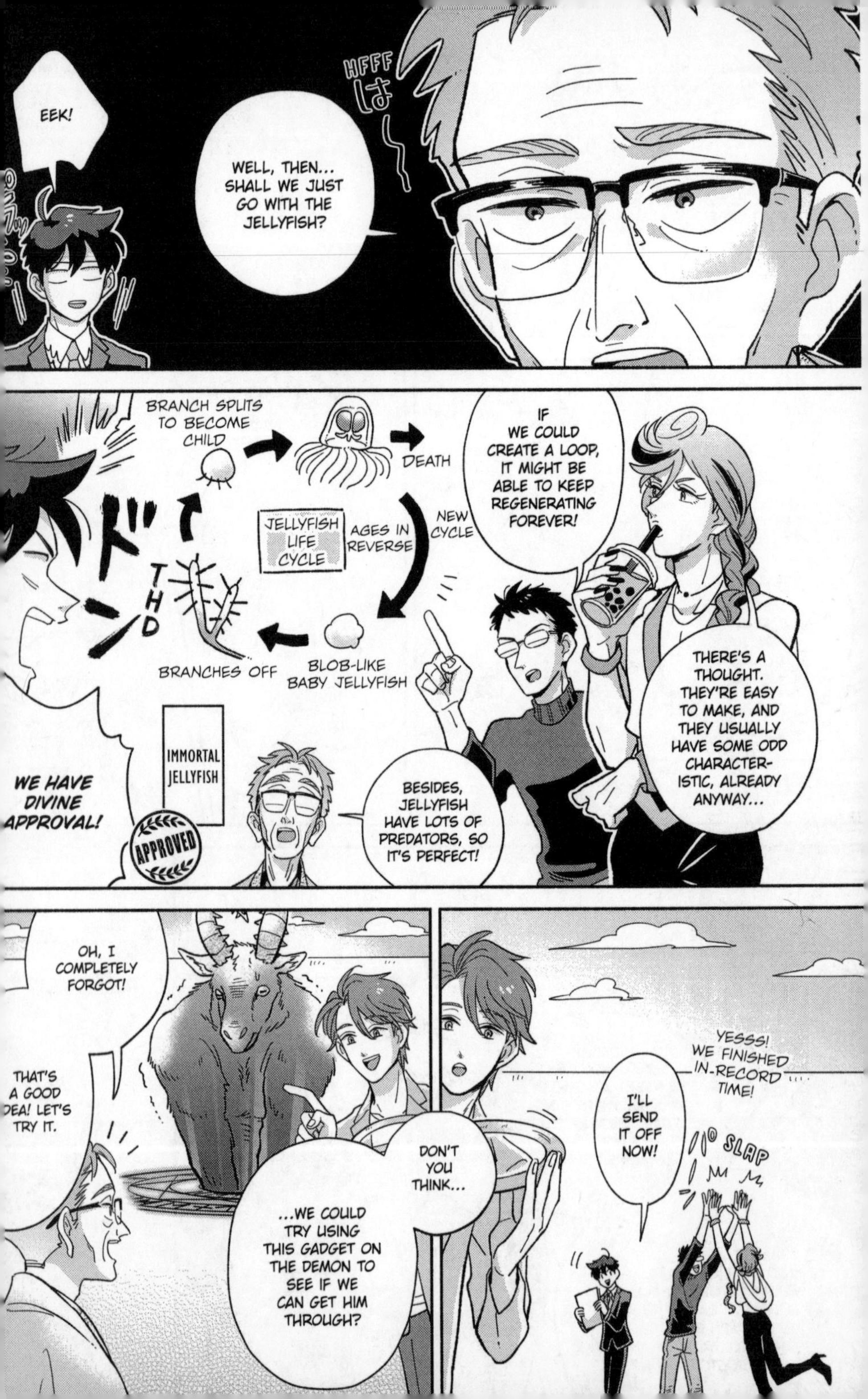
HFFF
はー
WELL, THEN... SHALL WE JUST GO WITH THE JELLYFISH?
EEK!
IF WE COULD CREATE A LOOP, IT MIGHT BE ABLE TO KEEP REGENERATING FOREVER!
THERE'S A THOUGHT. THEY'RE EASY TO MAKE, AND THEY USUALLY HAVE SOME ODD CHARACTER-ISTIC, ALREADY ANYWAY...
BRANCH SPLITS TO BECOME CHILD
DEATH
NEW CYCLE
JELLYFISH LIFE CYCLE
AGES IN REVERSE
BLOB-LIKE BABY JELLYFISH
BRANCHES OFF
BESIDES, JELLYFISH HAVE LOTS OF PREDATORS, SO IT'S PERFECT!
IMMORTAL JELLYFISH
APPROVED
WE HAVE DIVINE APPROVAL!
ドーン
THD
YESSS! WE FINISHED IN-RECORD TIME!
I'LL SEND IT OFF NOW!
SLAP
OH, I COMPLETELY FORGOT!
DON'T YOU THINK...
...WE COULD TRY USING THIS GADGET ON THE DEMON TO SEE IF WE CAN GET HIM THROUGH?
THAT'S A GOOD DEA! LET'S TRY IT.

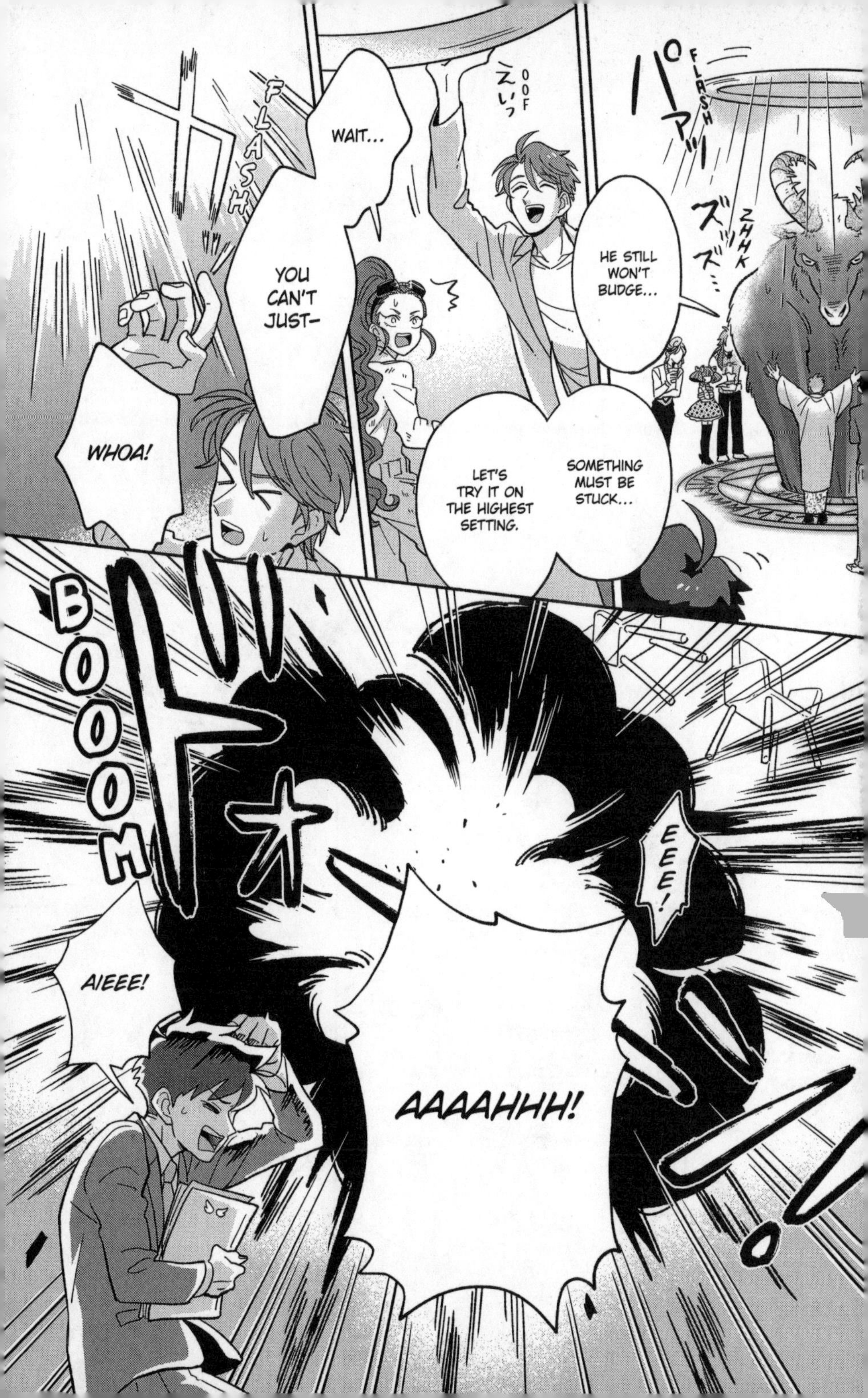
パァッ
FLASH
ズズ…
ZHHK
HE STILL WON'T BUDGE...
SOMETHING MUST BE STUCK...
LET'S TRY IT ON THE HIGHEST SETTING.
えいっ
OOF
WAIT...
YOU CAN'T JUST-
カッ
FLASH
WHOA!
EEE!
AAAAHHH!
BOOOM
AIEEE!

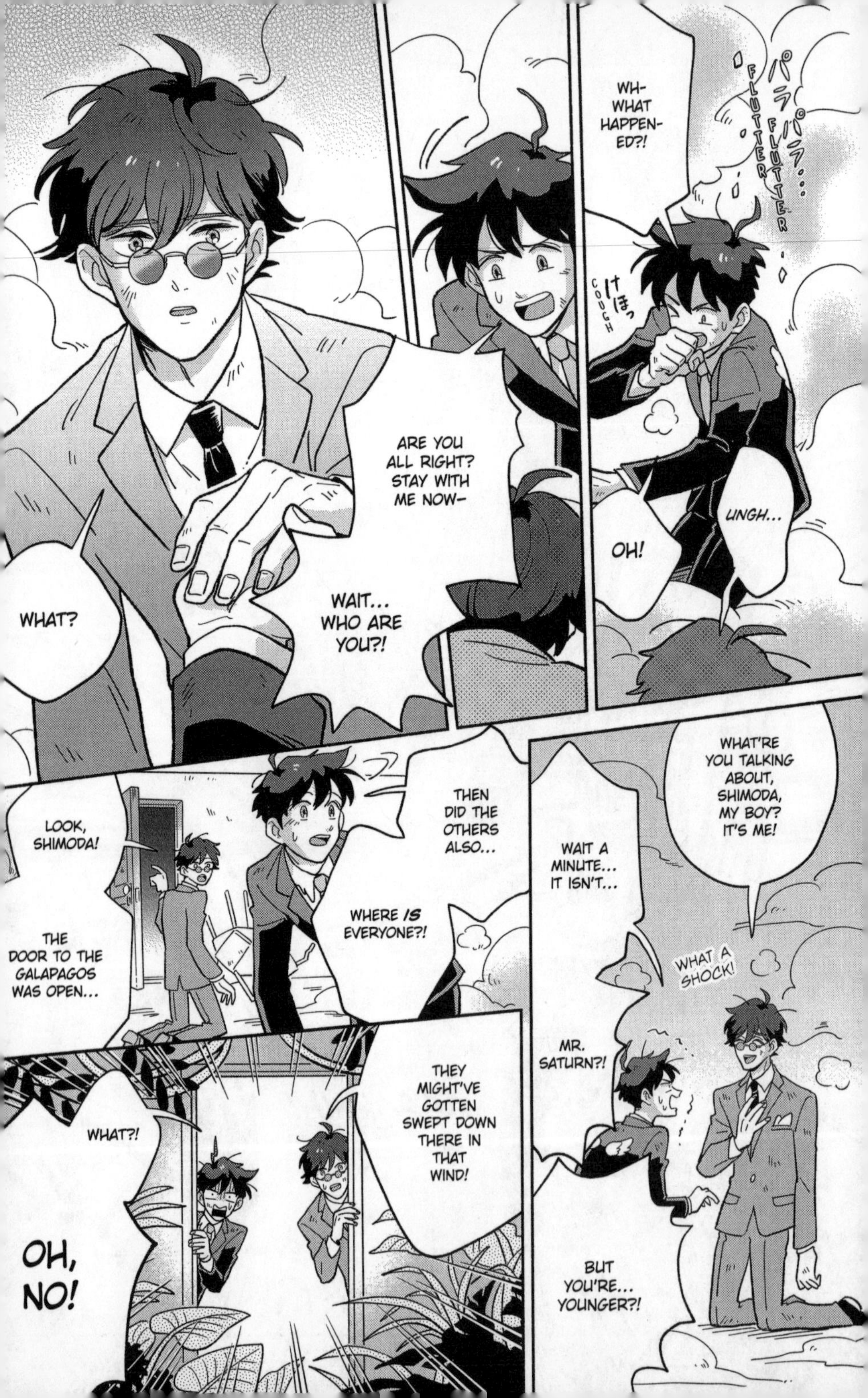
パラパラ…
FLUTTER FLUTTER
けほっ
COUGH
UNGH...
WH-WHAT HAPPEN-ED?!
OH!
ARE YOU ALL RIGHT? STAY WITH ME NOW–
WAIT... WHO ARE YOU?!
WHAT?
WHAT'RE YOU TALKING ABOUT, SHIMODA, MY BOY? IT'S ME!
WAIT A MINUTE... IT ISN'T...
WHAT A SHOCK!
MR. SATURN?!
BUT YOU'RE... YOUNGER?!
THEN DID THE OTHERS ALSO...
WHERE *IS* EVERYONE?!
LOOK, SHIMODA!
THE DOOR TO THE GALAPAGOS WAS OPEN...
THEY MIGHT'VE GOTTEN SWEPT DOWN THERE IN THAT WIND!
WHAT?!
OH, NO!

THE ENCYCLOPEDIA OF REAL ANIMALS 28

ANIMAL 69 | IMMORTAL JELLYFISH

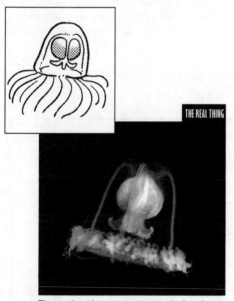

THE REAL THING

The northern Japanese variety can be found north of Ibaraki and Yamaguchi prefectures, while the southern species can be seen in Kagoshima Bay.

Photo: Minden Pictures/Aflo

The *benikurage*, or "scarlet jellyfish" in Japanese, was named for the bright red digestive organ inside of its transparent body.

When the jellyfish is attacked by predators or has just finished laying eggs, it forms a ball and sinks to the ocean floor. While most other jellyfish would die, the immortal jellyfish turns back into a polyp to start its life over again. This is a highly unusual phenomenon in which mature adult cells turn back into immature stem cells (cells that can differentiate into other types of cells). Though this creature has access to the elusive fountain of youth, its small size means that it is easily caught and eaten by predators. When first discovered, it was thought to be the only jellyfish that could turn back time, but other similar species have since been confirmed, including the *Laodicea undulata.*

[Name]	*Turritopsis dohrnii*
[Classification]	Class: Hydrozoa
	Order: Anthoathecata
	Family: Oceaniidae
	Genus: *Turritopsis*
[Habitat]	Tropical to warm oceans
[Length]	4-12 mm (0.2-0.4 in)

ANIMAL 70 GOAT

While the females of the species resemble sheep, male goats have straight coats, saber-shaped horns, and other unique characteristics.

THE REAL THING

Photo: Minden Pictures/Aflo

[Name]	*Capra*
[Classification]	Class: Mammalia
	Order: Artiodactyla
	Family: Bovidae
	Genus: *Capra*
[Habitat]	Western Eurasia to northern Africa
[Height]	45-130 cm (1.5-4.3 ft)

Living primarily in mountainous terrain, the goat eats grass and the tender shoots of trees. The males give off pheromones from their coats, which can induce ovulation and make the females go into heat. Even goat hair that has been cut off from the animal can have this stimulating effect.
A pheromone is a chemical that can cause a response in other members of the same species. Insects often use pheromones to signal or warn each other.

SPECIAL FEATURE JELLYFISH LIFE CYCLE

When asked to imagine a jellyfish, most people recall a partially transparent, umbrella-shaped creature. This, however, is the animal's final form, and it goes through several other stages prior to reaching this last phase.

Most of the jellyfish in the ocean are floating around in the form of eggs or larvae. Once a larva attaches to a hard surface, it grows into an anemone-shaped polyp. From there, the familiar umbrella shape begins to form, which eventually separates and becomes a fully mature jellyfish.

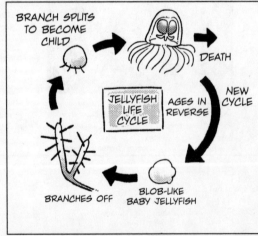

BRANCH SPLITS TO BECOME CHILD
DEATH
NEW CYCLE
JELLYFISH LIFE CYCLE
AGES IN REVERSE
BRANCHES OFF
BLOB-LIKE BABY JELLYFISH

The life cycle of the immortal jellyfish looks more like the process of recycling, but this varies between species.

References

Kodansha no Ugoku Zukan MOVE Tori Kenrouban. Supervised by Kazuto Kawakami. Japan: Kodansha Ltd., 2017.

Viegas, Jen. "Here's How a Bird Imitates a Laser Gun Perfectly." *Seeker.* 2014. https://www.seeker.com/heres-how-a-bird-imitates-a-laser-gun-perfectly-1769283340.html.

Coyne, Jerry. "The lyrebird: nature's finest sound mimic." *Why evolution is true.* 2014. https://whyevolutionistrue.com/2014/11/27/the-lyrebird-natures-finest-sound-mimic/.

Tsuchiya, Ken. *Tyrannosaurus wa Sugoi.* Supervised by Yoshitsugu Kobayashi. Japan: Bunshun Shinsho, Bungeishunju Ltd. 2015.

Kodansha no Ugoku Zukan MOVE Kyouryuu Kenrouban. Supervised by Yoshitsugu Kobayashi. Japan: Kodansha Ltd., 2017.

Christman, Steven P. "Geographic Variation for Salt Water Tolerance in the Frog *Rana sphenocephala.*" *Copeia,* vol. 1974, no. 3, American Society of Ichthyologists and Herpetologists, 1974, pp. 773-778.

Stangel, Judith, Doris Preininger, Marc Sztatecsny, and Walter Hödl. "Ontogenetic Change of Signal Brightness in the Foot-Flagging Frog Species *Staurois parvus* and *Staurois guttatus.*" *Herpetologica,* vol. 71, no. 1, BioOne Complete, 2015, pp. 1-7.

Kirk, Andrew. *Skeletons: The Extraordinary Form & Function of Bones.* Translated by Yuki Wada. Supervised by Hideto Fuse. Japan: Graphic-Sha Publishing Co., Ltd., 2017.

Hirayama, Ren. *Kame no Kita Michi: Koura ni Himerareta Niokunen no Seimei Shinka.* Japan: NHK Books, NHK Publishing Inc., 2007.

Yabe, Takashi. *Kodansha no Ugoku Zukan MOVE Hachuurui, Ryouseirui Kenrouban.* Supervised by Hideaki Kato. Japan: Kodansha Ltd., 2017.

Ohmuta, Ichiyoshi and Hidetoshi Kumazawa. *Yakushima Hatsu: Umigame no Namida Sono Seitai to Kankyou.* Japan: Ocean Engineering Research, Inc., 2011.

Nagashima, Hiroshi, Fumiaki Sugahara, Masaki Takechi, Rolf Ericsson, Yoshie Kawashima-Ohya, Yuichi Narita, and Shigeru Kuratani. "Evolution of the Turtle Body Plan by the Folding and Creation of New Muscle Connections." *Science,* vol. 325, American Association for the Advancement of Science, 2009, pp. 193-196.

Heiss, E., N. Natchev, D. Salaberger, M. Gumpenberger, A. Rabanser, and J. Weisgram. "Hurt yourself to hurt your enemy: new insights on the function of the bizarre antipredator mechanism in the salamandrid *Pleurodeles waltl.*" *Journal of Zoology,* vol. 280, issue 2, The Zoological Society of London, 2009, pp. 156-162.

Kodansha no Ugoku Zukan MOVE Doubutsu Kenrouban. Supervised by Juichi Yamagiwa. Japan: Kodansha Ltd., 2017.

"Motto Shiritai: Zukinazarashi." *Canada Theatre.* 2015-2017. https://www.canada.jp/stories/post-2854/.

Iwahori, Nobuharu. *Zukai Kankakuki no Shinka: Genshi Doubutsu kara Hito e Suichuu kara Rikujou e (BLUE BACKS).* Japan: Kodansha Ltd., 2011.

Kumon, Makoto. "Jikai ni Yoru Ongen Houkou Suitei." *Journal of the Society of Biomechanisms* 33, 4 (2009): pp. 243-249.

Birkhead, Tim. *Bird Sense: What It's Like to Be a Bird.* Translated by Yukiko Numajiri. Japan: Kawade Shobo Shinsha, Ltd., 2013.

Kobayashi, Narihikoto. *Fukurou ni Naze Hito wa Miserareru no ka Watashi no Fukurougoku.* Japan: Kodamasya, 2008.

Kroeger, R. A., H. D. Gruschka, T.C. Helvey, et al. "Low Speed Aerodynamics for Ultra-Quiet Flight." *The University of Tennessee Space Institute,* Tullahoma, Tennessee. 1972.

Kodansha no Ugoku Zukan MOVE Mizu no Naka no Ikimono. Supervised by Takashi Okutani. Japan: Kodansha Ltd., 2018.

Tashiro, Yoshiharu. *Pengin wa Naze Tobukoto wo Yameta no ka.* Art by Yasuhiro Murase. Japan: Jitsugyo no Nihon Sha Ltd., 1993.

Sparks, John and Tony Soper. *Penguins.* Translated by Masahiro Aoyagi and Kazuoki Ueda. Japan: Doubutsu Sha, 1997.

Hosokawa, Hiroaki. *Minna ga Shiritai Pengin no Himitsu.* Japan: Si Shinsho, SB Creative Corp., 2009.

Martin, Graham R. "Eye structure and foraging in King Penguins *Aptenodytes patagonicus.*" *Ibis,* vol. 141, British Ornithologists' Union, 1999, pp. 444-450.

Yoshida, Shigeto and Kazuo Okanoya. *Hadakadebanezumi—Joou, Heitai, Futon Gakari.* Japan: Iwanami Kagaku Library 151 Ikimono, Iwanami Shoten, 2008.

Science Magic Show. *How do naked mole-rats choose their queen?* Youtube, 20 September 2018, https://www.youtube.com/watch?v=q9Yr_jE5pUE&t=9s.

Watarai, Akiyuki, Natsuki Arai, Shingo Miyawaki, Hideyuki Okano, Kyoko Miura, Kazutaka Mogi, and Takefumi Kikusui, "Responses to pup vocalizations in subordinate naked mole-rats are induced by estradiol ingested through coprophagy of queen's feces." *PNAS,* vol. 115, no. 37, Proceedings of the National Academy of Sciences of the Unites States of America, 2018, pp. 9264-9269.

Kiyokawa, Yasushi and Yukari Takeuchi. "Honyuurui ni okeru Kihatsusei Pheromone no Doutei." *Kagaku to Seibutsu,* vol. 53, no. 10, Japan Society for Bioscience, Biotechnology, and Agrochemistry, 2015, pp. 681-688.

Mitteldorf, Josh and Dorion Sagan. *Cracking the Aging Code: The New Science of Growing Old - And What It Means for Staying Young.* Translated by Makoto Yaguchi. Japan: Shueisha Inc., 2018.

jfish. *Kurage no Fushigi - Umi wo Tadayou Kimyou na Seitai.* Supervised by Shin Kubota and Shunjiro Ueno. Japan: Shiritai! Science, Gijutsu-Hyohron Co., Ltd., 2006.

Miyake, Hiroshi and Dhugal Lindsay. *110 Shu no Kurage no Fushigi na Seitai Saishin Kurage Zukan.* Japan: Seibundo-shinkosha, 2013.

Kuwahara, Yasumasa. *Sei Pheromone.* Japan: Kodansha Sensho Mechie 91, Kodansha Ltd., 1996.

Akaike, Manabu and Yoshihiro Tanaka. *Chou no Pheromone, Kirin no Kairaku - Chotto Ecchi na Seibutsugaku.* Japan: Kodansha + α Bunko, Kodansha Ltd., 1998.

Kanzaki, Ryohei. *Cyborg Konchuu, Pheromone wo Ou.* Japan: Iwanami Kagaku Library 228, Iwanami Shoten, 2014.

*All websites were accessed on July 23, 2019.

Special thanks:

Editor/Yoshimi Takuwa-san (Institution for Liberal Arts, Tokyo Institution of Technology)

Kamome Shirahama-san
Saba-san
Ame Toba-san
Tomato-san

A Kodansha Comics Trade Paperback Original
Heaven's Design Team 4 copyright © 2019 Hebi-zou&Tsuta Suzuki/Tarako
English translation copyright © 2021 Hebi-zou&Tsuta Suzuki/Tarako
All rights reserved.

Published in the United States by Kodansha Comics, an imprint of
Kodansha USA Publishing, LLC, New York.

Publication rights for this English edition arranged through
Kodansha Ltd., Tokyo.

First published in Japan in 2019 by Kodansha Ltd., Tokyo
as *Tenchi sozo dezainbu*, volume 4.

ISBN 978-1-64651-131-0

Original cover design by SAVA DESIGN

Printed in the United States of America.

www.kodanshacomics.com

9 8 7 6 5 4 3 2 1
Translation and lettering: JM Iitomi Crandall
Additional translation: Jacqueline Fung
Additional lettering and layout: Belynda Ungurath
Editing: Jesika Brooks, Vanessa Tenazas
YKS Services LLC/SKY Japan, INC
Kodansha Comics edition cover design by My Truong

Publisher: Kiichiro Sugawara

Director of publishing services: Ben Applegate
Associate director of operations: Stephen Pakula
Publishing services managing editor: Noëlle Webster
Assistant production manager: Emi Lotto, Angela Zurlo
Logo and character art ©Kodansha USA Publishing, LLC